Capital Punishment

Mary E. Williams, *Book Editor*

Bruce Glassman, *Vice President*
Bonnie Szumski, *Publisher*
Helen Cothran, *Managing Editor*

CURRENT CONTROVERSIES

GREENHAVEN PRESS
An imprint of Thomson Gale, a part of The Thomson Corporation

THOMSON
™
GALE

Detroit • New York • San Francisco • San Diego • New Haven, Conn.
Waterville, Maine • London • Munich

LIBRARY OF CONGRESS CATALOGING-IN-PUBLICATION DATA

Capital punishment / Mary E. Williams, book editor.
    p. cm. — (Current controversies)
Includes bibliographical references and index.
    ISBN 0-7377-2200-2 (lib. : alk. paper) — ISBN 0-7377-2201-0 (pbk. : alk. paper)
    1. Capital punishment. I. Williams, Mary E. II. Series.
HV8694.C284 2005
364.66—dc22   2004047486

Printed in the United States of America

Contents

Chapter 2: Is Capital Punishment Administered Fairly?

No: Capital Punishment Is Administered Unfairly

Foreword

By definition, controversies are "discussions of questions in which opposing opinions clash" (Webster's Twentieth Century Dictionary Unabridged). Few would deny that controversies are a pervasive part of the human condition and exist on virtually every level of human enterprise. Controversies transpire between individuals and among groups, within nations and between nations. Controversies supply the grist necessary for progress by providing challenges and challengers to the status quo. They also create atmospheres where strife and warfare can flourish. A world without controversies would be a peaceful world; but it also would be, by and large, static and prosaic.

The Series' Purpose

The purpose of the Current Controversies series is to explore many of the social, political, and economic controversies dominating the national and international scenes today. Titles selected for inclusion in the series are highly focused and specific. For example, from the larger category of criminal justice, Current Controversies deals with specific topics such as police brutality, gun control, white collar crime, and others. The debates in Current Controversies also are presented in a useful, timeless fashion. Articles and book excerpts included in each title are selected if they contribute valuable, long-range ideas to the overall debate. And wherever possible, current information is enhanced with historical documents and other relevant materials. Thus, while individual titles are current in focus, every effort is made to ensure that they will not become quickly outdated. Books in the Current Controversies series will remain important resources for librarians, teachers, and students for many years.

In addition to keeping the titles focused and specific, great care is taken in the editorial format of each book in the series. Book introductions and chapter prefaces are offered to provide background material for readers. Chapters are organized around several key questions that are answered with diverse opinions representing all points on the political spectrum. Materials in each chapter include opinions in which authors clearly disagree as well as alternative opinions in which authors may agree on a broader issue but disagree on the possible solutions. In this way, the content of each volume in Current Controversies mirrors the mosaic of opinions encountered in society. Readers will quickly realize that there are many viable answers to these complex issues. By questioning each author's conclusions, students and casual readers can begin to develop the critical thinking skills so important to evaluating opinionated material.

Current Controversies is also ideal for controlled research. Each anthology in the series is composed of primary sources taken from a wide gamut of informational categories including periodicals, newspapers, books, United States and foreign government documents, and the publications of private and public organizations. Readers will find factual support for reports, debates, and research papers covering all areas of important issues. In addition, an annotated table of contents, an index, a book and periodical bibliography, and a list of organizations to contact are included in each book to expedite further research.

Perhaps more than ever before in history, people are confronted with diverse and contradictory information. During the Persian Gulf War, for example, the public was not only treated to minute-to-minute coverage of the war, it was also inundated with critiques of the coverage and countless analyses of the factors motivating U.S. involvement. Being able to sort through the plethora of opinions accompanying today's major issues, and to draw one's own conclusions, can be a complicated and frustrating struggle. It is the editors' hope that Current Controversies will help readers with this struggle.

"Although public support for capital punishment remains strong, concern about the possibility of wrongful executions is reflected in the increasing calls for a death penalty moratorium."

Introduction

One of the most prominent and influential U.S. Supreme Court cases involving capital punishment was the 1972 case *Furman v. Georgia*. Concluding that the death sentence in thirty-five states had been applied unfairly, the Court placed a moratorium on executions until new standards could ensure evenhandedness in the administration of capital punishment. The Court's specific concerns were that states had applied the death penalty in a way that violated the Eighth Amendment's prohibition against cruel and unusual punishment. Several justices cited factors such as racial discrimination, the poor quality of court-appointed lawyers for the accused, and the risk of executing the innocent as proof that the death penalty had become inhumane.

As a result of the *Furman* ruling, several states passed statutes designed to prevent arbitrariness and discrimination in death penalty cases. These statutes created significant capital-punishment reforms, including the abolition of mandatory death penalties, limiting state-level capital punishment to the crime of murder, and obligatory appeals of death sentences. The Supreme Court then reinstated the death penalty in 1976, enabling states to resume executions in 1977. During the 1980s and 1990s, a rise in the U.S. homicide rate apparently bolstered popular support for capital punishment. Polls reveal that since the mid-1990s, 60 to 75 percent of the American public has favored the death penalty, with many maintaining that it is the most just punishment for the crime of murder.

Recent events, however, have led to new questions about the fairness of the death penalty and renewed calls for a national moratorium on executions. Since 1977, more than 110 death-row inmates have been released after new information revealed that they had been erroneously convicted. Many of their stories are harrowing. Gary Gauger, for example, was wrongly convicted of murdering his parents on the basis of a coerced confession obtained by police after he was held for nearly twenty hours of questioning without food or access to an attorney. Gauger was acquitted in 1995 only after a law professor took over the case and presented evidence pointing to the real killers. Troy Lee Jones received a death sentence after being assigned a defense attorney who failed to interview potential witnesses, obtain a police report, or seek pretrial investigative funds. Jones spent fourteen years on death row before a state supreme court ruled that he should have a new trial. Ultimately, prosecutors dropped all charges against him. In 2001 Earl Washington Jr. was released from prison after DNA tests proved that he could not have committed the 1982 rape and murder that had led to his conviction and death sentence. A man with pronounced mental retardation, Washington had allegedly "quickly" confessed to the crime even though he could not describe the victim or identify where or how he had killed her.

As death penalty critics point out, innocent people can be sentenced to death for various reasons. Police misconduct, suppressed evidence, coerced confessions, inept legal representation, mistaken identification, false testimony, and juror prejudice can lead to wrongful convictions. Another contributing factor to the sentencing of innocents, many analysts contend, is institutional discrimination based on race, class, or social status. The wrongly convicted are often "outsiders"—minorities, the poor, nonconformists, or the mentally ill—who do not receive equitable treatment in the criminal justice system. Poor defendants are particularly disadvantaged, critics claim, because they cannot afford their own legal representation and may be assigned court-appointed lawyers who are inexperienced, overworked, or underpaid. Consequently, the American Bar Association (ABA)—echoing the sentiments expressed in the 1972 *Furman* decision—has called for a voluntary moratorium on executions "unless and until greater fairness and due process prevail in death penalty implementation."

A few state leaders have taken the ABA's plea to heart. In January 2000, after more than half of the condemned inmates in Illinois had been exonerated, then-governor George Ryan proclaimed a moratorium on all executions in that state. "I cannot support a system which, in its administration, has proven so fraught with error and has come so close to the ultimate nightmare, the state's taking of innocent life," Ryan stated. In May 2002 Maryland governor Paris Glendening also announced a suspension of the death penalty in his state—a moratorium which he feels should continue until a University of Maryland study on racial bias and capital punishment is completed and reviewed. Then in 2003, before leaving office, Governor Ryan stirred controversy by granting clemency to all of Illinois' death-row inmates, commuting his state's remaining death sentences to sentences of life without parole. "It [became] clear to me that when it came to the death penalty in Illinois, there was no justice in the justice system. . . . I am comfortable knowing that I did the right thing," Ryan maintains. As this volume goes to press, several other states have legislation pending that would temporarily suspend executions within their jurisdictions.

According to recent surveys, 63 percent of Americans favor a moratorium on executions until the fairness of capital trials can be determined, and 80 percent believe that an innocent person has probably already been executed. Consequently, some death penalty advocates are working to allay concerns by establishing new rules to ensure that those accused of murder receive adequate legal counsel. Some states, for example, have adopted systemic reforms, including assigning at least two lawyers to poor defendants, requiring lead attorneys to have extensive trial experience, and providing special training for judges who preside over death penalty cases.

On the other hand, many capital punishment supporters contend that the concerns about executing the innocent are unfounded. In the opinion of law professor Paul G. Cassell, the belief that wrongly sentenced inmates have been executed is a kind of "urban legend." Cassell insists that there is "no credible example of any innocent person executed in this country under the modern death-penalty system," but that "innocent people undoubtedly have died because of our mistakes in failing to execute." Moreover, death-penalty advocates are often skeptical about declarations of innocence by condemned prisoners whose convictions have been overturned. They maintain that exonerations of the allegedly "wrongly convicted" are typically based on irrelevant legal technicalities rather than solid evidence that proves innocence. In effect, they argue, many of the exonerated are actually guilty, but death penalty abolitionists create the illusion of numerous unjust sentences by spotlighting the few cases in which innocence was proven.

Many death penalty supporters believe, furthermore, that the possibility of executing the innocent does not justify suspending or abolishing capital punishment. They contend that society has a right to use the death penalty to deter potential murderers even if it leads to the execution of a few innocent people. As West Point instructor Louis P. Pojman argues, "If the basic activity or process is justified, then it is regrettable, but morally acceptable, that some mistakes are made. Fire trucks occasionally kill innocent pedestrians while racing to fires, but we accept those losses as justified by the greater good of the activity of using fire trucks." Columnist Samuel Francis agrees, maintaining that "certainty . . . is rarely available in contested criminal proceedings or any other human judgment." If perfect certainty were required in court trials, claims Francis, then even life imprisonment should be abolished because innocents can and do receive such sentences.

Although public support for capital punishment remains strong, concern about the possibility of wrongful executions is reflected in the increasing calls for a death penalty moratorium and in the writings of criminologists, lawmakers, and researchers. *Capital Punishment: Current Controversies* explores this topic as well as arguments concerning the ethics, fairness, and deterrent effects of the death penalty in the United States. The volume's various authors provide a thought-provoking examination of the enduring issues surrounding the death sentence.

Chapter 1

Is Capital Punishment Ethical?

Chapter Preface

Capital punishment has been sanctioned by most societies at some point in their history. The cultures of ancient Egypt, Assyria, and Greece, for example, all executed citizens for a variety of offenses, ranging from perjury to murder. Ancient Roman and Mosaic law, adhering to the rule of "an eye for an eye," endorsed execution as a form of retaliatory justice. Colonial America, which inherited its use of capital punishment from Europe, considered death to be the proper punishment for murder as well as for lesser crimes such as burglary and horse thievery.

It was not until the end of the eighteenth century, when Western criminologists and lawmakers came under the influence of the Enlightenment, that the ethics of capital punishment came into question. In the United States, policy makers adopted the belief that criminals—increasingly seen as sick rather than evil—could be rehabilitated. Prison then became the customary means of punishment, and many states outlawed the death penalty for lesser offenses. Currently, capital punishment in America is restricted to the crimes of deliberate murder and (with Congressional sanction) treason. Since the mid-1990s, a majority of the U.S. public—between 60 and 75 percent—has favored the death penalty for premeditated homicide. Still, disagreement about the ethics of capital punishment continues to draw the attention of activists, politicians, and the public.

Supporters of the death penalty maintain that execution is the only suitable punishment for those who have committed felony homicide. They contend that the standards of modern criminal justice require a murderer to face a penalty that is comparable to the damage caused by his or her crime. As author and lecturer Robert James Bidinotto argues, "The moral defense of the death penalty is the principle of justice. In the case of premeditated murder, capital punishment is the only punishment: it is the only punishment roughly proportionate to the harm that has been done to the murder victim. . . . Proportionate punishment for crimes is the moral keystone of any system of justice." Moreover, proponents claim, capital punishment affirms society's moral recognition that certain crimes are not to be tolerated.

Critics, however, contend that premeditated killing—by either a criminal or by the government—is unethical. While they grant that murderers should be sternly penalized, they believe that the state undermines its moral authority when it executes killers to proclaim that murder is wrong. According to some critics, capital punishment is motivated more by a desire for revenge than by a pursuit of justice. As social psychology professor Mark Constanzo maintains, vengeance is an understandable—but misguided—rationale for execution:

The desire to lash back at those who have harmed us. . . . is a powerful human motive that must be taken seriously, but it is not a sufficient justification for killing. Although individually we all feel the primitive urge to exact revenge against those who harm us, collectively we must strive to be more rational, fair, and humane than the criminals who commit the acts of violence or cruelty that we condemn.

Debates about the morality of the death penalty are likely to continue unabated for years to come. In the chapter that follows, several authors—including a U.S. Supreme Court justice, a police officer, and a death row inmate—present compelling arguments concerning the ethics of capital punishment.

Capital Punishment Is Just

by Dudley Sharp

About the author: *Dudley Sharp is vice president of Justice for All, a criminal justice reform organization in Houston, Texas.*

There is nothing quite like hanging out with your best friend. Jenny Ertman, 14, and Elizabeth Pea, 16, shared their hopes and dreams with each other. Like millions of other teenagers, they liked to have fun, to laugh and smile. One summer evening in Houston, Texas, they shared their last moments on earth together—their own murders.

They were late returning home and took a shortcut through the woods, next to some railroad tracks. They ran into a gang initiation. They were both raped: orally, anally, and vaginally. The gang members laughed about the virgin blood they spilled. When they had finished, they beat and strangled the girls. But Jenny and Elizabeth wouldn't die. With all their strength, with their souls still holding on to the beautiful lives before them, they fought for life.

The gang worked harder. The girls were strangled with belts and shoelaces, stomped on and beaten. Their dreams disappeared as life seeped away from their broken bodies.

Their parents are left to visit empty rooms, to cry upon the beds of their daughters and think what could have been. How beautiful Elizabeth would have been in her prom dress. Her corsage was replaced by the flowers on her grave.

And Jenny's future children, would their grandparents have spoiled them? You know the answer. The immutable joy of grandchildren's laughter was silenced by the cruel selfishness of murder.

Why the Death Penalty?

Sometimes, the death penalty is simply the most appropriate punishment for the vile crime committed. In such cases, jurors are given the choice between a death sentence and a variety of life sentences, depending upon the jurisdiction. It is never easy for juries to give a death sentence. Neither hatred nor revenge is part of their deliberations. The search for justice determines the punishment.

Dudley Sharp, "Do We Need the Death Penalty? It Is Just and Right," *World & I*, vol. 17, September 2002, p. 247. Copyright © 2002 News World Communications, Inc. Reproduced by permission.

The murder of the innocent is undeserved. The punishment of murderers has been earned by the pain and suffering they have imposed on their victims. Execution cannot truly represent justice, because there is no recompense to balance the weight of murder. For some crimes, it represents the only just punishment available on earth.

Attacks on Capital Punishment

Today, much more than justice is part of the death penalty discussion. Opponents are relentlessly attacking the penalty process itself. They insist that it is so fraught with error and caprice that it should be abandoned. At the very least, they say, America should impose a national moratorium so the system can be reviewed.

The leading salvo in those claims is that [at least] 101 innocent people have been released from death row with evidence of their innocence. The number is a fraud. Unfortunately, both the international media and, most predictably, the U.S. media have swallowed such claims and passed them along to the public.

Even many of our elected officials in Washington have blindly accepted those numbers. Sen. Patrick Leahy, chairman of the Senate Judiciary Committee, has said: "What we know is that nearly 100 innocent people have been released from death row since 1973."

The source for these claims is the Death Penalty Information Center (DPIC), the leading source of antideath penalty material in the United States. Richard Dieter, head of the DPIC, has admitted, in the June 6, 2000, *ABA Journal*, that his group makes no distinction between the legally innocent ("I got off death row because of legal error") and the actually innocent ("I had no connection to the murder") cases. Although the DPIC has attempted to revise its standards for establishing innocence, none of the various contortions even suggests actual innocence.

As everyone knows, the debate is about the actually innocent. To strengthen their case, death penalty opponents have broadened their "innocent" count by cases that don't merit that description. On June 20, [2002], for example, the Florida Commission on Capital Cases released its review of 23 death sentence cases that the DPIC had called into question. Its conclusion was that in only 4 of those cases were there doubts as to guilt.

Though the DPIC claims that 101 cases were released from death row with evidence of innocence, the actual number is closer to 30. That is 30 cases out of 7,000 sentenced to

> *"Sometimes, the death penalty is simply the most appropriate punishment for the vile crime committed."*

death since 1973. It appears that the death penalty may well be this country's most accurate criminal sanction, when taking into account the percentage of actual innocent convicted (0.4 percent) and the thoroughness of preventing those allegedly innocent from being executed (100 percent).

Of all the world's social and governmental institutions that put innocents at risk, I can find only one, the U.S. death penalty, that has no proof of an innocent killed since 1900. Can you think of another?

Saving Innocent Lives

Two other factors weigh into the innocence consideration. First, the death penalty remains the most secure form of incapacitation, meaning that executed murderers do not harm and murder again. Living murderers do, quite often. This is unchallenged. Second, although the deterrent effect of capital punishment has been unjustifiably maligned, the evidence is overwhelming that the potential for negative consequences deters or alters behavior. History and the social sciences fully support that finding.

Three major studies were released in 2001, all finding for the deterrent effect of the death penalty. One, out of Emory University, finds that "each execution results, on average, in 18 fewer murders—with a margin of error of plus or minus 10."

Another, out of the University of Houston, found that a temporary halt to executions in Texas resulted in an additional 90–150 murders, because of the reduction in deterrence. One author, Professor C. Robert Cloninger, states: "[Our] recent study is but another of a growing list of empirical work that finds evidence consistent with the deterrent hypothesis. It is the cumulative effect of these studies that causes any neutral observer to pause."

> *"For some crimes, [execution] represents the only just punishment available on earth."*

Death penalty opponents want us to believe that the most severe criminal sanction—execution—deters no one. However, if reason is your guide and you remain unsure of deterrence, you are left with the following consideration. If the death penalty does deter, halting executions will cause more innocents to be slaughtered by giving murderers an additional opportunity to harm and murder again. If the death penalty does not deter, executions will punish murderers as the jury deems appropriate, preventing them from harming any more victims. Clearly, ending or reducing executions will put many more innocents at risk.

The "Error" Rate

Another major factor in the debate was introduced in a study headed by James Liebman, a professor at Columbia University Law School. *A Broken System: Error Rates in Capital Cases* revealed that there was a 68 percent reversal rate in death penalty cases from 1973 to 1995. The error rate within that study has not been publicly discussed.

Professors Barry Latzer and James Cauthen of John Jay College of Criminal Justice found a 25 percent error within the study's calculations, bringing the reversal rate down to 52 percent. Unfortunately, they had to accept the accuracy of Liebman's assessments, because he refused to release his database. Case reviews in Florida, New Jersey, Utah, and Nevada have provided specific cause to challenge his data. Florida challenges any assessment of error in 33 percent of

the cases identified by Liebman, suggesting that the national "error" rate may be closer to 35 percent.

But even that number is suspect. The Supreme Court has stated that the death penalty system receives super

> *"The death penalty may well be this country's most accurate criminal sanction."*

due process. This means that the courts are extraordinarily generous in granting reversals in death penalty cases. In fact, the appellate courts are twice as likely to reverse the sentence in death penalty cases as they are the conviction.

Traditionally, death penalty opponents have stated that racism and poverty determine who receives the death penalty. Those arguments persist. What they fail to reveal is that white murderers are twice as likely to be executed as black murderers and are executed 12 months faster.

Some claim that the race of the victim determines the sentence. While those who murder whites dominate death row, it is also true that, overwhelmingly, whites are the victims in robberies, rapes, burglaries, and carjackings, which make up the majority of death penalty crimes.

No one disputes that the wealthy have an advantage in avoiding a death sentence. The United States executes about 0.1 percent of its murderers. Is there any evidence that it is less likely to execute the wealthier ones, based on the ratio of wealthier to poorer capital murderers? Surprisingly, no.

The Justice Factor

This brings me back to where I started: justice. Some say that executions show a contempt for human life, but the opposite is true. We would hope that a brutal rape may result in a life sentence. Why? We value freedom so highly that we take freedom away as punishment. If freedom were not valued, taking it away would be no sanction.

Life is considered even more precious. Therefore, the death penalty is considered the severest sanction for the most horrible of crimes. Even murderers tell us that they value life (their own) more than freedom. That is why over 99 percent of convicted capital murderers seek a life sentence, not a death sentence, during the punishment phase of their trials.

Even some of those traditionally against capital punishment have decided that some crimes are justly punished with death. Timothy McVeigh's 2001 execution was thought a just punishment by 81 percent of the American people, reflecting an all-time high of support.[1] When 168 innocents were murdered, in-

1. In 2001 McVeigh was executed for the 1995 bombing of the Murrah federal building in Oklahoma City, Oklahoma.

cluding 19 children whom McVeigh described as "collateral damage," the collective conscience of the American people reached an overwhelming consensus. A Gallup poll, released on May 20 [2002] shows that 72 percent supported the death penalty, with nearly half those polled saying the sanction is not imposed enough.

Why didn't I invoke the murder of 3,100 innocents on September 11 [2001]? Because the murder of one Jenny Ertman is enough—much too much. Which one of the murdered innocents was more valuable than another? Was one child blown apart in Oklahoma City not enough? Was a father forever lost on September 11 not enough? A son? A granddaughter?

Is it the numbers, at all? No, it is the realization that those innocent lives, so willfully ripped from us, represent individuals who contributed to someone's life and happiness. The sheer numbers of murders committed each year may numb us beyond what an individual murder can. But that is only because we must shield ourselves from the absolute horror represented by one innocent murdered. It is a matter of emotional self-preservation.

Often, in the most horrible of times, we find that the goodness in people stands out. At one point during the attack, Jenny was able to escape and run away. Elizabeth's cries brought Jenny back in a fruitless attempt to aid her friend. Love, friendship, and devotion overcame fear.

Of the six attackers who brutalized these girls for over an hour, five received the death penalty. The sixth was too young to prosecute for death. And why did five separate juries give death? Justice.

Capital Punishment Grants Reasonable Retribution

by Burton M. Leiser

About the author: *Burton M. Leiser is a professor of philosophy and law at Pace University in New York. He is also the author of* Liberty, Justice, and Morals: Contemporary Value Conflicts.

Timothy McVeigh, the terrorist who bombed the federal building in Oklahoma City in 1995, resulting in 168 deaths and untold anguish for the friends, relatives, and colleagues of the victims, is scheduled to be executed by the federal government about a month after I write these words.[1] The only regret he has expressed was, "Damn, I didn't knock the building down." Far from being remorseful about the children in a day care center in the building who were killed by the explosion he set off, he referred to them simply as "collateral damage." As for the survivors, he said, "I understand what they felt in Oklahoma City. I have no sympathy for them."

One Rational Justification

Of the four traditional justifications for punishment—reform, deterrence, incapacitation, and retribution—only one seems to be relevant to the McVeigh case and others like it:

• Reform is clearly not at issue here. The execution of a mass murderer, or of anyone else, for that matter, is not designed to improve his character or to persuade him to mend his evil ways.

• Deterrence is almost as irrelevant as reform in this case. There is ample evidence that critics of the death penalty are generally wrong in supposing that it is ineffective as a deterrent to other potentially violent criminals. Interviews with prisoners on death row prove only that some people are not deterred by the threat of death. No one has ever claimed that any penalty would effectively de-

---

1. McVeigh was executed on May 16, 2001.

ter every potential offender. A more meaningful inquiry would explore the relationship, if there is one, between fear of the death penalty and the fact that some people who have been tempted to commit serious crimes did not carry them out. In any event, deterrence alone would not be sufficient to justify McVeigh's execution. Potential mass murderers are not likely to deliberate over McVeigh's execution as they plan further acts of terrorism. Indeed, some terrorists welcome martyrdom. Others believe that, like many before them, they will either get away with their crimes because they will never be caught, or that if they are caught, their colleagues will engage in further acts of terrorism, taking hostages and demanding their release—a threat that has often been acceded to by the political authorities of many nations.

> *"[Retribution] is the only reasonable justification for the execution of most criminals against whom the death penalty is invoked."*

• Incapacitation is of course an absolute certainty when executions are carried out. Executed criminals are unable to pursue their criminal careers from beyond the grave. But terrorists and other evil people can be incapacitated with methods short of the death penalty. High security prisons are generally quite effective in preventing even the worst criminals from engaging in further serious mischief. If our purpose is simply to make an evil person harmless, death will certainly do the job, but it seems unnecessary since there are other ways of achieving the same result.

• Retribution, then, appears to be the only rational justification for the execution of Timothy McVeigh—assuming, of course, that capital punishment can be justified. Indeed, it is the only reasonable justification for the execution of most criminals against whom the death penalty is invoked. Reform is irrelevant, deterrence is speculative at best, and incapacitation can be achieved with far less controversy.

In the remainder of this article, I will examine the nature of retribution, its moral standing as a motive for criminal punishment, and the validity of using it as a rationale for inflicting capital punishment on violent criminals.

Is Vengeance Ours?

Retribution and revenge (or vengeance) bear some resemblance to one another, but some important distinctions must be noted. Revenge is essentially a private matter between the perpetrator and the victim or the victim's family. The avengers discussed in various parts of the Bible are of this type: individuals or family members seeking to exact private justice against a person they believed had wronged someone close to them. The blood feuds so vividiy portrayed in *Romeo and Juliet*, in tales from the Ozarks, and in the many stories of vendettas among Italian and Sicilian families derive from this desire for vengeance. They are based upon the assumption that the injured party or his or her clan has the right to punish the wrongdoer and to see that the harm done is exacted from the wrongdoer to a degree equal to or greater than that which he or she inflicted upon the victim. The remedy sought is essentially a private one: satisfaction of the desire of the injured parties to inflict evil upon the person or persons who harmed them or their loved one.

The law has often sanctioned private revenge. Ancient Middle Eastern law codes such as the code of Hammurabi contained provisions for the *lex talionis* (law of retaliation) and often employed language similar to several passages in the Hebrew Bible: a life for a life, an eye for an eye, a tooth for a tooth, and so on. The principal difference between those pre-biblical codes and the Bible itself is the fact that the pre-biblical codes sanctioned literally gouging out the perpetrator's eye or amputating a limb in retaliation for the loss of the eye or limb of the victim, while the biblical code appears instead to sanction some form of financial compensation for the victim's loss. In any event, the focus was always upon satisfaction of the victim of the crime or the tort. The law, as enforced by the king or his court, simply enabled the victim or the victim's family to mete out the penalty without interference from the legal system or the officials who administered it. The basic sense of the matter is very much like what we find in tort law, or the law of damages. A person who has lost an eye or a limb, for example, due to the negligence of his or her neighbor, is entitled to be paid for the loss at least to a degree equivalent to it. This is exceedingly difficult to do, of course,

> *"Retribution is a carefully calculated, reasoned, orderly process of exacting punishment."*

as it seems impossible to place a monetary value on an eye or a leg. The fact is, however, that judges and juries do exactly that every day of the week, assessing the value of eyes and legs and arms, and even lives, as best they can and imposing upon negligent automobile drivers, physicians, and manufacturers the duty to compensate their victims for losses sustained. In some cases, the court may add to the value of the limb itself the wages the victim has lost because of the injury, the medical expenses incurred, and the pain and humiliation he or she has suffered.

In contrast to such private or personal remedies, retribution is a concept that seems to have arisen with the development of the modern state and its enforcement of public criminal law. The sense that once an injustice has been done it must be corrected, made right, by a payment in kind by the wrongdoer was carried out by the state as the aggrieved party rather than the individual victim or his or her surrogates. The notion grew that the state itself was wronged by criminal behavior. Thus, cases came to be entitled *R. v. Smith*, i.e., The King (Rex) against Smith. Once the United States was formed as a republic without a king, criminal cases were entitled *State v. Jones, The People v. Smith*, or *Nebraska v. Owens*. Private individuals were no longer entitled to punish the wrongdoer.

Apprehension, trial, and punishment were all to be conducted by organs of the state itself. To some degree, they served as surrogates for the aggrieved parties. Note that the victims were no longer parties to the case. If they survived the damage the criminal had done them, they might serve as witnesses at trial, or bring a complaint to the authorities. The state, however, was considered to be the chief victim, for the perpetrators had broken its laws and shattered the peace of the realm. Through their actions, perpetrators had also brought fear and insecurity to all of the state's inhabitants and disturbed the equilibrium that prevails when members of a community live together in harmony and in accordance with the law. It was therefore the state's duty to punish them if it could satisfactorily establish that they were indeed at fault. Private vengeance, "taking the law into one's own hands," was forbidden and could result in criminal prosecution.

By the same token, the immediate victims of a crime could not provide amnesty or any other form of legal pardon to the criminals, for the injury was not theirs alone. The injury was inflicted upon the entire state collectively, and in a sense, upon each of its inhabitants. Although the prosecutor and the jury might give some consideration to pleas for mercy by the immediate victims, they were under no obligation to do so, and were entitled to ignore such pleas altogether.

The State's Business

Well-intentioned people sometimes urge crime victims to forgive the criminals who have victimized them. The immediate victims or their survivors may choose to act compassionately, if they wish, and they may in turn ask the state's representatives to treat the perpetrators mercifully. But they have no right to demand that the state do so, for it has its own agenda, its own priorities in dealing with criminals. And it has no obligation to accede to the wishes of individuals who have been harmed by the persons being prosecuted. The state's business is to protect its citizens from suffering preventable harm and exacting punishment from those who inflict such harm through their unlawful conduct.

It is not enough, however, to distinguish revenge and retribution on the ground that one is private and the other public. The drive for vengeance is a highly emotional determination to "get back at" the wrongdoer, while retribution is a carefully calculated, reasoned, orderly process of exacting punishment for the crime the perpetrator has committed. A vengeful father or brother may slaughter someone who is believed to have violated a female member of the family, without affording the accused a hearing and without giving due consideration to the appropriateness of the penalty relative to the injury allegedly sustained by the victim or

> *"Retribution is based . . . upon the sense that particular crimes warrant the imposition of certain penalties."*

24

others. Retribution is based upon the same basic concept: exacting a kind of payment from the wrongdoer for the crime committed. But the penalty for a given type of criminal behavior is considered before the particular case occurs,

"No crime is comparable to murder."

and is enacted into legislation by the authorities based upon a careful study of the law and after giving due consideration to the type of penalty appropriate for it. Thus, persons close to the victim do not set the penalty in the heat of passion. Instead, it is prescribed in a legal enactment after careful deliberation by the legislature, and is assessed by an impartial judge or jury only after due consideration of all of the relevant facts surrounding the case and in accordance with the law.

The Principles of Retribution

The basic principles behind retribution are these:
1. The state has the right to punish the wrongdoer for the crime he or she has committed.
2. The penalty should be proportionate to the crime.
3. So far as possible, the penalties imposed upon various persons for similar crimes should be equal.

Although it is impossible to be very precise in assessing penalties, because moral factors that are exceedingly difficult to quantify must be assessed, people generally have a sense of justice that enables them to agree, at least in a fairly rough way, as to the general parameters of penalties that they deem appropriate for various kinds of offenses.

There is general agreement, for example, that the proper penalty for overtime parking is a relatively small fine. The amount of such fines may vary from city to city because the seriousness of the offense varies. In the little village in which I live, the village council has determined that a ten-dollar fine is appropriate. In New York City, on the other hand, an overtime parking ticket may result in a fine of sixty dollars or more. Many factors enter into these calculations, including the relative difficulty of finding parking space in a particular community, the price of real estate and off-street parking (for it would hardly do to impose a fine so low that it is cheaper to pay the fine than to pay the fee of a parking lot or garage), and the desirability of encouraging people to patronize local merchants without making it too onerous for them to find suitable parking while they do so. On the other hand, everyone would surely agree that prison terms often to twenty years would be utterly disproportionate to the seriousness of the offense of overtime parking. Such prison terms would effectively discourage most overtime parkers and would get them off the streets. They would be seen, however, as a despotic abuse of governmental power disproportionate to our sense of justice.

Similarly, a fine of ten or twenty dollars for rape would be viewed as utterly inappropriate to the gravity of the crime. Indeed, such a "penalty" would amount to a license to commit the crime; it would even be less expensive than the going price of streetwalkers. Women would rightly feel outraged by a legislature that valued their bodily integrity so little as to create open season for sexual predators willing to pay a piddling fee. Because we feel that sexual violence causes such grievous injury and is so utterly despicable, we unhesitatingly impose heavy penalties upon those who engage in it.

Notice that this has little or nothing to do with deterrence, though fines and prison terms generally tend to deter such offenses, at least with most normal persons. If deterrence were our only object in setting penalties, we would make them as heavy as possible in order to deter potential violators. But we don't do that, because our sense of justice—our sense of proportionality—would be outraged by such a policy.

Retribution is based, then, upon the sense that particular crimes warrant the imposition of certain penalties. Those that are more severe in the harm they inflict upon their victims and upon society deserve harsher penalties than those that cause less damage or are perceived to be less morally iniquitous.

Due Process of Law

We have long taken it for granted that people are entitled to certain fundamental rights, enumerated in various political and philosophical works and in the founding documents of the United States as life, liberty, and property (or the pursuit of happiness). Possession of these rights implies a corresponding duty by the government not to interfere with them. However, under appropriate circumstances the Constitution (in the fifth and fourteenth amendments) recognizes that each of those fundamental rights may be forfeited, and provides that no person may be deprived of life, liberty, or property without due process of law. The obvious corollary of this provision is that with due process of law, a person may be deprived of property (e.g., by imposing a fine), liberty (e.g., by imprisonment), or life.

Our sense of justice and proportionality in punishment is embodied in the penal laws enacted by our state and federal legislatures, which have affixed varying degrees of penalties for the many varieties of harm that people can inflict upon the state. These penalties range from the least severe fines for minor violations to periods of incarceration for more serious crimes, and finally to the penalty of death for the gravest of all. Although many crimes once earned the perpetrator the penalty of death, relatively few such crimes remain on the books, at least in this country. Those few are among the most outrageous crimes known: the de-

> *"[We] ought to be offended by the suggestion that anything less than the death penalty is a suitable punishment for those who commit [monstrous] crimes."*

liberate, premeditated, wanton taking of innocent human life, terrorism, and others that entail gross violations of human rights and the security of the state and its citizens.

No crime is comparable to murder, for we see no right as more precious than the right to live one's life to the fullest. We find it impossible to imagine a greater evil than the deliberate extinction of a human life. A person whose life has come to an end is deprived forever of any pleasure, any happiness, any contact with other

> *"The state must be prepared to take the lives of those who violate their most fundamental obligations."*

people, any of the joys that life may offer; all those who loved the murder victim are forever deprived of the opportunity to express their love or to enjoy the companionship of their loved one; and the community loses the opportunity to benefit from the contributions that the ability, the talent, and the efforts of that person might have produced.

Just as our sense of proportionate justice is offended by the notion that a small fine would be an adequate penalty for the crime of rape, we are or ought to be offended by the suggestion that anything less than the death penalty is a suitable punishment for those who commit crimes as monstrous as those of Timothy McVeigh and others like him. McVeigh did far more than outrage the citizens of Oklahoma City. He destroyed close to two hundred human lives and all the potential that they might have enjoyed and contributed. The damage he did is incomparable and irreparable, both to those who died in the explosion he engineered and to those who loved them, as well as to the community whose laws he broke and whose tranquility he shattered. Consequently when he detonated his bomb, he forfeited all of the rights he had previously enjoyed, and the government that had nurtured and protected him was relieved of any duty it might have had to preserve and defend him. No penalty that anyone can exact from him can possibly begin to repair the damage he did. And it cannot satisfy or provide "closure" to the survivors of the devastation he caused. They will live the rest of their lives without "closure," for they will always remember and suffer from the losses that McVeigh inflicted upon them.

A Symbolic Statement

The execution of Timothy McVeigh is right and proper because it is the worst punishment our society can impose upon him without turning to barbarism and cruelty. The death penalty is a symbolic statement by our government that we have utter contempt for anyone who tramples upon our laws and violates the rights of our people to such a degree, and that we will not abide such a person's living in our midst. It is a declaration that any person who commits such a breach of our most fundamental norms is so unworthy as to have no right to live. And it announces to the world that the law must be obeyed, that people must bend their wills to obedience to the law, and that the state will use all measures necessary to see that they do.

The defense of human life is so central to the mission of every government that the state must be prepared to take the lives of those who violate their most fundamental obligations—that is, in retribution for their willful defiance of lawful authority as regards the preservation of human life and the maintenance of peace and security in their community. No other penalty can be remotely proportionate to the penalty of death for such crimes.

Capital Punishment Is Not Immoral

by Antonin Scalia

About the author: *Antonin Scalia is a justice of the Supreme Court of the United States.*

Editor's Note: This essay is adapted from remarks given at a conference sponsored by the Pew Forum on Religion and Public Life at the University of Chicago Divinity School.

Before proceeding to discuss the morality of capital punishment, I want to make clear that my views on the subject have nothing to do with how I vote in capital cases that come before the Supreme Court. That statement would not be true if I subscribed to the conventional fallacy that the Constitution is a "living document"—that is, a text that means from age to age whatever the society (or perhaps the Court) thinks it ought to mean.

The Arbiters of Evolving Standards

In recent years, that philosophy has been particularly well enshrined in our Eighth Amendment jurisprudence, our case law dealing with the prohibition of "cruel and unusual punishments." Several of our opinions have said that what falls within this prohibition is not static, but changes from generation to generation, to comport with "the evolving standards of decency that mark the progress of a maturing society." Applying that principle, the Court came close, in 1972, to abolishing the death penalty entirely. It ultimately did not do so, but it has imposed, under color of the Constitution, procedural and substantive limitations that did not exist when the Eighth Amendment was adopted—and some of which had not even been adopted by a majority of the states at the time they were judicially decreed. For example, the Court has prohibited the death penalty for all crimes except murder, and indeed even for what might be called run-of-the-mill murders, as opposed to those that are somehow characterized by a high degree of brutality or depravity. It has prohibited the mandatory imposition of the death penalty for any crime, insisting that in all cases the jury be permitted to consider all mitigating factors and to impose, if it wishes, a lesser sentence. And it has imposed an age limit at the time of the offense (it is currently seventeen) that is well above what existed at common law.

If I subscribed to the proposition that I am authorized (indeed, I suppose compelled) to intuit and impose our "maturing" society's "evolving standards of decency," this essay would be a preview of my next vote in a death penalty case. As it is, however, the Constitution that I interpret and apply

> *"The choice for the judge who believes the death penalty to be immoral is resignation."*

is not living but dead—or, as I prefer to put it, enduring. It means today not what current society (much less the Court) thinks it ought to mean, but what it meant when it was adopted. For me, therefore, the constitutionality of the death penalty is not a difficult, soul-wrenching question. It was clearly permitted when the Eighth Amendment was adopted (not merely for murder, by the way, but for all felonies—including, for example, horse-thieving, as anyone can verify by watching a western movie). And so it is clearly permitted today. There is plenty of room within this system for "evolving standards of decency," but the instrument of evolution (or, if you are more tolerant of the Court's approach, the herald that evolution has occurred) is not the nine lawyers who sit on the Supreme Court of the United States, but the Congress of the United States and the legislatures of the fifty states, who may, within their own jurisdictions, restrict or abolish the death penalty as they wish.

Part of "the Machinery of Death"

But while my views on the morality of the death penalty have nothing to do with how I vote as a judge, they have a lot to do with whether I can or should be a judge at all. To put the point in the blunt terms employed by Justice Harold Blackmun towards the end of his career on the bench, when he announced that he would henceforth vote (as Justices William Brennan and Thurgood Marshall had previously done) to overturn all death sentences, when I sit on a Court that reviews and affirms capital convictions, I am part of "the machinery of death." My vote, when joined with at least four others, is, in most cases, the last step that permits an execution to proceed. I could not take part in that process if I believed what was being done to be immoral.

Capital cases are much different from the other life-and-death issues that my Court sometimes faces: abortion, for example, or legalized suicide. There it is not the state (of which I am in a sense the last instrument) that is decreeing death, but rather private individuals whom the state has decided not to restrain. One may argue (as many do) that the society has a moral obligation to restrain. That moral obligation may weigh heavily upon the voter, and upon the legislator who enacts the laws; but a judge, I think, bears no moral guilt for the laws society has failed to enact. Thus, my difficulty with *Roe v. Wade*[1] is a legal rather than a moral one: I do not believe (and, for two hundred years, no one believed) that the Constitution contains a right to abortion. And if a state were to permit abortion on demand, I would—and could in good conscience—vote against all attempt to invalidate that law for the same reason that I vote against the invalidation of laws that forbid abortion on demand: because the Constitution gives the federal government (and hence me) no power over the matter. . . .

I pause here to emphasize the point that in my view the choice for the judge who believes the death penalty to be immoral is resignation, rather than simply ignoring duly enacted, constitutional laws and sabotaging death penalty cases. He has, after all, taken an oath to apply the laws and has been given no power to supplant them with rules of his own. Of course if he feels strongly enough he can go beyond mere resignation and lead a political campaign to abolish the death penalty—and if that fails, lead a revolution. But rewrite the laws he cannot do. This dilemma, of course, need not be confronted by a proponent of the "living Constitution," who believes that it means what it ought to mean. If the death penalty is (in his view) immoral, then it is (hey, presto!) automatically unconstitutional, and he can continue to sit while nullifying a sanction that has been imposed, with no suggestion of its unconstitutionality, since the beginning of the Republic. (You can see why the "living Constitution" has such attraction for us judges.)

Christian Tradition

It is a matter of great consequence to me, therefore, whether the death penalty is morally acceptable. As a Roman Catholic—and being unable to jump out of my skin—I cannot discuss that issue without reference to Christian tradition and the Church's Magisterium.

The death penalty is undoubtedly wrong unless one accords to the state a scope of moral action that goes beyond what is permitted to the individual. In my view, the major impetus behind modern aversion to the death penalty is the equation of private morality with governmental morality. This is a predictable (though I believe erroneous and regrettable) reaction to modern, democratic self-government.

> *"Government—however you want to limit that concept— derives its moral authority from God."*

Few doubted the morality of the death penalty in the age that believed in the divine right of kings. Or even in earlier times. St. Paul had this to say (I am quoting, as you might expect, the King James version):

Let every soul be subject unto the higher powers. For there is no power but of

---

1. *Roe v. Wade* is the 1973 U.S. Supreme Court decision that legalized abortion.

God: the powers that be are ordained of God. Whosoever therefore resisteth the power, resisteth the ordinance of God: and they that resist shall receive to themselves damnation. For rulers are not a terror to good works, but to the evil. Wilt thou then not be afraid of the power? Do that which is good, and thou shalt have praise of the same: for he is the minister of God to thee for good. But if thou do that which is evil, be afraid; for he beareth not the sword in vain: for he is the minister of God, a revenger to execute wrath upon him that doeth evil. Wherefore ye must needs be subject, not only for wrath, but also for conscience sake. (Romans 13:1–5)

This is not the Old Testament, I emphasize, but St. Paul. One can understand his words as referring only to lawfully constituted authority, or even only to lawfully constituted authority that rules justly. But the core of his message is that government—however you want to limit that concept—derives its moral authority from God. It is the "minister of God" with powers to "revenge," to "execute wrath," including even wrath by the sword

> *"The more Christian a country is the less likely it is to regard the death penalty as immoral."*

(which is unmistakably a reference to the death penalty). Paul of course did not believe that the individual possessed any such powers. Only a few lines before this passage, he wrote, "Dearly beloved, avenge not yourselves, but rather give place unto wrath: for it is written, Vengeance is mine; I will repay, saith the Lord." And in this world the Lord repaid—did justice—through His minister, the state.

The Effect of Secular Democracy

These passages from Romans represent the consensus of Western thought until very recent times. Not just of Christian or religious thought, but of secular thought regarding the powers of the state. That consensus has been upset, I think, by the emergence of democracy. It is easy to see the hand of the Almighty behind rulers whose forebears, in the dim mists of history, were supposedly anointed by God, or who at least obtained their thrones in awful and unpredictable battles whose outcome was determined by the Lord of Hosts, that is, the Lord of Armies. It is much more difficult to see the hand of God—or any higher moral authority—behind the fools and rogues (as the losers would have it) whom we ourselves elect to do our own will. How can their power to avenge—to vindicate the "public order"—be any greater than our own?

So it is no accident, I think, that the modern view that the death penalty is immoral is centered in the West. That has little to do with the fact that the West has a Christian tradition, and everything to do with the fact that the West is the home of democracy. Indeed, it seems to me that the more Christian a country is the less likely it is to regard the death penalty as immoral. Abolition has taken its firmest hold in post-Christian Europe, and has least support in the churchgoing United States. I attribute that to the fact that, for the believing Christian, death is no big deal. Intentionally killing an innocent person is a big deal: it is a grave sin, which causes one to lose his soul. But losing this life, in exchange for the next? The Christian attitude is reflected in the words Robert Bolt's play has Thomas More saying to the headsman: "Friend, be not afraid of your office. You send me to God." And when Cranmer asks whether he is sure of that, More replies, "He will not refuse one who is so blithe to go to Him." For the nonbeliever, on the other hand, to deprive a man of his life is to end his existence. What a horrible act!

Besides being less likely to regard death as an utterly cataclysmic punishment, the Christian is also more likely to regard punishment in general as deserved. The doctrine of free will—the ability of man to resist temptations to evil, which God will not permit beyond man's capacity to resist—is central to the Christian doctrine of salvation and damnation, heaven and hell. The post-Freudian secularist, on the other hand, is more inclined to think that people are what their history and circumstances have made them, and there is little sense in assigning blame.

Of course those who deny the authority of a government to exact vengeance are not entirely logical. Many crimes—for example, domestic murder in the heat of passion—are neither deterred by punishment meted out to others nor likely to be committed a second time by the same offender. Yet opponents of capital punishment do not object to sending such an offender to prison, perhaps for life. Because he deserves punishment. Because it is just.

Government and Divine Authority

The mistaken tendency to believe that a democratic government, being nothing more than the composite will of its individual citizens, has no more moral power or authority than they do as individuals has adverse effects in other areas as well. It fosters civil disobedience, for example, which proceeds on the assumption that what the individual citizen considers an unjust law—even if it does not compel him to act unjustly—need not be obeyed. St. Paul would not agree. "Ye must needs be subject," he said, "not only for wrath, but also for conscience sake." For conscience sake. The reaction of people of faith to this tendency of democracy to obscure the divine authority behind government should not be resignation to it, but the resolution to combat it as effectively as possible.

> *"Government carries the sword as 'the minister of God' to 'execute wrath' upon the evildoer."*

We have done that in this country (and continental Europe has not) by preserving in our public life many visible reminders that—in the words of a Supreme Court opinion from the 1940s—"we are a religious people, whose institutions presuppose a Supreme Being." These reminders include: "In God we trust" on our coins, "one nation, under God" in our Pledge of Allegiance, the opening of sessions of our legislatures with a prayer, the opening of sessions of my Court with "God save the United States and this Honorable Court," annual Thanksgiving proclamations issued by our President at the direction of Congress, and constant invocations of divine support in the speeches of our political leaders, which often conclude, "God bless America." All this, as I say, is most unEuropean, and helps explain why our people are more inclined to understand, as St. Paul did, that government carries the sword as "the minister of God," to "execute wrath" upon the evildoer.

> *"Can one possibly say with a straight face that nowadays [the death penalty] would 'rarely if ever' be appropriate?"*

A brief story about the aftermath of [the terrorist attack of] September 11 [2001], nicely illustrates how different things are in secularized Europe. I was at a conference of European and American lawyers and jurists in Rome when the planes struck the twin towers. All in attendance were transfixed by the horror of the event, and listened with rapt attention to the President's ensuing address to the nation. When the speech had concluded, one of the European conferees—a religious man—confided in me how jealous he was that the leader of my nation could conclude his address with the words "God bless the United States." Such invocation of the deity, he assured me, was absolutely unthinkable in his country, with its Napoleonic tradition of extirpating religion from public life. It will come as no surprise from what I have said that I do not agree with the encyclical *Evangelium Vitae* and the new Catholic catechism (or the very latest version of the new Catholic catechism), according to which the death penalty can only be imposed to protect rather than avenge, and that since it is (in most modern societies) not necessary for the former purpose, it is wrong. That, by the way, is how I read those documents—and not, as Avery Cardinal Dulles would read them, simply as an affirmation of two millennia of Christian teaching that retribution is a proper purpose (indeed, the principal purpose) of criminal punishment, but merely adding the "prudential judgment" that in modern circumstances condign retribution "rarely if ever" justifies death. I cannot square that interpretation with the following passage from the encyclical:

> It is clear that, for these [permissible purposes of penal justice] to be achieved, the nature and extent of the punishment must be carefully evaluated and decided upon, and ought not go to the extreme of executing the offender except in cases of absolute necessity: in other words, when it would not be possible otherwise to defend society. Today, however, as a result of steady improvements in the organization of the penal system, such cases are very rare, if not practically nonexistent. . . .

How in the world can modernity's "steady improvements in the organization of the penal system" render the death penalty less condign for a particularly heinous crime? One might think that commitment to a really horrible penal system (Devil's Island, for example) might be almost as bad as death. But nice clean cells with television sets, exercise rooms, meals designed by nutritionists, and conjugal visits? That would seem to render the death penalty more, rather than less, necessary. So also would the greatly increased capacity for evil—the greatly increased power to produce moral "disorder"—placed in individual hands by modern technology. Could St. Paul or St. Thomas even have envisioned a crime by an individual (as opposed to one by a ruler, such as Herod's slaughter of the innocents) as enormous as that of [Oklahoma City bomber] Timothy McVeigh or of the men who destroyed three thousand innocents in the World Trade Center? If just retribution is a legitimate purpose (indeed, the principal legitimate purpose) of capital punishment, can one possibly say with a straight face that nowadays death would "rarely if ever" be appropriate?

Disagreeing with the Catholic Church

So I take the encyclical and the latest, hot-off-the-presses version of the catechism (a supposed encapsulation of the "deposit" of faith and the Church's teaching regarding a moral order that does not change) to mean that retribution is not a valid purpose of capital punishment. Unlike such other hard Catholic doctrines as the prohibition of birth control and of abortion, this is not a moral position that the Church has always—or indeed ever before—maintained. There have been Christian opponents of the death penalty, just as there have been Christian pacifists, but neither of those positions has ever been that of the Church. The current predominance of opposition to the death penalty is the legacy of Napoleon, Hegel, and Freud rather than St. Paul and St. Augustine. I mentioned earlier Thomas More, who has long been regarded in this country as the patron saint of lawyers, and who has recently been declared by the Vatican the patron saint of politicians (I am not sure that is a promotion). One of the charges leveled by that canonized saint's detractors was that, as Lord Chancellor, he was too quick to impose the death penalty.

I am therefore happy to learn from the canonical experts I have consulted that the position set forth in *Evangelium Vitae* and in the latest version of the Catholic catechism does not purport to be binding teaching—that is, it need not be accepted by practicing Catholics, though they must give it thoughtful and respectful consideration. It would be remarkable to think otherwise—that a couple of paragraphs in an encyclical almost entirely devoted not to crime and punishment but to abortion and euthanasia was intended authoritatively to sweep aside (if one could) two thousand years of Christian teaching.

> *"I do not find the death penalty immoral."*

So I have given this new position thoughtful and careful consideration—and I disagree. That is not to say I favor the death penalty (I am judicially and judiciously neutral on that point); it is only to say that I do not find the death penalty immoral. I am happy to have reached that conclusion, because I like my job, and would rather not resign. And I am happy because I do not think it would be a good thing if American Catholics running for legislative office had to oppose the death penalty (most of them would not be elected); if American Catholics running for Governor had to promise commutation of all death sentences (most of them would never reach the Governor's mansion); if American Catholics were ineligible to go on the bench in all jurisdictions imposing the death penalty; or if American Catholics were subject to recusal when called for jury duty in capital cases.

I find it ironic that the Church's new (albeit non-binding) position on the death penalty—which, if accepted, would have these disastrous consequences—is said to rest upon "prudential considerations." Is it prudent, when one is not certain enough about the point to proclaim it in a binding manner (and with good reason, given the long and consistent Christian tradition to the contrary), to effectively urge the retirement of Catholics from public life in a country where the federal government and thirty-eight of the states (comprising about 85 percent of the population) believe the death penalty is sometimes just and appropriate? Is it prudent to imperil acceptance of the Church's hard but traditional teachings on birth control and abortion and euthanasia (teachings that have been proclaimed in a binding manner, a distinction that the average Catholic layman is unlikely to grasp) by packaging them—under the wrapper "respect for life"—with another uncongenial doctrine that everyone knows does not represent the traditional Christian view? Perhaps, one is invited to conclude, all four of them are recently made-up. We need some new staffers at the Congregation of Prudence in the Vatican. At least the new doctrine should have been urged only upon secular Europe, where it is at home.

Capital Punishment Is Necessary

by Andrew Jones

About the author: *Andrew Jones was a second-year political science student at the University of California at Los Angeles when he wrote this essay.*

It is no triumph that death sentences are routinely carried out, or even that such a device is necessary within our society. Yet the fact remains that society does require a death penalty, and to believe that the topic is one-sided or easily answered would be a fatal mistake. It is best to note the absolutes of the death penalty—first, that once it is carried out, there is no reversing the outcome. It seems an obvious point, but it is worth remembering, as it warns us that state-sanctioned executions must never be taken lightly.

Just as firm is the fact that in most cases, the death penalty is a matter of justice and equality. With most crimes, the purposes of the punishment are to rehabilitate the convict and to send a warning to others who would commit similar crimes. In contrast, the death penalty intends neither to rehabilitate nor dissuade others from capital crimes.

A Matter of Justice

Certainly, the threat of the ultimate penalty may give pause to a small percentage, but most capital cases involve a defendant who is far from rational enough to weigh the costs and benefits of his action.

Still, this misconception of the death penalty as a deterrent is one limp argument constantly trotted out against capital punishment. Many people ask, "If the death penalty is working, why isn't the murder rate falling?"

The answer is that the death penalty is a matter of justice and societal preservation. Some crimes [are] so abhorrent, the convict does not deserve to continue living. We do not live completely in the days of Hammurabi's "eye for an eye," but neither have we come close to a crime-free utopia which would allow the end of the death penalty. Instead, we compromise, reserving execution for the most serious crimes and filtering the decision through a jury of 12 peers and a presiding judge.

The Need for Caution

It cannot be denied that in many states, capital punishment is completely broken or barely functioning. The Illinois death penalty moratorium enacted in 1999 was an intelligent response to one state's miserable record in the application of justice. The student journalists who worked to free a number of wrongly convicted men on the state's death row may have been sharp, but they were far from young Alan Dershowitzes.[1]

This raises the question: how did these poor slobs slip through the cracks for all these years? The evidence which originally "convicted" them was in several cases extremely thin, based merely on eyewitness accounts from unreliable witnesses who had other

> *"Society does require a death penalty."*

motives. Thus, it may be a wise move for each state to emphasize extreme caution in imposing the death penalty.

Certainly it is within their rights for a state or municipality to focus their prosecution exclusively on the aspects of a case which will prove most likely to convict a defendant. This is all well and good for non-capital cases, where, if a wrongful conviction results, the innocent may rot unjustly in jail for many years—but at least no one is executed.

But when a prosecutor in a capital case intentionally ignores strong evidence that could exonerate a defendant or presses ahead despite gaping holes in his case, leading to a questionable conviction, the result is negative public perception of an integral part of the justice system.

The Success of Texas

The mere fact, however, that same states are under moratoriums does not mean that the system is broken nationwide. Take the example of Texas: every liberal within shouting distance certainly does. Texas, so it seems, is a bloodthirsty, crude and inhuman sort of state.

Liberals know this because they read sad stories about the people on death row, such as Karla Faye Tucker. She claimed to find religion while on death row and proceeded to "rehabilitate" herself, at least as judged by her fellow inmates and prison guards. In these teary tales, little mention was made of the brutal crime which landed Tucker on death row in the first place. Namely, she was convicted of murdering two innocents with a pick-axe.

To conclude that because Texas executes more people than any other state, it is doing something wrong, would ignore the circumstances in Texas relative to

---

1. Alan Dershowitz is a renowned criminal defense lawyer and Harvard Law School professor.

the rest of the nation. Texas puts more people to death because of many factors: it has the second-largest population in the Union, has a high crime rate compared to other states, and most saliently, has a justice system which does not drag its feet in carrying out sentences.

It is assumed, and rightly so, that people on death row are there to be executed for their heinous crimes right away without having to spend decades waiting for a resolution. In reality, Texas is not rushing convicts through the process. A fact-based comparison reveals that the average time for convicts on death row is quite similar in Texas and the largest state in the nation.

In the period since the 1978 Supreme Court reversal of its previous death penalty ban, the average time for convicts on death row in California has been 14 years, 10 months. Texas, supposedly a veritable charnel-house, averages a wait of 10.61 years. Now the obvious difference: in the post-1978 period, California, the nation's most populous state, has executed all of 9 men, while 591 are waiting on death row. In Texas, 242 men and women have been put to death, with 446 awaiting their fate. What should we make of this?

It is evident, by average time served, that Texas is giving convicts more than enough time in which to exhaust every possible legal avenue, just as in California. The main difference seems to be that when convicts have used all their legal channels, the state carries out the sentence. So apparently, Texas' crime is this: following procedure in carrying out death sentences.

Hypocrites in Reverse

Another rather obvious argument used by opponents is a stilted portrayal of death penalty supporters. An image is presented of Bible-thumping evangelical Christians, "attacking" a "woman's right to choose" while simultaneously howling for criminals to be put to death. This is rich hypocrisy, right? These crazy right-wing zealots want some people to live, but other people to die!

Well, if such a thing is hypocrisy, then pro-choice/anti–death penalty supporters are simply hypocrites in reverse. But consider this: who's most innocent? The unborn child, or a merciless killer? Speaking relatively, of which the secular left is so fond, those right-wing zealots do seem to have reason and logic on their side. The fetal child we know is innocent; conversely, we can be certain that death row convicts have done something to get themselves into their current situation. Therefore, if someone has to die, it would seem that we would choose the guiltiest person.

While no advocate of the death penalty enjoys the idea or triumphs in the latest execution, simply shrugging at the horror of some crimes makes a mockery of equal protection under the law, and more importantly, the primacy of justice within our community. The death penalty enjoys such strong support—66 percent even after the recent stumbles in some states—because most people recognize its important role.

Capital Punishment Cannot Be Justified

by Sunil Dutta

About the author: *Sunil Dutta is a sergeant of the Los Angeles, California, police department.*

A few months before the birth of Israel, my family lost our ancestral home in the village of Kanjrur-Duttan, a village where Duttas had lived since the time of Emperor Babar. Kanjrur-Duttan happened to be on the wrong side of the line when India was divided in two (Hindu India and Muslim Pakistan) by British colonialists. The entire Hindu village fled in the dark of the night to escape being massacred by a rampaging mob of Muslim goons who were looting, raping, and murdering. Some did not make it, and were caught and slaughtered.

My great-grand uncle became a dispenser of retributive justice. He joined a roving gang of Hindu vigilantes in the border town of Dera Baba Nanak, where he extracted revenge for the murder of his mother and sisters. He killed many Muslim refugees who were trekking defenselessly in the opposite direction from my family—towards the newly created Pakistan from the Hindu-majority India. During my visit to India . . . , I sat across from him and asked if he felt remorse for what he had done during the time when the entire Indian subcontinent had been submerged into a bloodbath in which almost one million people died. He avoided my gaze and kept puffing at his cigarette. I persisted, "Do you ever think that people you killed were also innocent refugees, just like you and the family members we lost?" The old man looked down and defiantly said, "I may have killed some innocent people, but there must have been some sinners in there too!"

When people play God and dispense the Ultimate Justice, they create Himalayan blunders. Whether they are avenging the blood of their family members by slitting their enemies' throats, blowing them up with bombs, or passing orders to execute criminals while sitting on their judge's throne, human beings cannot morally justify taking another human's life.

Sunil Dutta, "Humans Playing God: Capital Punishment and Its Follies," *Tikkun*, vol. 17, July/August 2002, p. 17. Copyright © 2002 by the Institute for Labor and Mental Health. Reproduced by permission of *Tikkun*: A Bimonthly Jewish Critique of Politics, Culture & Society. www.tikkun.org.

Chapter 1

A Serious Failure in Humanity

As a police officer, I often see the results of human depravity. I see incidents of such brutal behavior that my compassion dissolves like a candle flame swept by a tornado. I vividly remember responding to a double homicide scene. . . . The bodies on the grass were covered with white sheets. As soon as the news helicopters hovering above us left, detectives pulled the sheets off to look at the victims. An elderly woman with a ghostly expression stared at me through hollow eyes. Her neck was almost severed. Her skin was burnt and peeling; her body was giving off smoke. A blood-soaked, semi-burnt shirt was sticking to the torso of her husband. Though his body was badly burnt, the watch on his left wrist was still working.

The murderer had viciously executed his frail victims by slitting their throats, then started a fire to cover up the crime. The gentle couple, loved by their neighbors, had been married for the last fifty years. Now they were dead. I stood silently, shaken by human savagery that no other animal could match.

The crime-scene photographer walked slowly to me and whispered, "I hope they find the guy and hang him!" She sees a lot in her job, but the brutality of the crime and the elderly age of the victims had visibly shaken her. I didn't have the courage to tell her that executing the depraved killers would not turn back the clock and erase this blot on the sheer fabric of humanity. As I looked at the young photographer, I thought, would I have the courage to look into the eyes of the victims' daughter and self-righteously proclaim that the death penalty is immoral? Could I emphatically say that the cold-blooded monster who planned this robbery and viciously murdered these defenseless people could or should be rehabilitated? No. It would be presumptuous of me to tell the victims' families that I feel their pain. It would be even more preposterous to ask them to forgive the murderer and not root for capital punishment.

Nevertheless, although I am deeply aware of the suffering that murder causes, I don't believe the death penalty can be justified. When I find myself faced with murder, I think about my great-uncle, who used senseless murder to justify senseless murder. The practice of capital punishment, particularly by our "justice system," reveals a serious failure in our humanity. We no longer burn witches or keep slaves or have monarchs dictate our lives. Capital punishment is similarly anachronistic.

I am not some soft-hearted ignoramus arguing for going easy on murderers. As a police officer, I am sometimes confronted by vicious people who have so lost their human-

> *"Human beings cannot morally justify taking another human's life."*

ity that they don't belong in any neighborhood. Some are such cold-blooded killers and others bring such misery to the world around them that they should be locked up forever. I want the people who calculatingly and brutally murder others to pay severely for their heinous crimes. Wanting to keep dangerous people out of society is different, however, from wanting to respond to violence with violence. No society can reach a peaceful existence if its people resolve their problems with violence.

Playing God

I have heard many arguments in favor of capital punishment. For example, some people argue that if I kill someone, I give up my right to live. That principle would qualify as a moral argument only if it were applied evenly. However, we do not sentence every murderer to death. Why isn't a reckless drunk driver who kills an entire family not sentenced to death? Because murders are different from each other, is the response—some are more cruel than others. But how do we quantitatively measure the heinousness of a murder? When mistake-prone humans send some criminals to the death chamber and others to prison are we not appropriating God's authority? What could be more immoral?

Not only do we play the role of God by judging who will die and who will live, by supporting the death penalty we send out the dangerous message to impressionable minds that violence is a way to resolve problems. "Thou shalt not kill" cannot be taught by the state-sponsored execution of criminals. To tell others not to kill by killing someone makes a mockery of the message. We need only to look around the world to remember that subservience to violence as a way to resolve problems has brought us perpetual misery and suffering: just look at Israel, Kashmir, East Timor, Rwanda, Serbia . . .

> *"We no longer burn witches or keep slaves or have monarchs dictate our lives. Capital punishment is similarly anachronistic."*

Capital Punishment Is Flawed

Death penalty support in law-enforcement comes from a deeply-held conviction by police officers that it is a deterrent. Demagogues exploit the fear of crime in the community and use their support for capital punishment as a badge of honor. As a police officer myself, I can emphatically state that many of my colleagues are wrong: the death penalty has no deterrent effect on crime. Capital punishment fails to deter those who commit crimes of passion. Capital punishment also has no dissuading power over criminals who are opportunistic, calculating, or overcome by drugs. A person taking a chance that he will not be caught for the crime he is planning to commit does not discriminate between the death penalty and life in prison without parole. Killing a criminal will prevent him from committing another crime—but so will putting him behind bars forever.

The only practical justification for the death penalty is revenge and punishment. I am not one to defend the actions of murderers. After seeing the pain and loss faced by the victims' families and the cruelty of remorseless killers, I do not find merit in the argument that criminal behavior can be explained away by childhood abuse or a lack of opportunities and therefore excused. I know count-less people who grew up in miserably wretched conditions and turned out to be caring adults. I also cannot fault a victim's family's demand for revenge. Only those who have lost their family members at the hands of vicious reprobates have the right to make such judgements. However, even as a means of revenge, the death penalty is an absolute failure. Candlelight vigils, media coverage, and an end-

> *"No society can reach a peaceful existence if its people resolve their problems with violence."*

less judicial process turns the criminal into a celebrity while the victim's family seethes with resentment, sometimes for decades! Not only does the criminal be-come glorified, the taxpayer-subsidized court costs are horrendous. Victims are re-victimized repeatedly as the loss of their dear ones is downplayed and they are portrayed as despicable people because some of them want the execution to proceed. This sort of revenge is not sweet. Despite the hopes of most pro-death penalty victims, executing criminals does not necessarily bring resolution and healing to the victim's family. In a calculated act so depraved that even sick people would deplore it, Reynaldo Rodriguez walked into the wealthy suburban home of his ex-girlfriend Maria Calderon in Simi Valley and systematically killed three of her family members and wounded two others. After his heinous crime, he drove to a campground in Los Padres National Forest and killed him-self. Maria Calderon's feelings reveal the profound flaw in capital punishment. She said to the *Los Angeles Times*, "I would have much rather he stayed alive. That way he could face the justice system and live with the fact that he mur-dered three people, and suffer what we're suffering. Now he took his own life—and he's not suffering anymore."

Miscarriages of Justice

Even if we were to accept the arguments in favor of capital punishment, the clearest reason to forego killing criminals comes from the inevitable miscar-riage of the punishment itself. I shudder at the fact that ninety-four innocent in-dividuals in the last decade were released from death row. They had been wrongfully condemned to death for crimes they did not commit. Some were minutes from execution. For each person exonerated, how many innocent people have we executed? This utter disgrace should make members of the criminal justice system hang their heads in shame. I cannot even imagine the anguish of a wasted life, the years away from friends and family, the disrepute and shame suffered by these poor souls who spent precious moments of their lives locked away in a maximum security prison for crimes they did not com-mit. What does the sword hanging over one's head do to the psyche of a wronged person who awaits the hand of the executioner while the appeals pro-cess is being exhausted? Frank Lee Smith was convicted of a 1985 rape and murder and condemned to death row. Smith died in prison after spending fifteen years there. His innocence was proven by DNA tests after his death! This is only one of many poignant examples that cries out loud against capital punishment.

In many of these cases, nothing in the legal appeals process helped uncover the innocence of these wrongly convicted individuals. Instead, it was investigations conducted by journalists or college students, or the confessions of the true perpetrators of these crimes that helped to exonerate the innocent. In fact, the justice system has at times worked to wrongly criminalize the innocent. Reckless prosecutors and police lab chemist teams like Robert Macy and Joyce Gilchrist of Oklahoma have been criticized for playing with the rules to convict people in murder trials. This makes a mockery of the system when professional enforcers of the law mangle the spirit of the law to get convictions, forcing outsiders to rescue the hapless victims of the criminal justice system.

People also make mistakes; research shows that even eyewitnesses are unable to recall events accurately. Yet we brazenly act as if we were God and condemn people to death, calmly ignoring that we are mistake-prone humans. Furthermore, our history is replete with stories of governments framing people they did not like. Individuals such as Geronimo Pratt can attest to the effectiveness with which innocent people can be framed by a determined government. Criminal cops such as Rafael Perez ride roughshod over prosecutors and juries and railroad people into prison or worse. Corruption in FBI crime labs, lying forensic analysts, biased juries, and prosecutors bending to local politics make a dangerous mixture, making the legal process highly unsafe for those on the lower socio-economic stratum of the society. I am not saying that a majority of people on death row are innocent; most are brutal killers who deserve to be there. However, even if a minute fraction of individuals on death row are innocent, it is immoral to support capital punishment. When our government executes an innocent person in our name, all of society is responsible for the death of that innocent person.

At least the members of death row in the United States had the opportunity to go to trial. To see the logical extension of this willingness to kill in the name of the state we need only look to Israel, which in [2002] has begun an even more brazen and barbaric application of capital punishment: the selective assassination by the Israeli government of those suspected of being involved in terrorist activities. It is a disgrace that a government can indulge in such a sinister practice. Even in the United States, an argument to execute hard-core gang members in the inner-city because that would prevent them from killing others would jolt the conscience of the most callused hard-on-crime person. The pre-emptive executions of "sus-

> *"'Thou shalt not kill' cannot be taught by the state-sponsored execution of criminals."*

pected" terrorists by the Israeli government are based on similarly fallacious reasoning. What about proving someone's guilt before meting out the ultimate punishment? Not only do such executions backfire and lead to more violence against the Israeli people, they result in a complete loss of moral authority for the state; we should take heed from this example of the inherent immorality of the state playing God.

Alternatives to the Death Penalty

People have asked me whether I would support capital punishment if the criminal is absolutely identified beyond a shadow of a doubt. What if the wickedness of the crime shocks the conscience of everyone? The dastardly bombing in Oklahoma by Timothy McVeigh and the evil mass murder [on] September [11, 2001], of people in the World Trade Center come to mind. Is it moral and practical to execute a terrorist whose sole reason for existence is causing pain and suffering? Well, I don't think that capital punishment would make such terrorists rethink the shallowness of their reasoning and understand the insanity of their behavior. Instead, we would make them martyrs. Capital punishment is not a deterrent to these terrorists, but a goad. It is more important to look to social and political circumstances to prevent such monumental catastrophes from happening.

Instead of using the death penalty to express society's rage at wanton murder, we would be better off forcing remorseless and callous criminals to confront their depravity and make them realize how much pain they cause to others. It would be even more useful to turn our energies away from revenge on the perpetrators of crime and concentrate them instead on community support for the victims, who are often neglected as the criminal justice system focuses on retribution. Those of us who oppose the death penalty should never concentrate our efforts solely on the manifold problems of the death penalty or, as some do, on the humanity of the killer. We must pay equal attention to compassionate support for the families and other loved ones of the victims. We must feel the loss, agony, and anger of the survivors, and build social and institutional support for them. It is as immoral to ignore the pain of the victims as it is to support capital punishment.

An effective alternative to the death penalty exists. Life in prison without parole is moral, practical, and far less expensive than the complicated process that leads to the death chamber. With life imprisonment, the cold-blooded murderer is removed from society and immediately forgotten, so that attention can be turned to the victims and their needs.

Revenge may bring momentary satisfaction, but only the potential to reach into someone's callused heart can bring healing. We cannot be a civilized society while we indulge in hatred and consign forgiveness to the sidelines. Anyone can be a knee-jerk reactionary and demand blood; it takes enormous courage to forgive the depraved who have caused us such enormous pain and sorrow.

Capital Punishment Does Not Grant Reasonable Retribution

by Marvin E. Wolfgang

About the author: *Marvin E. Wolfgang is a professor of law and criminology at the University of Pennsylvania.*

There is no rationale of punishment or disposition of a convicted offender that requires the death penalty. No logic of any rationale leads ineluctably to the death penalty. What are these rationales? Retribution, expiation, the utilitarian notion of deterrence, rehabilitation, social protection, or defense. We know they are not mutually exclusive except in abstract analysis, perhaps not even in that.

Weak Arguments

Several of these I should like to dispense with quickly because either the argument of the rationale clearly does not lead to the death penalty, or the evidence required to support the argument for the death penalty is weak, inadequate, or inconclusive. Death is not expiatory for the offender, for expiation implies that the offender has atoned for his guilt and is now cleansed in this life so he is free to accept the grace of God or a God-surrogate in the name of the state. Rehabilitation also requires life to continue so the former offending person can be restored to a life of social conformity. Deterrence is an unproven case. The Committee on Deterrent and Incapacitative Effects, of the National Research Council, National Academy of Science, concluded, after extensive research on crime in general and the death penalty in particular, that "in summary, the flaws . . . lead the Panel to conclude that the results of the analyses on capital punishment provide no useful evidence on the deterrent effect of capital punishment."

What is left? Social protection and retribution. But social protection is so closely linked to deterrence and the utilitarian position that we need not pursue it further. Moreover, the social protection argument can lead to the undesirable consequences of executing potentially "dangerous" violent offenders and those who, as in the case of the Soviet penal code of the late 1920s and early 1930s, are "socially dangerous" to the state, even though they may not have committed any other specifically designated capital crime.

Retribution would appear to contain the most reasonable logic leading to the death penalty. Part of the reasoning in retribution theory includes [English philosopher Thomas] Hobbes's notion of establishing an equilibrium, of restoring the state of being to what it had been before the offensive behavior had been committed. Strict homeostasis cannot be achieved with

> *"No logic of any rationale leads ineluctably to the death penalty."*

the death penalty for, as we all know, the victim of a killing cannot be restored. Nor is the abstract sense of equilibrium satisfied by execution, that is, the *lex talionis*, eye for an eye, tooth for a tooth. For retribution requires pain equal to that inflicted on the victim, plus an additional pain for committing the crime, crossing the threshold from law-abiding to law-violative behavior.

The Opposition to Corporal Punishment

The state's killing of a convicted offender, especially under the medically protective circumstances now used, is not likely to cause him as much pain as he inflicted on his victim. Even if the pain to each were the same, the second requirement of retribution is not met—namely, the pain to be inflicted for the crime per se. What then would meet the requirement? A torturous execution? Perhaps, but that solution conflicts with other attitudes in our society, particularly those concerned with physical assaults by or in the name of the state. Apparently, Western society considers corporal punishment an anathema of civilization. We permit the police to shoot at fleeing felons under certain circumstances, but even this act is discouraged unless life is endangered. Physical force may be used to arrest a suspect. But once a suspect is arrested, we mount glorious attacks against any physical abuse of arrestees, detainees, and defendants. We decry inadequate diets and urge good medical care for prisoners. The philosophy of our health delivery system is such that we must present our sacrifice to the rationalization for death in good physical condition. The state has made efforts to reduce the suffering of death in most exquisite ways.

Thus, there is a strong cultural opposition to corporal punishment. Western society today would not tolerate, I am sure, cutting off limbs, gouging out eyes, or splitting the tongue. Even for murder, there would be opposition to "partial execution" (i.e., cutting off legs, cutting of the penis, etc.). If we cringe at the thought of eliminating part of the corporal substance, is it logical to eliminate the total corpus?

Rational Retribution

A principal part of the rationale of retribution is proportional sentencing. Cesare Beccaria, Jeremy Bentham, and other rationalists recognized the principle. The "just desserts" or "commensurate desserts" model amply anticipates it. Beccaria's scales of seriousness of crime and severity of sanction were meant to be proportional. Equal punishment for equal crime does not mean that the punishment should be exactly like the crime but that the ratios of sanction severity should have a corresponding set of ratios of crime seriousness.

Moreover, punishment can or should be expressed in equivalences rather than in the same physical form of the crime. For example, we do not prescribe state-inflicted injuries for offenders who have injured but not killed their victims. It is not banal to argue this point because it is critical to the logic of capital punishment. If the victim has been assaulted and then treated by a physician and discharged or is hospitalized, the state does not exact the same penalty for the offender. We do not in the name of the state stab, shoot, throw acid, maim, or mug persons convicted of such aggravated assaults. Where, then, is the rational logic for retention of the death penalty for inflicting death?

Instead, equivalences in pain are sought in kind, not in physical exactitude. The common commodity of pain in our democratic society is deprivation of liberty over time, measured in days, months, and years. Other forms of deprivation are subsumed under this deprivation. It is but a reasonable extension of the equivalences between deprivation of liberty for crimes less than murder and the same deprivation for longer periods of time for the crime of homicide.

In the Beccarian mode, more can be said about the "pains of imprisonment." Death eliminates all. It does away with guilt, frustration, aspiration achievement disparities, desires for unattained and unattainable things, anxieties, and fears. By execution, the state deprives itself of the functioning of these self-inflicted punishments and of those punishments derived from the deprivation of liberty. Death ends all pain, and the offender is punished no more.

Capital Punishment Is Immoral

by Camille D'Arienzo

About the author: *Camille D'Arienzo, a Catholic sister, is president of the Brooklyn Regional Community of the Sisters of Mercy of the Americas and president of the Leadership Conference of Women Religious.*

The inmate seated at the head of the table in the small counseling room at the U.S. Federal Penitentiary in Allenwood, Pennsylvania, wore chains about his torso and feet. The tears that splattered his manacled hands resting on the table before him were a sign of his remorse for the crime that had placed him on death row.

"If only I knew why I killed Andrew," he said over and over again. "He was no threat to me. Why did I do that? Why did I take his life? I know God has forgiven me, but I can't forgive myself."

My friend Edward Doherty and I had made the four-hour trip from New York in response to a letter addressed to our Cherish Life Circle—a group of sisters, priests, and laypeople who circulate the Declaration of Life, which expresses the signer's absolute opposition to capital punishment.

The inmate requested two things of our circle: prayers—for himself, for his victim Andrew Marti, and for the Marti family—and a spiritual guide to accompany him during the final phase of his life.

Deep Remorse

David Paul Hammer has spent 21 of his 40 years on earth behind bars. He was in solitary confinement when he strangled the prisoner assigned to his cell.

He asked us: "Why did you decide to take this long trip to visit me?"

"It was the tone of your letter, David," I replied. "You took full responsibility for Andrew's murder and the other crimes you've committed before that. It was your deep remorse that brought us to you."

Ed explained that remorse is the first step on the road to repentance. Repen-

Camille D'Arienzo, "Stop This in Memory of Me," *U.S. Catholic*, vol. 65, June 2000, p. 29. Copyright © 2000 by Claretian Publications. Reproduced by permission.

tance paves the way for forgiveness and the possibility of reconciliation and inner peace so needed by this tortured killer.

David's first letter expressed his desire to die as a way of bringing peace to Marti's family. Ed suggested that living a converted life, rather than surrendering it to the state, would provide him with a better avenue for reconciliation with Marti's family.

"I can't believe God wills your execution," he said. Ed reminded David of the story of the prodigal son, assuring him that God's capacity to forgive is far greater than any evil anyone is capable of committing. As graced as this day was, it never seemed more so than when David expressed a desire for Confession. Ed was able to offer the sacrament.

All Life Is Sacred

But a person's conversion, while most desirable, is not the reason for opposing executions. Not every murderer repents of his or her crime. Opposing capital punishment is not about rewarding those who do; it is the expression of a fierce conviction that all life—not only innocent life—is sacred.

Pope John Paul II has refined church teaching on the death penalty, moving it from approval to condemnation, as happened previously with warfare and slavery. He has repeatedly called for an end to the death penalty and inspired others to work for a moratorium on capital punishment.

With human redemption at the heart of the Easter mystery, how is it that good men and women who share the same faith and are nourished by the same Eucharist are so divided on this issue?

Appreciation of the sacredness of all life rightfully encourages believers to protect and defend it. While wanting to do the right thing, outrage and fear influence people's sense of justice, as much as do longings for forgiveness and redemption.

With each plea from the pope and other spiritual leaders, the church invites us to take another look at our convictions in view of the instruction Jesus gave to his disciples at the first Eucharist: "Do this in remembrance of me." In every circumstance of our lives we cry out for grace and mercy when we ask: "What ought we to do in remembrance of Jesus?"

[In 1995], during the trial of Susan Smith, the South Carolina woman who drowned her two young sons, a billboard on a major Staten Island, New York, thoroughfare personified one man's thirst for vengeance. He depicted an extended arm holding the severed head of Smith. In large black letters next to the painting were these words: "Susan Smith murdered her two babies. I say cut her @&#* head off."

Beneath the billboard three women and two men stood holding a statement that read: "Hatred and revenge destroy the human spirit."

Which message is better proclaimed in memory of Jesus?

Capital Punishment Harms Society

by John D. Bessler

About the author: *John D. Bessler is an attorney and an adjunct professor of law at the University of Minnesota Law School. He is also the author of* Death in the Dark: Midnight Executions in America.

The September 11, [2001,] terrorist attacks on New York City's World Trade Center buildings profoundly affected everyone. The images of smoke billowing from the twin towers, people plummeting hundreds of feet to their deaths, and then the collapse of the skyscrapers themselves, are gruesome and unforgettable. The coordinated terrorist plot, with hijacked planes also crashing into the Pentagon and in Pennsylvania, claimed thousands of lives even as the attacks steeled the world's resolve to fight international terrorism. As we mourn the loss of life, one question that will remain unanswered for some time is the extent to which the terrorist attacks will affect America's domestic anti–death penalty movement, which appeared to be gaining strength in the months before that fateful day.

In the aftermath of the hijackings and the mailing of deadly letters containing anthrax spores, the American people face a host of new challenges. How do we defend ourselves against future terrorist attacks while protecting the constitutional rights of Arab Americans? How do we bring Osama bin Laden[1] and terrorists in al Qaeda to justice, yet not kill hundreds of innocent Afghan civilians in the process? And how should we administer justice to those who killed, harbored terrorists, or facilitated the terrorist attacks who are not themselves killed in the military campaign in Afghanistan? Openly or in secret? The answers to these questions are not trivial, for the whole world is watching what we do and how we conduct ourselves. Just what kind of example will America's government set for the rest of the world?

---

1. Saudi exile and radical Islamist leader Osama bin Laden is believed to have orchestrated the September 11, 2001, terrorist attacks.

John D. Bessler, "America's Death Penalty: Just Another Form of Violence," *Phi Kappa Phi Forum*, vol. 82, Winter 2002, p. 13. Copyright © 2002 by *Phi Kappa Phi Forum*. Reproduced by permission.

Although the world changed on September 11, my firm conviction is that we must not allow acts of terrorism to change our aspirations for a nonviolent society and a lasting global peace. The terrorists, of course, must be brought to justice, but on the home front and abroad Americans must act to reduce violence and human suffering, which are all too often a root cause of violence. In other words, as we tighten airport security and make the U.S. mail safe for everyone to use, we also must take concrete steps to reduce gun crimes and poverty; to address the global threat of chemical, biological, and nuclear weapons; and to eliminate the use of land mines. The death penalty—already abolished in Europe—needs to be done away with as well.

The Death Penalty in a Violent Society

While many people are sure to call for the death penalty's widespread use after the September 11 terrorist attacks, my own opposition to capital punishment remains unchanged. For me, even in the post–September 11 world, America's death penalty continues to be just another form of violence in an already too-violent society. The problems with the death penalty—the conviction of the innocent, racial discrimination in its application, and the abysmal quality of representation most death-row inmates received at their trials—are legion and have certainly not changed since September 11, and no past or future terrorist attack will affect those realities. Elected officials such as Illinois Governor George Ryan had compelling reasons before September 11 to call for a moratorium on executions, and none of those reasons has gone away. Indeed, so long as the death penalty exists, there will be men like Anthony Porter, one of many death-row inmates recently exonerated in Illinois alone, who are sent to death row in error.

When crimes of violence such as murder, rape, and assault are committed, any just system of laws obviously demands that the perpetrators be punished. This makes perfect sense. Maintaining public safety is one of the government's most important obligations, and justice requires that criminals be held accountable for their actions. Just as Osama bin Laden and terrorist networks around the globe cannot be allowed to continue to operate, anyone who murders, rapes, stabs, or shoots someone must go to prison after guilt is established.

> *"America's death penalty continues to be just another form of violence in an already too-violent society."*

The whole purpose of incarcerating criminals is, after all, to eliminate the risk of future acts of violence in society at large.

What makes no sense to me is for a government that already has a criminal in custody to use violence—that is, the death penalty—to try to reduce violence. Using capital punishment only sends the misguided message to members of society that killing already-incarcerated criminals can somehow solve the problem of violence in American life. Statistics and history, in fact, show that just the opposite is true; when the death penalty is used, it tends to brutalize society, not make our lives any safer. While American death-penalty laws may give some a false sense of security, only incarcerating offenders and taking steps to prevent violence will make us safer in the end. Timothy McVeigh's[2] execution did not put a stop to acts of terrorism on American soil, just as death-penalty laws do not stop homicides in Dallas or Houston and did not deter suicidal fanatics from hijacking commercial airliners and killing thousands of innocent people in a single day.

> *"When the death penalty is used, it tends to brutalize society, not make our lives any safer."*

I prefer life-without-parole sentences to the death penalty because capital punishment has a corrosive influence on any society, and there is no evidence that the death penalty really does anything to fight crime. In fact, a recent study commissioned by the *New York Times* examined FBI data and found that death-penalty states' average murder rates consistently exceeded those of non-death-penalty states. The study reached the very disturbing conclusion that, over the last twenty years, death-penalty states' homicide rates have been, on a per capita basis, an astonishing 48 percent to 101 percent higher than in non-death-penalty states. Of America's twelve non-death-penalty states, ten have murder rates that are below—often far below—the national average.

The State of Minnesota, where I live, for instance, abolished capital punishment in 1911 and yet has one of the lowest violent-crime rates in the country. While the national homicide rate was 6.3 murders per 100,000 people in 1998, Minnesota's rate that year was less than half that figure; in contrast, active death-penalty states such as Texas and Louisiana regularly have some of the country's highest murder rates. I think anyone who fairly considers the evidence should be extremely troubled by the fact that, year after year, America's death-penalty states have higher homicide rates than do non-death-penalty states. Obviously, many factors can affect a state's homicide rate. However, these compelling statistics—indeed, logic itself—compel the conclusion that the death penalty is, at bottom, really nothing more than part of a culture (still prevalent in many places) that condones the use of violence.

Executions Out of Sight

That executions are brutalizing to American society was actually clear at least more than a century ago. Indeed, in the 1830s, American states began moving executions out of public squares because of . . . the general disorder that often prevailed at them. This trend started in northeastern states and then gradually spread to all parts of the country. Midday executions on the public commons

2. McVeigh was convicted for his role in the 1995 bombing of the Oklahoma City federal building, which killed 168 people.

were, over the next hundred years, gradually replaced by after-dark executions that, by the late 1930s, universally took place behind prison walls. State laws specifically limited attendance at executions to a few official witnesses, and county sheriffs and prison wardens regularly barred children and women from attending them. In the twentieth century, new laws were passed throughout the country forbidding television cameras from filming these events.

Because civic leaders saw public executions as corrupting morals, many states even passed laws in the nineteenth century forbidding newspapers from printing any details of executions. Public executions, it was recognized, often drew pick-pockets and drunken spectators, and state legislators concluded that if executions were creating unintended consequences, so too were newspaper accounts of hangings. Thus, in many locales such as Arkansas, Minnesota, New York, and Virginia, only the bare fact that a criminal was executed could be printed or published. Any reporter who violated one of these laws and described an execution in print could be criminally prosecuted and jailed.

To further restrict public access to information about executions, many states actually mandated by law—as some still do—that executions take place "before sunrise." The constitutionality of one of these laws, dubbed by its contemporaries as the "midnight assassination law," was upheld by the Minnesota Supreme Court in 1907. That court ruled that the "evident purpose of the act was to surround the execution of criminals with as much secrecy as possible, in order to avoid exciting an unwholesome effect on the public mind." Executions "must take place before dawn, while the masses are at rest," the court held, to give effect to the law's "purpose of avoiding publicity."

The modern-day contention by some that executions deter crime better than life-without-parole sentences is thus totally at odds with both American history and the facts. If executions were such a wonderful deterrent, why would the government choose to hide them from public view and even pass laws to prohibit the dissemination of news about them?

Today, most American executions still receive very little media attention, with the exception of higher-profile ones such as Timothy McVeigh's. Of the 313 executions that were carried out in the United States from 1977 to 1995, more than 82 percent of them actually took place between 11:00 P.M. and 7:00 A.M., when most people are asleep. More than 50 percent of those executions took place between midnight and 1:00 A.M., with laws in Louisiana and Delaware specifically requiring that executions take place between midnight and 3:00 A.M. Because they are conducted in private, American executions are, to most people, mere abstractions, not tangible events that would seem more real if they were broadcast on the nightly news. Ironically, while we see horrific film footage on CNN of the

> *"Year after year, America's death-penalty states have higher homicide rates than do non-death-penalty states."*

Taliban[3] executing a civilian in an Afghan soccer stadium, American executions, without exception, remain hidden from public view.

Although executions are kept out of sight by state legislators and the federal government, it must never be forgotten that when a democratic government takes a life, it does so on behalf of its citizens. The United States of America is, after all, governed by "We, the People." Our own elected representatives pass death-penalty laws, ordinary Americans sit on juries that impose death sentences, and the public's money pays for lethal-injection machines and executioners' salaries. What I find so troubling about the death penalty is that our most valued democratic institutions (the judiciary, the Congress and state legislatures, and the executive branch) all sanction (and are tainted by) the very same horrific act—senseless killing—that we so rightfully decry when terrorists or murderers commit their crimes.

> *"In the 1830s, American states began moving executions out of public squares because of . . . the general disorder that often prevailed at them."*

Curtailing Violence by Committing Violence?

In the wake of terrorist attacks, workplace shootings, carjackings, or gun violence . . . effective measures can and should be taken to curtail violence. More sophisticated computer systems to track offenders, beefed-up security at public places, and better regulation of firearms are all steps that we can take to make the United States a safer place in which to live and work. Although lethal injections have largely sanitized executions, it cannot be doubted that the death penalty is a form of violence. Whether carried out by firing squad, hanging, electrocution, the gas chamber, or lethal injection, the result is the same: the killing of human life.

In wartime or when someone acts in self-defense to preserve his or her own life, the use of violence can be justified to protect life. World War II, for example, was fought to stop Nazi aggression and end the Holocaust. But when a government already has someone in prison, what purpose is served by an execution? All an execution does is inject more violence into a society. Because the government should be setting an example for its people, executions are especially counterproductive. The need for public safety and what should be any government's goal—that is, a nonviolent society—can be easily reconciled by making life-without-parole sentences the maximum penalty allowed by law for murder.

The amount of violence in American society, whether on the streets or as seen on prime-time television, is astonishing. We see hijacked planes piloted into the World Trade Center and bursting into flames; we see murder scenes with yellow police tape on the evening news; and family-friendly television program-

3. The Taliban, a Muslim sect, ruled Afghanistan between 1996 and 2001.

ming often seems to be a rare commodity. The media, acting under the guarantees of the First Amendment, must be allowed to report and expose acts of violence. However, the sheer amount of violence we face does not mean that we should inject even more violence into our lives by using the death penalty. Indeed, everyone from parents to our nation's lawmakers must play a role in shaping a better, more nonviolent future for our children.

When our country's governors or judges sign death warrants for people already confined in prison, they send the wrong message to our nation's youth. Do we really want some of our most educated members of society, who should be role models of the highest order, telling our children that killing locked-up criminals is the way to solve problems? We certainly do not hold up executioners as role models for our children, yet when executions occur aren't all members of our society in some way responsible for what those executioners are doing? It is, after all, our own laws that allow executions to happen within our borders. If anything, the death penalty only perpetuates the mistaken notion that state-sanctioned executions can somehow curtail violent crime in the United States. Just as the NAACP [National Association for the Advancement of Colored People] successfully crusaded against lynching in the last century, it is time for all of us in this century to work to do away with state-sponsored executions.

> *"The death penalty does nothing more than validate the use of senseless violence, which is not a wise or sensible thing to do."*

If America is to have a safer society, we must stop seeing the death penalty as a "crime-fighting" tool, which it clearly is not. Instead, we must start seeing capital punishment for what it is: just another form of violence in our society. Thus, as we grapple with the thorny issues of how to bring heavily armed terrorists in Afghanistan to justice, America's domestic political agenda cannot be allowed to stand still. The abolition of America's death penalty is, in fact, one way already within our grasp to reduce violence. Instead of putting needles into criminals who are brain-damaged, mentally retarded, or who do not share our value for human life, our crime-fighting efforts should focus on real solutions such as tougher gun-control laws, stiffer penalties for violent offenders, better child-protection laws, and combating truancy to keep kids in school and out of gangs.

In the final analysis, the death penalty does nothing more than validate the use of senseless violence, which is not a wise or sensible thing to do in the first place. As Martin Luther King, Jr., warned: "The ultimate weakness of violence is that it is a descending spiral, begetting the very thing it seeks to destroy." America's death penalty, inflicted after murders have already been committed, only creates more violence and represents yet another roadblock that we must dismantle if we are ever to realize King's dream of a nonviolent society based on the principles of equality and respect for human life.

Execution Is Inhumane

by Robert Murray

About the author: *In 1992 Robert Murray was sentenced to death for two murders he committed with his brother in 1991. He is imprisoned in Arizona's Eryman Complex.*

The idea of death and dying is never far from my mind. Before coming to death row, I hadn't given much thought to my own demise. I've come very close to death a couple of times, but they were mere moments.

Now not only does the state of Arizona intend to kill me; they want me to participate in the process by deciding the method they will use. It's a strange form of polite behavior. For years, state officials have determined every aspect of my existence. Now, in a sudden burst of good manners, they want to add a bit of civility to my death by offering me a choice.

They've given me two methods to consider: lethal injection and lethal gas. I often imagine myself in the gas chamber and try to guess at the difference between dying there and dying by lethal injection. But I just keep coming back to the outcome. I wanted to ask someone's advice about which method I should choose, but dead is dead, and the handful of people I might have consulted are testaments to this finality.

The Easy Way to Die?

Lethal injection is now paraded about as the easy way to die. Most of the public is under the impression that since lethal injection seems simple and painless it somehow makes killing more acceptable. Witnesses to injection executions come away with the illusory perception that a patient has fallen asleep. Typical witness testimony goes something like this:

"Well, he just seemed to fall asleep."

"Could you better describe the event?"

"We were standing there, and suddenly the curtain opened and there he was, just lying there."

"What happened next?"

"Well, like I said, he was just lying there looking at the ceiling. His lips were moving a little, and he . . . well, you know, he just closed his eyes and went to sleep. I wasn't expecting it to be so easy and fast. He just went to sleep."

Easy as going to sleep. I have thought about this for literally hundreds of hours. Easy as falling asleep. I guess everybody wants to die as easily as they fall asleep.

The state of Arizona has given me a description of the two methods of execution from which I am allowed to choose:

> One (1) pound of sodium cyanide is placed in a container underneath the gas chamber chair. The chair is made of perforated metal which allows the cyanide gas to pass through and fill the chamber. A bowl below the chair contains sulfuric acid and distilled water. A lever is pulled and the sodium cyanide falls into the solution, releasing the gas. It takes the prisoner several minutes to die. After the execution, the excess gas is released through an exhaust pipe which extends about 50 feet above the Death House.

> Inmates executed by lethal injection are brought into the injection room a few minutes prior to the appointed time of execution. He/she is then strapped to a gurney-type bed and two (2) sets of intravenous tubes are inserted, one (1) in each arm. The three (3) drugs used include: Sodium Pentothal (a sedative intended to put the inmate to sleep); Pavulon (stops breathing and paralyzes the muscular system); and Potassium Chloride (causes the heart to stop). Death by lethal injection is not painful and the inmate goes to sleep prior to the fatal effects of the Pavulon and Potassium Chloride.

These descriptions do not begin to illustrate the overall reality of an execution. The claim "Death by lethal injection is not painful . . ." is far from accurate, and "going to sleep" with an overdose of sodium pentothal isn't all it's cracked up to be. It's death by any definition. The pain lies in the years, months, days, hours, minutes, and seconds leading up to the moment of execution. The pain lies in choosing your own method of execution. Going to sleep while strapped to a table is the least of it; in fact, it ends a great deal of pain—the terror, nightmares, and constant internal struggles.

The Movement for Humane Executions

The gas chamber was introduced to Arizona in the 1930s. Before that, the state hanged people. Nooses from every execution were saved and displayed in glass cases on the walls of the witness chamber of the death house. Hanging was discontinued after a woman was accidentally decapitated in 1930.

On April 6, 1992, at 12:18 A.M., Donald Harding was pronounced dead after spending a full eleven minutes in the state's gas chamber. It was Arizona's first execution in twenty-nine years, and state officials were somewhat out of practice. The spectacle of Harding gasping in the execution chamber was a little too hard for people to handle. In response, a movement grew to make executions more "humane."

Suddenly there was a new political crisis. People were outraged. Politicians took to the stump. State execution was cruel, ghastly, horrid. It took a prisoner eleven minutes to cough up his life to the gas. Of course, if executions could be made to seem more humane, that was something else altogether.

It was a wonderful political banner to wave come election time: Arizona would continue to execute people, but they would be nice executions. The politicians went about their task with glee. They preserved their right to kill people by coming up with a new way to kill people. Lethal injection was their new champion, and champion it they did.

Seven months after Harding's execution, a new law was born: "Any person sentenced to death prior to November 23, 1992, is afforded a choice of execution by either lethal gas or lethal injection. Inmates receiving death after November 23, 1992, are to be executed by lethal injection."

As it happened, my brother Roger and I were sentenced to death on October 26, 1992. We were among the lucky few who were given a Hobson's choice about how we should die.

Offering prisoners a "humane" execution seems to be the latest strategy to keep capital punishment alive. But the notion that any execution could be humane eludes me. People today seem generally happy with the idea of lethal injection, as long as it is done in a neat, sanitary, easy-to-watch fashion. I'm not sure what this says about our society. However, I am sure most people don't grasp the reality of the "sleeping" death of which they so widely approve. Indeed, many witnesses leave an execution with a serene look on their faces, as if they'd just seen a somewhat pleasant movie. To my mind, it's actually the witnesses who are falling asleep at injection killings, lulled by the calmness of it all.

> *"The pain lies in the years, months, days, hours, minutes, and seconds leading up to the moment of execution."*

The Airplane Analogy

As I see it, death by injection is very like being tossed out of an airplane. Suppose I'm told that on November 3, someone will escort me from my cell, take me up in an airplane, and, at three o'clock in the afternoon, toss me out without a parachute. After a few minutes, my body will hit a target area, killing me immediately. It's an easy, instant, painless death. The impact of hitting the ground after falling several thousand feet will kill me as instantly and effectively as lethal injection.

Killing inmates by tossing them out of airplanes would of course be unacceptable to the public. But why? It's as fast and effective as lethal injection. The terror of falling two minutes isn't all that different from the terror of lying strapped to a table; and neither is physically painful. There's a similar waiting process before each execution. If an airplane is used, you wait for the time it takes the aircraft to take off and reach the target area at the proper altitude. For lethal injection, you wait in the death house until everything's ready and all possibility of a stay of execution has been exhausted. In an airplane, a cargo door is opened; in the death house, a curtain across the viewing window is drawn back. In an airplane, you are thrown to an absolute death and witnesses watch your body fall. In the death house, you are strapped to a gurney and witnesses watch state officials inject you with sodium pentothal. In both cases, death is sudden and final.

> *"The notion that any execution could be humane eludes me."*

To me they are the same. I will feel the same powerful emotions and chaotic anxiety either way. But the public would never describe my death by falling from an aircraft as "simply falling asleep." They would be outraged. Politicians would rush to give speeches about giving prisoners a "choice," and the law would be changed.

The public would cry out, not because the prisoner died an agonizing and painful death but because most people feel that the anxiety of being tossed from an aircraft without a parachute would be too terrible for an inmate to bear, and the spectacle of death would be too terrible for observers to bear. In this case, the public would be forced to understand the emotions an inmate feels before execution; when lethal injection is used, all such emotions are hidden behind a veil that is not drawn aside until the moment before death.

This airplane analogy is as close as I can come to illustrating the fallacy of the humane execution. There is much more to death by injection than just falling asleep, beginning with the long wait on death row (where execution is a constant presence), the terror of being taken to the death house, the helpless panic of being strapped to a table, and finally the sense of utter loss as the curtain is opened. All of the fear and anxiety of falling from an aircraft is present when the injection begins. Both are horrible by any measure. And neither is anything like falling asleep.

Chapter 2

Is Capital Punishment Administered Fairly?

Capital Punishment and Fairness: An Overview

by Kenneth Jost

About the author: *Kenneth Jost is a staff writer for* CQ Researcher, *a weekly report on current issues.*

The American Bar Association (ABA) has no official position on capital punishment. But [since 1998], the 600,000-member group has favored a moratorium on executions until states comply with a set of policies intended to ensure that death penalty cases are "administered fairly and impartially" and to "minimize the risk that innocent persons may be executed."

In promoting the moratorium at [an] ABA annual meeting . . . outgoing President Martha Barnett termed the existing death penalty system "absolutely unacceptable." In a letter to Congress, the Tallahassee, Fla., lawyer urged lawmakers to pass two bills—the Innocence Protection Act and the National Death Penalty Moratorium Act—as "immediate steps" to improve the fairness of the system.

Death penalty opponents say the fairness issues are helping shift public opinion in ways that the broad attacks on capital punishment failed to do. "It's not . . . that people are discovering that the death penalty is morally wrong," [death penalty opponent Richard] Dieter says, "but more a practical assessment that . . . innocent lives may be lost, that there is much that remains arbitrary and unfair about the death penalty."

Debating the Charges of Unfairness

Supporters of the death penalty sharply dispute the accusations of unfairness. "Capital trials are . . . among the fairest trials in the world," says [criminal justice professor Barry Latzer] "The procedural protections are heightened. All of the parties—the lawyers, the prosecutors, the judges—are all aware of the stakes. The prosecutors are the most experienced, and the defense lawyers are increasingly being certified to handle those cases."

However, critics say a variety of factors demonstrate the unfairness of the system. Death penalty defenders dispute each of the points.

For one thing, Dieter notes that death sentences are "much more likely" to be imposed in murder cases with white victims than in those with African-American victims. [Pro-death-penalty activist Dudley] Sharp acknowledges the statistic, but explains that whites are much more likely than blacks to be victims of the kinds of murders punishable by death—murders with aggravating factors such as robbery or carjacking or killings of police officers.

Death penalty opponents also emphasize the stark geographical disparities in the use of capital punishment. They note that 80 percent of the executions since 1976 have taken place in one region of the country—the South—with more than half from just three states: Texas, Virginia and Florida. In addition, Dieter says that 40 percent of the federal cases in which U.S. attorneys have sought the death penalty have come from just five of the country's 94 federal districts.

Supporters blame geographic disparities on delaying tactics of death penalty opponents themselves. "Opponents want no enforcement of capital punishments," Sharp of Justice for All says, "and it is their efforts that continue to encourage any disparity which exists between states."

Critics also say the death penalty is more likely to be imposed on indigent defendants with court-appointed lawyers. "If you can afford good quality representation, you're much less likely to get the death penalty," Dieter says. But Sharp says there is "no systemic evidence that wealthier capital murderers are less likely to be executed than poorer [ones]."

Some death penalty supporters do acknowledge a problem in uneven legal representation. Latzer, for one, calls for "more money for defense counsel" in capital cases. Death penalty critics note that court-appointed lawyers are paid well under $100 an hour in most jurisdictions.

A Nationwide Moratorium?

To critics, the various fairness issues point to the need for a nationwide moratorium on executions. "The evidence has accumulated to a degree that we should stop what we're doing," Dieter says. The number of people freed from death rows, he says, amount to "a national alert that we're taking too many risks. We should stop and find out whether this system is irredeemably broken or whether it can be fixed."

Death penalty supporters, however, note that under the current system there is already a long time—an average of 12 years—between conviction and execution. "On average, every death row inmate already has a nearly 12-year moratorium on their individual case during appeals," Sharp says.

Questioning the true motive behind the moratorium proposals, he says, "The nationwide effort for a moratorium on executions is a prelude to doing away with the death penalty altogether."

Capital Punishment Is Applied Unfairly

by Steven W. Hawkins

About the author: *Steven W. Hawkins is executive director of the Washington, D.C.–based National Coalition to Abolish the Death Penalty.*

When the Supreme Court struck down death penalty laws in 1972, former Justice Potter Stewart compared the arbitrariness of the death penalty to the freakishness of being struck by lightning.

Thirty years later, were he still alive, Justice Stewart would probably appreciate his choice of words. In the past five years, an average of 78 people a year have been executed in the United States; in 1995, according to the National Center for Health Statistics, 76 Americans were struck by lightning.

Americans who support the death penalty think it should be reserved for the worst of the worst. The reality of capital punishment, however, shows that it is reserved for racial minorities, people who are retarded or mentally ill, and those who cannot afford to hire a good attorney. It is also all too often reserved for people who are factually innocent of the crime for which they were convicted and sentenced to be executed.

Doubt that the death penalty is racist? Consider this: 55 percent of the inmates who make up America's death row population are people of color (43 percent of death row inmates are black). Two of every three juvenile offenders on death row are people of color, as are a majority of retarded inmates.

Furthermore, the race of the victim plays a role in who ends up on death row. Nationwide, just half of murder victims are white, yet four out of every five people executed in the United States have died for killing white people.

Signs of Unfairness

Of course, the numbers do not paint a complete picture. Racial minorities have been the victims of particularly cruel and vindictive wrongful prosecutions, particularly in the South. Consider the case of Clarence Brandley, who spent 10 years on death row in Texas for a crime he did not commit.

Brandley was the head janitor at a high school where a young white female student was found strangled. When police arrived at the crime scene and saw Brandley, a black man, and another janitor, who was white, one officer reportedly declared, "One of you is gonna hang for this. Since you're the nigger, you're elected." Brandley was freed from prison when all charges against him were dropped after a Department of Justice and FBI investigation uncovered trial misconduct.

> *"Racial minorities have been the victims of particularly cruel and vindictive wrongful prosecutions."*

Doubt that the death penalty is reserved for people who are retarded or mentally ill? Since executions were allowed to resume in 1976, we've executed 44 mentally retarded inmates. (And that is a conservative number. Many inmates are not evaluated for mental retardation before they are executed.)[1]

These 44 inmates include Morris Mason of Virginia who, on his way to the death chamber, turned to a prison worker and said, "You tell Roger [another death row inmate] when I get back, I'm going to show him I can play basketball as good as he can." Ricky Rector of Arkansas separated his pecan pie from his last meal and left it on the windowsill of his prison cell. He wanted to eat it after the execution.

The Importance of the Trial Attorney

Doubt that the death penalty discriminates against those who cannot afford a good attorney? Consider the case of Ronald Keith Williamson, who was convicted in Oklahoma and sentenced to death for murder and rape in 1988.

Williamson's conviction was tossed out because of ineffectiveness of counsel; a federal appellate court wryly noted that his attorney failed to investigate and present to the jury the fact that another man had confessed to the rape and murder. It was a case of you get what you pay for—the attorney had received only $3,200 for his defense. Later, DNA evidence would exonerate Williamson.

Of course, that is just the tip of the iceberg. We've seen capital murder suspects represented by drunken lawyers, sleeping lawyers, biased lawyers, inexperienced lawyers, lawyers who were later disbarred, and lawyers who would be institutionalized due to mental illness.

Aden Harrison Jr., a black man, had as his court-appointed counsel 83-year-old James Venable, who had been an imperial wizard of the Ku Klux Klan for more than 15 years. Judy Haney's court-appointed lawyer was so drunk during the trial in 1989 that he was held in contempt and sent to jail. The next day, both client and attorney came out of the cellblock and the trial resumed. George McFarland's attorney slept through much of the trial. He objected to hardly

---

1. In June 2002, the U.S. Supreme Court banned the execution of the mentally retarded.

anything the prosecution did, and every time he opened his eyes, a different witness was on the stand.

As Supreme Court Justice Ruth Ginsburg put it, "People who are well represented at trial do not get the death penalty. I have yet to see a death penalty case among the dozens coming to the Supreme Court on eve-of-execution stay applications in which the defendant was well represented at trial."

Ensnaring Innocents

Doubt that the death penalty ensnares innocent Americans in its complicated legal web? More than 100 people have been freed from death row due to actual innocence, while close to 800 people have been executed. This means that for every eight people we are executing, one person is completely exonerated.

Think of it this way. What if a prescription drug cured eight of every nine people who took it but killed the ninth? What if an airline carrier successfully completed eight of every nine flights it launched, but the ninth resulted in mechanical failure?

What if you are able to successfully reboot your computer eight of every nine tries, but the rest of the time, it crashes and destroys your document? As a society that depends upon a functioning criminal justice system, should we have confidence when that same justice system sends innocent people to death row?

"More often than we want to recognize, some innocent defendants have been convicted and sentenced to death."

As Supreme Court Justice Sandra Day O'Connor put it, "If statistics are any indication, the system may well be allowing some innocent defendants to be executed. More often than we want to recognize, some innocent defendants have been convicted and sentenced to death."

Kirk Bloodsworth of Maryland and Clyde Charles of Louisiana should know. Bloodsworth spent nine years in prison—two on death row—before DNA testing of old evidence proved him innocent of the only crime for which he had ever been arrested, the brutal rape and murder of a nine-year-old girl. While he was in prison, his mother passed away, and Bloodsworth was forced to view the body while wearing shackles. The real child predator and killer remains unidentified.

Charles spent 19 years at Angola in Louisiana, one of the country's most notorious prisons. He fought for 9 years to get DNA testing done. The results proved that Charles could not have committed the crime, and he was released.

His children grew into adults while he was in prison, and both his parents died; he also caught tuberculosis and developed diabetes. The same DNA test that exonerated Charles identified the real criminal—who had since been arrested for committing other crimes against innocent victims while the wrong man was in jail.

Some death penalty proponents quibble over the number of people who have been found to have been factually innocent. The exact number isn't really what's important. What's important is that not one of us—death penalty opponents or proponents—would conclude that executing even one innocent person constitutes acceptable criminal justice policy in the United States.

Who Is Listening?

Arguments against the death penalty are easy to make, but is anyone listening? The bad news is that most Americans continue to support capital punishment in theory. The good news is when you start to probe, there is a growing sense of unease and ambivalence.

For example, 80 percent of voters want to abolish or significantly reform the death penalty system. Sixty-nine percent of voters are more worried about executing an innocent person than executing the guilty. And 64 percent of voters—including 50 percent of Republican voters—want to suspend executions until issues of fairness can be resolved.

The fact is that people are beginning to respond to concerns about the system. Across the United States, a healthy and vibrant moratorium movement is gathering steam. Elected bodies in 73 municipalities have passed resolutions in favor of a moratorium.

Two governors, Republican George Ryan in Illinois and Democrat Parris Glendening in Maryland, have each declared a moratorium. Some 14 states have debated moratorium legislation; in New Hampshire, the legislature passed a bill abolishing the death penalty, only to see it vetoed by the governor.

In Nevada and Maryland, bills imposing a moratorium passed one chamber, only to be defeated in the other. In New Mexico, a bill to abolish the death penalty failed in the Senate by one vote. [In the future], we can expect many more moratorium bills to be debated—as well as bills calling for outright abolition.

Let's face it. The death penalty experiment in America has been tried and found wanting. It is time for the lethal injection gurney to go the way of the stake, the guillotine, and the gallows. It is time to relegate this gruesome practice to the dustbin of history. Our common decency demands no less.

Error Pervades the U.S. Capital Punishment System

by James S. Liebman et al.

About the author: *James S. Liebman is a professor of law at Columbia University's Law School.*

There is growing awareness that serious, reversible error permeates America's death penalty system, putting innocent lives at risk, heightening the suffering of victims, leaving killers at large, wasting tax dollars, and failing citizens, the courts and the justice system.

Our June 2000 Report [*A Broken System*] shows how often mistakes occur and how serious it is: 68% of all death verdicts imposed and fully reviewed during the 1973–1995 study period were reversed by courts due to serious errors.

Analyses presented for the first time [in *A Broken System, Part II*] reveal that 76% of the reversals at the two appeal stages where data are available for study were because defense lawyers had been egregiously incompetent, police and prosecutors had suppressed exculpatory evidence or committed other professional misconduct, jurors had been misinformed about the law, or judges and jurors had been biased. Half of those reversals tainted the verdict finding the defendant guilty of a capital crime as well as the verdict imposing the death penalty. 82% of the cases sent back for retrial at the second appeal phase ended in sentences less than death, including 9% that ended in not guilty verdicts.

Why Are There So Many Mistakes?

Part II of our study addresses two critical questions: Why does our death penalty system make so many mistakes? How can these mistakes be prevented, if at all? Our findings are based on the most comprehensive set of data ever assembled on factors related to capital error—or other trial error.

Our main finding indicates that if we are going to have the death penalty, it should be reserved for the worst of the worst: *Heavy and indiscriminate use of the death penalty creates a high risk that mistakes will occur.* The more often officials use the death penalty, the wider the range of crimes to which it is applied, and the more it is imposed for offenses that are not highly aggravated, the greater the risk that capital convictions and sentences will be seriously flawed.

Most disturbing of all, we find that the conditions evidently pressuring counties and states to overuse the death penalty and thus increase the risk of unreliability and error include *race, politics* and *poorly performing law enforcement systems.* Error also is linked to overburdened and underfunded state courts. . . .

Pressures Associated with Overuse of the Death Penalty

Four disturbing conditions are strongly associated with high rates of serious capital error. Their common capacity to pressure officials to use the death penalty aggressively in response to fears about crime and regardless of how weak any particular case for a death verdict is, may explain their relationship to high capital error rates.

• *The closer the homicide risk to whites in a state comes to equaling or surpassing the risk to blacks, the higher the error rate.* Other things equal, reversal rates are twice as high where homicides are most heavily concentrated on whites compared to blacks, than where they are the most heavily concentrated on blacks.

• *The higher the proportion of African-Americans in a state—and in one analysis, the more welfare recipients in a state—the higher the rate of serious capital error.* Because this effect has to do with traits of the population at large, not those of particular trial participants, it appears to be an indicator of crime fears driven by racial and economic conditions.

> *"Serious, reversible error permeates America's death penalty system, putting innocent lives at risk."*

• *The lower the rate at which states apprehend, convict and imprison serious criminals, the higher their capital error rates.* Predicted capital error rates for states with only 1 prisoner per 100 FBI Index Crimes are about 75%, holding other factors constant. Error rates drop to 36% for states with 4 prisoners per 100 crimes, and to 13% for those with the highest rate of prisoners to crimes. Evidently, officials who do a poor job fighting crime also conduct poor capital investigations and trials. Well-founded doubts about a state's ability to catch criminals may lead officials to extend the death penalty to a wider array of weaker cases—at huge cost in error and delay.

• *The more often and directly state trial judges are subject to popular election, and the more partisan those elections are, the higher the state's rate of serious capital error.*

Additional Findings

Heavy use of the death penalty causes delay, increases cost, and keeps the system from doing its job. High numbers of death verdicts waiting to be reviewed paralyze appeals. Holding other factors constant, the process of moving capital verdicts from trial to a final result seems to come to a halt in states with more than 20 verdicts under review at one time.

Poor quality trial proceedings increase the risk of serious, reversible error. Poorly funded courts, high capital and non-capital caseloads, and unreliable procedures for finding the facts all increase the chance that serious error will be found. In contrast, high quality, well-funded private lawyers from out of state significantly increase a defendant's chance of showing a federal court that his death verdict is seriously flawed and has to be retried.

Chronic capital error rates have persisted over time. Overall reversal rates were high and fairly steady throughout the second half of the 23-year study period, averaging 60%. When all significant factors are considered, state high courts on direct appeal—where 79% of the 2349 reversals occurred—found significantly more reversible error in recent death verdicts than in verdicts imposed earlier in the study period. Other things equal, direct appeal reversal rates were increasing 9% a year during the study period.

> *"[Sixty-eight percent] of all death verdicts . . . were reversed by courts due to serious errors."*

State and federal appeals judges cannot be relied upon to catch all serious trial errors in capital cases. Like trial judges, appeals judges are susceptible to political pressure and make mistakes. And the rules appeals judges use to decide whether errors are serious enough to require death verdicts to be reversed are so strict that egregious errors slip through. We [examined] four illustrative cases in which *the courts approved the convictions and death sentences of innocent men* despite *a full set of appeals.* These case studies show that judges repeatedly recognized that the proceedings were marred by error but affirmed anyway because of stringent rules limiting reversals.

The lower the rate at which a state imposes death sentences—and the more it confines those verdicts to the worst of the worst—the less likely it is that serious error will be found. The fewer death verdicts a state imposes, the less overburdened its capital appeal system is, and the more likely it is to carry out the verdicts it imposes. The more often states succumb to pressures to inflict capital sentences in marginal cases, the higher is the risk of error and delay, the lower is the chance verdicts will be carried out, and the greater is the temptation to approve flawed verdicts on appeal. Among the disturbing sources of pressure to overuse the death penalty are political pressures on elected judges, well-founded doubts about the state's ability to convict serious criminals, and the race of the state's residents and homicide victims. . . .

Policy Options

The harms resulting from chronic capital error are costly. Many of its evident causes are not easily addressed head-on (*e.g.*, the complex interaction of a state's racial make-up, its welfare burden and the efficacy of its law enforcement policies). And indirect remedies are unreliable because they demand self-restraint by officials who in the past have succumbed to pressures to extend the death penalty to cases that are not highly aggravated. As a result, some states and counties may conclude that the only answer to chronic capital error is to stop using the death penalty, or to limit it to the very small number of prospective offenses where there is something approaching a social consensus that only the death penalty will do.

In other states and counties, a set of carefully targeted reforms based upon careful study of local conditions might seek to achieve the central goal of limiting the death penalty to "the worst of the worst"—to defendants who can be shown without doubt to have committed an egregiously aggravated murder without extenuating factors. Ten reforms that might help accomplish this goal are:

- Requiring proof beyond *any* doubt that the defendant committed the capital crime.
- Requiring that aggravating factors substantially outweigh mitigating ones before a death sentence may be imposed.
- Barring the death penalty for defendants with inherently extenuating conditions—mentally retarded persons, juveniles, severely mentally ill defendants.
- Making life imprisonment without parole an alternative to the death penalty and clearly informing juries of the option.
- Abolishing judge overrides of jury verdicts imposing life sentences.
- Using comparative review of murder sentences to identify what counts as "the worst of the worst" in the state, and overturning outlying death verdicts.
- Basing charging decisions in potentially capital cases on full and informed deliberations.
- Making all police and prosecution evidence bearing on guilt vs. innocence, and on aggravation vs. mitigation available to the jury at trial.
- Insulating capital-sentencing and appellate judges from political pressure.
- Identifying, appointing and compensating capital defense counsel in ways that attract an adequate number of well-qualified lawyers to do the work.

The Time Is Ripe

Over decades and across dozens of states, large numbers and proportions of capital verdicts have been reversed because of serious error. The capital system is collapsing under the weight of that error, and the risk of executing the innocent is high. Now that explanations for the problem have been identified and a range of options for responding to it are available, the time is ripe to fix the death penalty, or if it can't be fixed, to end it.

Racism Influences the Administration of the Death Penalty

by Jan Boudart

About the author: *Jan Boudart is a researcher, writer, and former volunteer for the Center on Wrongful Convictions.*

There is an inextricable link between the racism in our criminal justice system and the existence of the death penalty itself.

During slavery the criminal code unabashedly authorized harsher punishments for Blacks (both slave and free) than for whites. In addition crimes against whites, in a legal sense, were considered more serious. Before passage of the Fourteenth Amendment in 1868, many state laws expressly authorized discrimination.

Even after slavery was abolished, there was a culture of acceptance for the lynching of freedmen in the South, but also on occasion in the North. Partly due to the work of Ida B. Wells, lynching became an embarrassment to the United States and particularly to the states where it was carried out.

A Racist Death Penalty

A racist death penalty with quick legal execution became an effective substitute, i.e. it worked to intimidate and subordinate the Black community and made killing African Americans respectable. According to a source quoted by Leon F. Litwack in his book *Been in the Storm So Long: The Aftermath of Slavery* (1979), "The best men in the State admit that no jury would convict a white man for killing a freedman, or fail to hang a Negro who had killed a white man in self-defense."

These issues of control and domination persist. Prosecutors have the power of discretion to decide when the death penalty will be pursued, just as whites formerly decided who would be lynched.

When in 1990 and again in 1994 the U.S. House of Representatives presented a Fairness in Death Sentencing Act, state Attorneys General and prosecutors in death-penalty states countered with absurdly contradictory refutations. They argued that racial discrimination "did not exist so the act was unnecessary," while at the same time saying "racial discrimination in the use of the death penalty was inevitable and impossible to prevent, detect, or remedy."

Further, they threatened that to redress the discrimination meant quotas or abolition of the death penalty altogether. (Surely, if such a choice were demanded, the death penalty would have to be abolished.)

Enter the electoral process. The spurious arguments of the prosecutors carried considerable weight with legislators who feared their support

> *"There is an inextricable link between the racism in our criminal justice system and the existence of the death penalty itself."*

of the act "could lessen the viability of the death penalty in their states." Read, "May prevent my reelection."

Thus we can see that our past, as a nation dependent on African slave labor, today saddles us with the death penalty when the whole rest of the Western World has rejected it. It is noteworthy that from its roots as a weapon of blatant and legal domination over the slave population, the death penalty has evolved into the more subtle and legal domination that we observe today.

In spite of the obvious racism with which the death penalty is administered, Kentucky is the only state that has passed a "Racial Justice Act" that lets defendants use statistical evidence to show race was a factor in their death sentence.

Hidden Bias

Race is almost always cited as a factor in the plethora of studies on how the death penalty is imposed in various American jurisdictions.

An Illinois study by [Glenn] Pierce and [Michael] Radelet dated March 20, 2002, very conservative in its methods and its conclusions, is a good example. The authors observe that a hidden chain of decisions leads to imposition of the death penalty. Their data begins where the prosecutor must decide whether to seek the death penalty against a certain defendant. But by that time the defendant has already been indicted and subject to decisions by police, sheriff, sheriff's detectives, a defense lawyer, etc.

Racism is hidden throughout the process. Nevertheless, Pierce and Radelet came to the conclusion that in Illinois the prosecutor will decide to seek the death penalty based on the race of the victim, not the defendant. Studies from other states show that in many jurisdictions the victim's race is a major influence on whether the death penalty will be sought.

Race and the death penalty was the subject of the much respected 1998 [David] Baldus study. In a paper rich in history and detail, one table summarizes the effect of race in the administration of the death penalty.

Three sets of data—prosecutors seeking the death penalty, jurors imposing it, and overall death sentencing rates—from thirty-two states that used the death penalty are listed, and their results broken down into various time periods. The picture is complex; but the upshot is that the race of the victims was vastly more significant than that of the accused.

The conclusions of the Baldus study expressed considerable disappointment that all levels of justice shy away from addressing racism in death penalty administration. But the problem is intractable at the level of the justice system, because racism is systemic in culture, education, employment, even environmental factors.

The conclusions of the Baldus 1998 study raise some intriguing insights as to why racism in death penalty administration has become a near-intractable problem. The reasons are hidden in history (as sketched above) and in the chain of decisions that lead eventually to the death penalty and the execution of a defendant.

Jury Selection and Race

Jury selection with its peremptory challenges is key to the technical reasons why the percentage of African Americans gets so high on death row.[1] Regarding the Supreme Court decision in *Batson v. Kentucky*,[2] Harvard's Charles Ogletree commented that the Court misunderstands how both prosecutors and defense lawyers feel about jury selection. Both sides regard race, age and gender discrimination as "rational, ethical and necessary strategies to protect the interest of their clients."

I disagree with Ogletree on how much the Court respects and fears the power of the American legal system to defend the traditions of jury selection. If you read the Supreme Court decision on *Batson v. Kentucky*, you will see more weasel language in less space than was previously possible.

The Court was clearly afraid to take a stand for the Constitution they are charged to uphold. Only one justice, Thurgood Marshall, made a clear, but extremely radical stand: "The decision today will not end the racial discrimination that peremptories inject into the jury-selection process. That goal can be accomplished only by eliminating peremptory challenges entirely."

"Race is almost always cited as a factor in the plethora of studies on how the death penalty is imposed."

Such a course of action would eliminate the effects of more than 200 years of history and tradition. Peremptory challenges are a treasured bailiwick of both prosecution and defense.

1. Peremptory challenges allow judges and lawyers to disqualify jurors because of their backgrounds or prior knowledge of the case.   2. In the 1986 case of *Batson v. Kentucky*, the Supreme Court ruled that prosecutors could not use race-based peremptory challenges to keep members of the defendant's race off the jury.

And the Honored Justices are correct in assuming that jury selection on the basis of race is important. (Women on the jury showed no significant difference from men.) Baldus 2001 argues that non-Blacks are more prone than Black jurors to convict and call for the death sentence. This being so, prosecutors in Pennsylvania and Texas work very hard to keep African Americans off their juries and defense lawyers do the same to get them on. . . .

The McMahon Tape

Notorious jury-selection instruction tapes or manuals, which have ostensibly been discredited and which were written for the prosecution, were created in [Pennsylvania and Texas]. The defense has used them as a mirror image of how to influence jury selection. But the techniques work better for the prosecution.

For example, the McMahon tape[3] has been extant in Pennsylvania since 1986. To paraphrase, it recommends the selection of successful-looking whites with "a predisposition toward . . . capital punishment and [who] accept as right and just the Government's evidence and arguments in favor of a death sentence."

These instructions are for the guilt-innocence phase of the prosecution not the sentencing phase. The prosecution's targets for elimination are "'(B)lacks from the low-income areas,' because they may feel 'resentment for law enforcement [and] . . . authority.'" Also dangerous are the well-educated: "doctors, lawyers, law students, social workers and teachers (unless they are 'fed up' with their black students)."

> *"Prosecutors in Pennsylvania and Texas work very hard to keep African Americans off their juries."*

McMahon follows this with advice on how to avoid being accused of racial bias, that is, how to formulate non-race reasons for having struck every possible Black jury member. The McMahon tape has surely influenced the fact that, although Pennsylvania's minority population is eleven percent, only Louisiana has a higher percentage of African Americans on death row.

I think Pennsylvania has a problem. . . .

Jury Shuffling

"Jury shuffling" has been a common practice in Texas and was one of the techniques used to select a white jury for Thomas Miller-el in 1986. Here's how it worked. Show and tell (*voir dire*, the jury selection process) begins when the week's jury pool (*venire* persons) appears.

The prosecution, represented by Janie Cockrell, had each *venire* person on a card. When she found out which of the choices look like African Americans, she shuffled the deck so they would be the last interviewed. That way she hoped that

---

3. A reference to a prosecutor-training videotape created by former Philadelphia, Pennsylvania, District Attorney Jack McMahon.

the jury would be chosen before the interviewers got to them. (After a week of show and tell, the jury pool is sent home and a new group comes on Monday.)

Justice Kennedy said the prosecutor applied this process at least three times in the selection of Miller-el's trial jury. She did it twice on her own and once after viewing the order shuffled into place by the defense.

In addition, the prosecutor would describe the process of death by injection in great detail before asking Black *venire* persons if they approved of the death penalty. She did not precede the same question given to whites with that gruesome introduction. Using this strategy, Cockrell could claim that Black *venire* persons were unsatisfactory, not because they were Black, but because they opposed the death penalty.

Also, without telling the African Americans the law on minimum convictions (five years) she would ask them what they thought a minimum sentence should be for murder. When they said twenty years, she would strike their name for cause, attributing to them the likelihood that upon hearing a case that only merited five years, they would not want to impose such a light sentence.

For whites her procedure was to explain the minimum sentence and then say something like, "If you hear a case, to your way of thinking [that] calls for and warrants and justifies five years, you'll give it?"

The statistical proof that executions occur most often when the murder victim was white, that Black defendants are more likely to be given the death sentence, and that African Americans are systematically denied their right to serve on juries indicate that African Americans do not have equal protection under the law. In employment practices, service in public facilities, and other areas where African Americans have rebelled in favor of their human rights, they have achieved more success than in their constitutional right to justice.

Capital Punishment Should Be Reformed to Protect the Innocent

by Patrick Leahy

About the author: *Patrick Leahy is the Democratic senator from Vermont.*

Editor's Note: The following viewpoint was originally delivered as testimony before the U.S. Senate on November 18, 2002, in support of the Innocence Protection Act. As of this writing, the act had not passed.

For more than 2 years, I have been working hard with Members on both sides of the aisle, in both Houses of Congress, to address the horrendous problem of innocent people being condemned to death within our judicial system. This is not a question of whether you are for or against the death penalty. Many of the House Members and Senate Members who have joined this effort are in favor of the death penalty. I suspect the majority of them are in favor of it. It goes to the question of what happens if you have an innocent person who is condemned to death.

Our bill, the Innocence Protection Act [IPA], proposes a number of basic commonsense reforms to our criminal justice system; reforms that are aimed at reducing the risk that innocent people will be put to death.[1]

We have come a long way since I first introduced the IPA in February 2000. At that time, we had four Democratic cosponsors. Now there is a broad consensus across the country among Democrats and Republicans, supporters and opponents of the death penalty, liberals, conservatives, and moderates, that our death penalty machinery is broken. We know that putting an innocent person on death row is not just a nightmare, it is not just a dream, it is a frequently recurring reality.

---

1. As of this writing, the bill had not passed.

Patrick Leahy, testimony before the United States Senate, Washington, DC, November 18, 2002.

Sentenced to Death by Mistake

Since the 1970s, more than 100 people who were sentenced to death have been released, not because of some technicality, but because they were innocent, because they had been sentenced to death by mistake. One wonders how many others were not discovered and how many innocent people were executed.

These are not just numbers, these are real people. Their lives are ruined. Let me give an example: Anthony Porter. Anthony Porter was 2 days from execution in 1998 when he was exonerated and released from prison. Why? Not because the criminal justice system worked. He was exonerated and released because a class of journalism students, who had taken on an investigation of his case, found that he did he not commit the crime. They also found the real killer. A group of students from a journalism class did what should have been done by the criminal justice system in the first place.

Ray Krone spent 10 years in prison. Three of those ten years were on death row waiting for the news that he was about to be executed. Then, [in 2002], through DNA testing, he was exculpated and the real killer was identified. These are two of the many tragedies we learn about each year.

These situations result not only in the tragedy of putting an innocent person on death row, but they also leave the person who committed the crime free. Everything fails. We have the wrong person in prison. But we have not protected society or the criminal justice system because the real criminal is still out running free. Often times, the actual perpetrator is a serial criminal.

> *"Putting an innocent person on death row is not just a nightmare ... it is a frequently recurring reality."*

Today, Federal judges are voicing concerns about the death penalty. Justice Sandra Day O'Connor has warned that "the system may well be allowing some innocent defendants to be executed." Justice [Ruth Bader] Ginsburg has supported a State moratorium on the death penalty. Another respected jurist, Sixth Circuit Judge Gilbert Merritt, referred to the capital punishment system as "broken," and two district court judges have found constitutional problems with the Federal death penalty.

The Innocence Protection Act

We can agree there is a grave problem. The good news is that there is also a broad consensus on one important step we have to take—we must pass the Innocence Protection Act.

That is why I wanted to let my colleagues know what is happening. As the 107th Congress draws to a close, the IPA is cosponsored by a substantial bipartisan majority of the House and by 32 Senators from both sides of the aisle, including, most recently, Senator Bob Smith of New Hampshire. A version of the bill has been reported by a bipartisan majority of the Senate Judiciary Committee. And the bill enjoys the support of ordinary Americans across the political spectrum.

What would the Innocence Protection Act do? As reported by the committee, the bill proposes two minimum steps that we need to take—not to make the system perfect, but simply to reduce what is currently an unacceptably high risk of error. First, we need to make good on the promise of modern technology in the form of DNA testing. Second, we need to make good on the constitutional promise of competent counsel.

DNA Testing

DNA testing comes first because it is proven and effective. We all know that DNA testing is an extraordinary tool for uncovering the truth, whatever the truth may be. It is the fingerprint of the 21st Century. Prosecutors across the country rightly use it to prove guilt. By the same token, it should also be used to do what it is equally scientifically reliable to do: to establish innocence.

Just like fingerprints, in many crimes there are no fingerprints; in many crimes there is no DNA evidence.

Where there is DNA evidence, it can show us conclusively, even years after a conviction, where mistakes have been made. And there is no good reason not to use it.

Allowing testing does not deprive the State of its ability to present its case, and under a reasonable scheme for the preservation and testing of DNA evidence, it should be possible to preserve the evidence.

The Innocence Protection Act would therefore provide improved access to DNA testing for people who claim that they have been wrongfully convicted.

[In November 2002], prosecutors in St. Paul, MN, vacated a 1985 rape conviction after a review of old cases led to DNA testing that showed they had the wrong man—and also identified the actual rapist. Think how much better society would have been had they caught the real rapist 17 years ago. The district attorney wanted to conduct DNA testing in two other cases, but the evidence in those cases had already been destroyed. She has called on law enforcement agencies to adopt policies requiring retention of such evidence, and that is what our bill would call for.

> *"Where there is DNA evidence, it can show us conclusively, even years after a conviction, where mistakes have been made."*

The Need for Competent Counsel

Many cases have no DNA evidence to be tested, just as in most cases there are no fingerprints. In the vast majority of death row exonerations, no DNA testing has or could have been involved.

So the broad and growing consensus on death penalty reform has another top priority. All the statistics and evidence show that the single most frequent cause of wrongful convictions is inadequate defense representation at trial. The biggest thing we can do is to guarantee at least minimum competency for the defense in a capital case.

This bill offers States extra money for quality and accountability.

They can decline the money but then the money will be spent on one or more organizations that provide capital representation in that State. One way or another, the system is improved.

> *"All of the statistics and evidence show that the single most frequent cause of wrongful convictions is inadequate defense representation at trial."*

More money is good for the states. More openness and accountability is good for everyone. And better lawyering makes the trial process far less prone to error.

When I was a State's Attorney in Vermont, I wanted those I prosecuted to have competent defense counsel. I wanted to reach the right result in my trials, whatever that was, and I wanted a clean record, not a record riddled with error. Any prosecutor worth his or her salt will tell you the same; any prosecutor who is afraid of trying his cases against competent defense counsel ought to try a new line of work, because the whole system works better if both prosecutor and defense counsel are competent. That is what I wanted when I was prosecuting cases because I wanted to make sure justice was done.

The Constitution requires the Government to provide an attorney for any defendant who cannot afford one. The unfortunate fact is that in some parts of the country, it is better to be rich and guilty than poor and innocent, because the rich will get their competent counsel, but those who are not rich often find their lives placed in the hands of underpaid court-appointed lawyers who are inexperienced, inept, uninterested, or worse.

We have seen case after case of sleeping lawyers, drunk lawyers, lawyers who meet with their clients for the first time on the eve of trial, and lawyers who refer to their own clients with racial slurs.

Part of the problem, I think, lies with some state court judges who do not appear to expect much of anything from criminal defense attorneys, even when they are representing people who are on trial for their lives. Good judges, like good prosecutors, want competent lawyering for both sides. But some judges run for reelection touting the number and speed of death sentences they have handed down. For them, the adversary system is a hindrance.

The problem of low standards is not confined to elected State judges. [In 2002] a bare majority of the Supreme Court held that it was okay for the defendant in a capital murder trial to be represented by the same lawyer who represented the murder victim. Most law students would automatically say that is a conflict of interest, but our Supreme Court said that was all right. And [in 2001] a Federal appeals court struggled with the question whether a defense lawyer who slept through most of his client's capital murder trial provided effective assistance of counsel.

Fortunately, a majority of the court eventually came to the sensible conclusion that "unconscious counsel equates to no counsel at all," basically reversing what a State court said when it said the Constitution guarantees a person counsel. It does not guarantee they will stay awake.

No law can guarantee that no innocent person will be convicted. But surely we can do better than this. Surely we can demand more of defense counsel than that they simply show up for the trial and remain awake. When people in this country are put on trial for their lives, they should be defended by lawyers who meet reasonable standards of competence and who have sufficient funds to investigate the facts and prepare thoroughly for trial. As citizens, we expect that of our prosecutors. We ought to expect the same thing of our defense attorneys. That is all we ask for in the IPA.

Responding to Critics' Arguments

I have heard four arguments against the bill. One wonders, with all these people from the right to the left, all these editorial writers and Members of Congress from both parties supporting the IPA, what that tells us.

First, critics claim that the bill is an affront to States' rights. As a Vermonter, and as a former State prosecutor, I agree that States' rights are very important. States should have the right to set their own laws, free of Federal preemption at the behest of special interests. They should have the right to set their own budgets, free of unfunded mandates. And their reasonable expectations of Federal funding for criminal justice and other essential programs should be met, rather than bankrupting State governments because of Federal tax policy.

The IPA is entirely consistent with these principles of State sovereignty. It leaves State laws, including the death penalty laws, in place. It offers States new funding for their criminal justice systems. And there was a provision added during the committee process establishing a student loan forgiveness program for prosecutors and public defenders, something that a lot of State governments say would help recruit and retain competent young lawyers.

> *"We have seen case after case of sleeping lawyers, drunk lawyers, . . . and lawyers who refer to their own clients with racial slurs."*

This is one of those cases, like in the civil rights era, where the rhetoric of States rights is being abused as a code for the denial of basic justice and accountability. Some States have made meaningful reforms, but many have not. They have had more than a quarter of a century and 100 death row exonerations to get their act together, but they have failed. As many in this body argued in 1996, when promoting legislation to speed up executions, justice delayed is justice denied. I agree with that. We cannot wait forever while innocent lives are in peril.

I have heard a second argument against the IPA, which is that society cannot afford to pay for these reforms. The truth, however, is that we cannot afford to do otherwise if we want to maintain confidence in our criminal justice system. The costs of providing DNA testing and competent counsel are relatively small, especially when you compare them to the costs of retrials that are necessitated by the lack of adequate counsel at trial, or the cost of locking up innocent people for years or even decades. I am all for efficiency, but the greatest nation on Earth should not be skimping on justice in matters of life or death.

I have heard a third argument from a vocal minority of State prosecutors. They claim the bill would make it unduly difficult, if not impossible, to seek the death penalty. That is a shocking claim. When I prosecuted cases, I felt very comfortable prosecuting those cases under the laws of our State because of two things: I knew that all the evidence we had, including potentially exonerating evidence, had been given to the defendant. And I knew I was working in a well-functioning adversarial system with effective representation on the other side. That is the way it is supposed to work.

When I hear a prosecutor say that the IPA reforms—enabling DNA testing and securing adequate defense representation—would make it almost impossible for him to do his job, it makes me wonder what he thinks that job is.

Innocence Denial

Finally, there is one more argument against the bill which is rarely stated out loud. I call it the "innocence denial" argument. We saw this in the Earl Washington case in Virginia where, despite conclusive DNA evidence to the contrary, the Commonwealth for years clung to the hopelessly unreliable and implausible confession of a mentally retarded man. We see it in claims that "the system is working" when an innocent man is released after years on death row due to the work of journalism students. And we see it in the often-repeated insistence that, no matter how many people have been exonerated, no one can prove that an innocent person has actually been executed.

The innocence deniers will never concede there is a problem. But with 100 known instances of the system failing—and those are only the ones we know about—it would be surprising if there were not more unknown cases of innocent people being sentenced to death.

The IPA was passed out of committee in the Senate and is supported by a majority of the House. We ought to pass it before more lives are ruined.

As a prosecutor, I never had any hesitation to seek the severest penalties our State could provide for people who committed serious crimes. When I look at some of the cases I have reviewed over recent years, when I see shoddy evidence, or when I see evidence that was not looked at because it might have pointed to someone else, I wonder, why wouldn't society want a better system? Passing the IPA will help fix these problems and give greater credibility to our criminal justice system.

The Mentally Disadvantaged Should Not Be Sentenced to Death

by Michael B. Ross

About the author: *Michael B. Ross has been on Connecticut's death row since June of 1987. His case is under appeal.*

> The death penalty is an absolute punishment. If it is to be imposed at all, it should be imposed on people whose sense of responsibility and judgment is such that they fully appreciated the seriousness of what they were doing.

These words by David Bruck, a lawyer who has represented numerous capital defendants, appeared in the *International Herald Tribune* on June 23, 1987. Most people not only agree with the sentiment expressed but believe that only the most cunning and culpable of criminals are executed in this country—that the mentally ill and mentally retarded are explicitly excluded. Far too often, however, they are wrong.

As things now stand, mentally disadvantaged defendants often have to rely on a defense referred to as "diminished capacity." This simply means that such defendants may have known right from wrong but did not have full control over their actions, resulting in an inability to refrain from acts that people of average abilities could resist or simply would not commit.

The Problem with the "Diminished Capacity" Defense

Two basic problems face capital defendants trying to prove diminished capacity in court. The first is the skepticism with which most people view such a defense. All people are assumed to be normal and fully responsible for their actions, so it is the defendants' burden to prove otherwise.

Many people mistakenly believe that they can just look at a defendant and tell if he or she has a significant mental disorder. Even when a competent psychia-

Michael B. Ross, "Don't Execute Mentally Disturbed Killers," *The Humanist*, January/February 1999.

trist has diagnosed a mental illness or mental retardation, juries tend to dismiss the diagnosis if the defendant "looks normal."

There are several reasons for this. First, there is a general lack of confidence in psychiatric testimony. Second, there is a pervasive feeling that psychiatrists testifying for the defense will give whatever diagnosis is desired—and that psychiatrists testifying for the state are somehow more credible and less likely to be "bought." Third, it is generally assumed that a person whose life is on the line will feign a mental disorder and be able to fool even the best-trained psychiatrist. And finally, even if the defendant is proven to be mentally disturbed, it is often felt that she or he is somehow "getting away" with the crime. These feelings present formidable obstacles for any mentally disadvantaged defendant to overcome.

The second basic difficulty with proving diminished capacity has to do with the nature of capital crimes themselves. Often these are terrible crimes of a disturbing and heinous nature, and the trials can become extremely emotionally charged, leading many jurists to ignore even clear cases of a mental disorder.

The U.S. Supreme Court has mandated that mental disorders are mitigating factors, but this has not prevented mentally disadvantaged people from ending up on death row. It is estimated that 10 percent of all current death-row inmates are mentally ill and another 10 percent are mentally retarded. That translates to more than 600 mentally disadvantaged defendants currently under sentence of death in this country today. Some have already been executed.

Cases Involving Mentally Disadvantaged Defendants

Varnell Weeks was executed in Alabama for murder. Weeks had been diagnosed as being severely mentally ill and suffering from a "longstanding paranoid schizophrenia." Psychiatrists testifying for both the defense and prosecution agreed that he suffered from pervasive and bizarre religious delusions. Weeks believed that he was God, that his execution was part of a millennial religious scheme to destroy humankind, and that he would not die but, rather, would be transformed into a giant tortoise and reign over the universe.

An Alabama judge acknowledged that Weeks believed he was God in

> *"It is estimated that 10 percent of all current death-row inmates are mentally ill and another 10 percent are mentally retarded."*

various manifestations and that he was a paranoid schizophrenic who suffered delusions. The judge's ruling went on to say that Weeks was "insane" according to "the dictionary generic definition of insanity" and what "the average person on the street would regard to be insane." However, the judge ruled that the electrocution could proceed because Weeks' ability to answer a few limited questions about his execution proved that he was legally "competent."

Morris Mason was executed in Virginia for murdering an elderly woman during an alcoholic rampage. She was burned to death after Mason had raped her, nailed her to a chair by the palms of her hands, and set the house on fire. Mason had a long history of mental illness and, prior to his arrest, had spent time in three state mental hospitals where he was diagnosed as mentally retarded and suffering from paranoid schizophrenia. In the week before the killing, he had twice sought help from his parole officer for his uncontrollable drinking and drug abuse. The day before the crime, he had asked to be placed in a halfway house but no openings were available.

> *"The death penalty . . . should clearly be limited to the most vicious, premeditated crimes. The acts of mentally disadvantaged criminals clearly do not qualify."*

Johnny Frank Garrett was executed in Texas for the rape and murder of an elderly man. He was chronically psychotic and brain-damaged. One psychiatrist who examined Garrett described him as "one of the most psychiatrically impaired inmates" she had ever examined. Another said he had "one of the most virulent histories of abuse and neglect . . . encountered in over twenty-eight years of practice."

The late U.S. Supreme Court Justice Thurgood Marshall once wrote:

> At a time in our history when the streets of the nation's cities inspire fear and despair, rather than pride and hope, it is difficult to maintain objectivity and concern for our fellow citizens. But the measure of a country's greatness is its ability to retain compassion in times of crises.

If the death penalty is to be maintained, it should clearly be limited to the most vicious, premeditated crimes. The acts of mentally disadvantaged criminals clearly do not qualify. This distinction can be recognized by introducing verdicts of "guilty but mentally ill" and "guilty but mentally retarded," which would prohibit the death penalty in such cases and automatically impose sentences of life without the possibility of parole. This would offer some measure of protection to the mentally disadvantaged while guaranteeing the protection of the public. This is clearly the most logical and compassionate thing to do.

Abolitionists Distort Data to Make Capital Punishment Seem Unfair

by Michael Tremoglie

About the author: *Michael Tremoglie is a former police officer who writes about criminal justice policy. He lives in Philadelphia, Pennsylvania.*

In March 1979, a Graterford (Pa.) prison guard was murdered brutally by an inmate. The inmate—at the time he murdered the guard—already was serving a life sentence for the triple murder of two infants and an elderly woman.

In 1994, an inmate who already was serving two life sentences in the Philadelphia Industrial Correctional Center was sentenced to three more after he was convicted of stabbing three prison guards.

In 1995, two death-row inmates at the Florida State Prison in Starke were killed by their fellow inmates.

In 1999, a Beeville (Texas) prison guard was killed by an inmate already serving a sentence for murder.

More examples could be cited, but it would be pointless. The fact is that murderers who already are imprisoned murder again. According to the latest Department of Justice (DOJ) information, of those sentenced to be executed, 65.7 percent had been convicted of a prior felony. Nearly one in 10 had been convicted of a prior homicide, and 4 percent either were in prison or escaped from prison when they murdered again.

Liberal Media Censorship

Those who say capital punishment is not a deterrent, or who say life imprisonment is an effective substitute, should examine these facts. Unfortunately, this information is not readily available because of the de facto censorship by liberal media that only publish the canards of those who want to abolish capital punishment.

Michael Tremoglie, "Capital Punishment Canards," *Insight on the News*, vol. 190, March 4, 2003, p. 52.

One such canard proffered is that scores of innocent people have been executed. Maryland Attorney General J. Joseph Curran recently announced that he wants to end capital punishment in his state because of this. He cited a study by the Death Penalty Information Center (DPIC), an abolitionist group that claims 102 people sentenced to be executed have been exonerated.

The exonerated persons DPIC cited include:

• Ricardo Aldape Guerra, who was convicted in the murder of a Houston cop in 1982 and was exonerated in 1997 when evidence indicated he may have been only the accomplice;

• Steve Manning, who was convicted for an Illinois homicide in 1993. He saw his conviction dismissed in 1998. In 2000 the district attorney chose not to retry Manning, primarily because he already was serving two life sentences;

> *"The disinformation campaign by [death-penalty] abolitionists is quite effective, and they are well-funded."*

• Clarence Smith, who was reconvicted in a federal court in 1998 of crimes that included the death for which he was acquitted in a state court.

These are not who most of us think of when we think of innocent people. There are other inconsistencies in the DPIC report, but the media do not mention any of them. The mainstream liberal media prefer to be the myrmidons of capital-punishment abolitionists. The liberal media are their accomplices.

Abolitionist Deceit

Another abolitionist canard is the 1993 U.S. Supreme Court case of *Herrera v. Collins*. According to the death-penalty abolitionists, the Supreme Court held that "new evidence of innocence to stop an execution was unconstitutional." The Supreme Court made no such statement, yet this canard is repeated routinely in colleges and by the solons of public policy. Actor Mike Farrell of the TV show *MASH*, an anti-capital-punishment crusader, made this claim while giving a speech before the Iowa Legislature in 1998.

The disinformation campaign by abolitionists is quite effective, and they are well-funded. Politicians, entertainers, academicians and even so-called conservative journalists, all of whom can influence public policy, are unaware of pro-capital-punishment data. Of course, this is exactly what the abolitionists desire. The result is that policymakers such as the Maryland attorney general believe abolitionist claims.

Ironically, despite the deceit, Americans approve of capital punishment. A Gallup poll in October 2002 indicated that Americans favor the death penalty by a ratio of almost 3-to-1 (70 percent in favor compared with 25 percent in opposition). A 2000 Zogby poll revealed that 78 percent of Italian-Americans and 75 percent of Asian-Americans favored capital punishment. Among Hispanics, Zogby found 73 percent supported the death penalty, while 71 percent of Arab-

Americans advocated capital punishment. Even 64 percent of this country's African-Americans, the group supposedly most "discriminated" against by capital punishment, favor it.

The Vilest Canard

This racial-discrimination claim is the vilest canard. Abolitionists claim blacks are sentenced to be executed in disproportion to their numbers in the general population. What capital-punishment abolitionists conveniently omit is that blacks make up a disproportionate number of the country's murder victims. According to DOJ data, "Racial differences exist, with blacks disproportionately represented among homicide victims and offenders. Blacks were six times more likely than whites to be murdered in 1999." Unlike college admissions, capital punishment does not consider race.

The capital-punishment abolitionists—along with most liberals—attempt to divide America. They will cleave the races, the classes, the genders or the faithful so that they can obtain control. There are some legitimate grounds to want to abolish capital punishment. However, the liberals tend to present their case using propaganda and deceit.

Those who oppose capital punishment are chasing a chimera. Furthermore, what makes their ideas risky is that in their quest for cosmic justice, there indeed will be innocent people killed. It was people such as these crusaders to whom Edmund Burke alluded when, in 1791, he wrote a letter to the Chevalier de Rivarol in which he stated, "The men who today snatch the worst criminals from justice will murder the most innocent persons tomorrow."

Reports About Errors in the U.S. Capital Punishment System Are Biased

by Paul G. Cassell

About the author: *Paul G. Cassell is a professor of law at the University of Utah.*

[In June 2000] avowed opponents of the death penalty caught the attention of [then vice president] Al Gore among others when they released a report purporting to demonstrate that the nation's capital punishment system is "collapsing under the weight of its own mistakes." Contrary to the headlines written by some gullible editors, however, the report proves nothing of the sort.

At one level, the report is a dog-bites-man story. It is well known that the Supreme Court has mandated a system of super due process for the death penalty. An obvious consequence of this extraordinary caution is that capital sentences are more likely to be reversed than lesser sentences are. The widely trumpeted statistic in the report—the 68% "error rate" in capital cases—might accordingly be viewed as a reassuring sign of the judiciary's circumspection before imposing the ultimate sanction.

Deceptive Factoids

The 68% factoid, however, is quite deceptive. For starters, it has nothing to do with "wrong man" mistakes—that is, cases in which an innocent person is convicted for a murder he did not commit. Indeed, missing from the media coverage was the most critical statistic: After reviewing 23 years of capital sentences, the study's authors (like other researchers) were unable to find a single case in which an innocent person was executed. Thus, the most important error rate—the rate of mistaken executions—is zero.

What, then, does the 68% "error rate" mean? It turns out to include any reversal of a capital sentence at any stage by appellate courts—even if those courts ultimately uphold the capital sentence. If an appellate court asks for additional findings from the trial court, the trial court complies, and the appellate court then affirms the capital sentence, the report finds not extraordinary due process but a mistake. Under such curious scorekeeping, the report can list 64 Florida postconviction cases as involving "serious errors," even though more than one-third of these cases ultimately resulted in a reimposed death sentence, and in not one of the Florida cases did a court ultimately overturn the murder conviction.

> *"[Researchers] were unable to find a single case in which an innocent person was executed."*

To add to this legerdemain, the study skews its sample with cases that are several decades old. The report skips the most recent five years of cases, with the study period ostensibly covering 1973 to 1995. Even within that period, the report includes only cases that have been completely reviewed by state appellate courts. Eschewing pending cases knocks out one-fifth of the cases originally decided within that period, leaving a residual skewed toward the 1980s and even the 1970s.

During that period, the Supreme Court handed down a welter of decisions setting constitutional procedures for capital cases. In 1972 the court struck down all capital sentences in the country as involving too much discretion. When California, New York, North Carolina and other states responded with mandatory capital-punishment statutes, the court in 1976 struck these down as too rigid. The several hundred capital sentences invalidated as a result of these two cases inflate the report's error totals. These decades-old reversals have no relevance to contemporary death-penalty issues. Studies focusing on more recent trends, such as a 1995 analysis by the Criminal Justice Legal Foundation, found that reversal rates have declined sharply as the law has settled.

A Simplistic Assumption

The simplistic assumption underlying the report is that courts with the most reversals are doing the best job of "error detection." Yet courts can find errors where none exist. About half of the report's data on California's 87% "error rate" comes from the tenure of former Chief Justice Rose Bird, whose keen eye found grounds for reversing nearly every one of the dozens of capital appeals brought to her court in the 1970s and early 1980s. Voters in 1986 threw out Bird and two of her like-minded colleagues, who had reversed at least 18 California death sentences for a purportedly defective jury instruction that the California Supreme Court has since authoritatively approved.

The report also relies on newspaper articles and secondhand sources for factual assertions to an extent not ordinarily found in academic research. This approach produces some jarring mistakes. To cite one example, the study claims William Thompson's death sentence was set aside and a lesser sentence imposed. Not true. Thompson remains on death row in Florida today for beating Sally Ivester with a chain belt, ramming a chair leg and nightstick into her vagina and torturing her with lit cigarettes (among other depravities) before leaving her to bleed to death.

These obvious flaws in the report have gone largely unreported. The report was distributed to selected print and broadcast media nearly a week in advance of [the June 2000] embargo date. This gave ample time to orchestrate favorable media publicity, which conveniently broke 24 hours before the Senate Judiciary Committee began hearings on capital-sentencing issues.

The report continues what has thus far been a glaringly one-sided national discussion of the risk of error in capital cases. Astonishingly, this debate has arisen when, contrary to urban legend, there is no credible example of any innocent person executed in this country under the modern death-penalty system. On the other hand, innocent people undoubtedly have died because of our mistakes in failing to execute.

Real Mistakes

Colleen Reed, among many others, deserves to be remembered in any discussion of our error rates. She was kidnapped, raped, tortured and finally murdered by Kenneth McDuff during the Christmas holidays in 1991. She would be alive today if McDuff had not narrowly escaped execution three times for two 1966 murders. His life was spared when the Supreme Court set aside death penalties in 1972, and he was paroled in 1989 because of prison overcrowding in Texas. After McDuff's release, Reed and at least eight other women died at his hands. [Then] Gov. George W. Bush approved McDuff's execution in 1998.

While no study has precisely quantified the risk from mistakenly failing to execute justly convicted murderers, it is undisputed that we extend extraordinarily generosity to murderers. According to the National Center for Policy Analysis, the average sentence for murder and non-negligent manslaughter is less than six years. The Bureau of Justice Statistics has found that of 52,000 inmates serving time for homicide, more than 800 had previously been convicted of murder. *That* sounds like a system collapsing under the weight of its own mistakes—and innocent people dying as a result.

Racism Does Not Influence the Administration of the Death Penalty

by John Perazzo

About the author: *John Perazzo is the author of* The Myths That Divide Us: How Lies Have Poisoned American Race Relations.

Maryland Governor Parris Glendening recently joined an ever-growing list of public officials and social activists to question the manner in which the death penalty is administered to convicted murderers in the US. Upon learning that nine of Maryland's thirteen current death-row inmates are black, Glendening expressed his concern about possible racial bias in the justice system and promptly suspended executions in his state.

Mr. Glendening has plenty of company in holding this position. The NAACP [National Association for the Advancement of Colored People] Legal Defense and Education Fund, for instance, asserts that "history and current practice continue to show that the death penalty is steeped in a tradition of racism and cannot, for that reason, be applied in a fair manner." According to Amnesty International, "The United States legal system is riddled with deeply ingrained racial and ethnic divisions. The prejudices of some police, jurors, judges and prosecutors reflect contemporary racial and ethnic divisions in US society and nowhere is racial discrimination more evident, or more deadly, than in the application of the death penalty." The National Coalition to Abolish the Death Penalty which is comprised of the American Civil Liberties Union, the National Urban League, and some 140 other organizations complains that capital punishment is overwhelmingly reserved for racial minorities. Representative John Conyers emphatically agrees.

Louis Farrakhan goes even further, stating that "the unfair use of the death penalty to punish the black male is in fact a systematic genocidal tool being institutionalized to significantly decrease the black population." In 1996, Rev.

Jesse Jackson co-authored the book *Legal Lynching: Racism, Injustice, and the Death Penalty.* At a recent Chicago rally, Jackson compared the inherent racism underlying capital punishment to the inherent racism that once supported the institution of slavery. "You couldn't really fix slavery," said Jackson. "You couldn't modify it. . . . We had to abolish the slavery system. Let's abolish the death penalty."

The Racism Myth

If all the aforementioned charges were true, there would indeed be good reason to consider outlawing capital punishment. Certainly we cannot tolerate separate standards of justice based on race. Remarkably, however, none of the charges are true. While there may be valid moral and ethical reasons to oppose the death penalty, racial inequity is simply not one of them.

Consider the pertinent facts. According to the Bureau of Justice Statistics, whites who are arrested for

> *"While there may be valid . . . reasons to oppose the death penalty, racial inequity is simply not one of them."*

murder or non-negligent manslaughter are actually more likely than their black counterparts to be sentenced to death (1.6 percent vs. 1.2 percent). Of those inmates under death sentences, whites are actually likelier than blacks to have their sentences carried out (7.2 percent vs. 5.9 percent). These disparities are not huge, and the purpose here is not to suggest that they indicate bias against whites; the point is that in no way do they support the notion of bias against blacks.

Contrary to the rhetoric of our contemporary racial arsonists and "civil rights" organizations, scholars have known for quite some time that capital punishment is not applied in a racist manner. In his 1987 book *The Myth of a Racist Criminal Justice System*, Professor William Wilbanks cites an important study which found that between 1977 and 1984, white killers were actually more likely to get the death penalty than were black killers. Even more to the point, Wilbanks notes that "whites who had killed whites were more likely than blacks who had killed whites to be on death row, [and] whites who killed blacks were more likely to reach death row than blacks who killed blacks." In other words, even a full generation ago the anti-capital punishment crowd's most popular contention was already nothing more than a hollow fable.

Race Plays No Significant Role

More recently, in their 1997 book *America in Black and White*, Stephan and Abigail Thernstrom point out that "black offenders over the past generation have not been sentenced to death at a higher rate than white offenders. No careful scholarly study in recent years has demonstrated that the race of the defendant has played a significant role in the outcome of murder trials." The Thernstroms also note that while fully 58 percent of prisoners currently serving sentences for murder are black, only 40 percent of inmates on death row are black. That is, relative to the rate at which black offenders commit murder, they are sentenced to death in disproportionately low numbers.

Finally, if courts were unfairly imposing the death penalty against black defendants who deserved more leniency, we would expect to find that blacks on death row have cleaner criminal records than their white counterparts. But in fact, the exact opposite is true. Blacks awaiting execution are 10 percent likelier to have had felony convictions, and 20 percent likelier to have had homicide convictions, prior to the crimes that propelled them to death row.

Is it possible that Governor Glendening is unaware of these thorny but vital facts? If so, is it not irresponsible of him to parade the haunting, oft-unfurled banner of racism before the eyes of the American people once again? Haven't our perceptions of reality already been compromised enough by the nonsense of demagogues in recent decades?

Claims About Innocents on Death Row Are Exaggerated

by Ramesh Ponnuru

About the author: *Ramesh Ponnuru is a writer for the* National Review, *a conservative journal of opinion.*

A terrible injustice was done to Ray Krone. In 1992, he was sentenced to death for the murder of Kim Ancona, a Phoenix cocktail waitress. He spent three years on Death Row before his first conviction was overturned. On retrial, he was sentenced to life in prison. All the while, he maintained that he was innocent. Eventually, DNA analysis proved that he was telling the truth: Another man had committed the crime. In April of [2002], Krone was freed.

In Washington, D.C., Sen. Russ Feingold marked the occasion. Krone, the Wisconsin Democrat said, was "the hundredth person to be released from Death Row in the modern death-penalty era"—since, that is, the Supreme Court allowed the practice to resume in 1976. "How many innocent Americans today sit in their prison cells wrongly accused, counting down the days until there are no more?" Feingold asked. "There have now been 100 exonerations and 766 executions since the early 1970s. In other words, for every seven to eight Death Row inmates executed by the states or federal government, one has been found innocent and released from Death Row. . . . One risk, one error, one mistake, is one too many. But 100 mistakes, proven mistakes, qualifies as a crisis. And a crisis calls for action." Feingold wants a national moratorium on the death penalty. Failing that, he favors his colleague Patrick Leahy's Innocence Protection Act, which backers say would improve the administration of the death penalty.

The Exonerated Are Not Always Innocent

Krone's case is certainly disturbing. But have there really been 100 such "proven mistakes," as Feingold put it, in the last quarter century? The senator, like the many others who make this claim, relies on the "Innocence List" compiled by the Death Penalty Information Center [DPIC], a group that opposes capital punishment. According to its list, the total number of people who spent time on Death Row but were later exonerated is [as of 2002] up to 102.

But most of the cases on the list are very different from that of Ray Krone. Nobody is going to make a TV movie anytime soon about Jonathan Treadaway, another of DPIC's "Cases of Innocence." Treadaway was convicted in 1975 for sodomizing and murdering a six-year-old boy. His palm prints were found outside the victim's bedroom window, and he said that he could not explain their presence. Pubic hairs on the victim's body were similar to his.

But the Arizona supreme court reversed his conviction. The trial court had admitted evidence that Treadaway had committed sexual acts with a 13-year-old boy three years before the murder. The court held that to be irrelevant without "expert medical testimony" that this act demonstrated a continuing propensity to commit such acts. The court also ordered that at Treadaway's retrial, his statements about the palm prints not be admitted. Treadaway had made those statements voluntarily, but without being advised of his Miranda rights or waiving those rights. Finally, the court excluded some evidence that three months before the murder, Treadaway had been found naked in a young boy's bedroom trying to strangle the boy.

Treadaway didn't get off Death Row because it was proven that the cops had the wrong man. Technicalities spared him.

Jeremy Sheets, another of DPIC's "innocents," got off Death Row because the key witness against him couldn't testify. That was his best friend, Adam Barnett, who told the police that the two of them—both white men—had been angry about all the white women they knew who were dating black men. To get even, they kidnapped and raped a black high-school student. Barnett said that Sheets had then stabbed her to death. Barnett committed suicide in jail. Sheets was sentenced to death on the basis of Barnett's taped confession (and Sheets's own testimony, which the jury found unbelievable). The Nebraska supreme court reversed his conviction because Sheets's lawyer had not been able to cross-examine the dead Barnett. Sheets walked.

The lead police investigator in the case called the result a "travesty," but it was probably the right legal call. What it wasn't was an "exoneration" of Sheets.

> *"[Jonathan] Treadaway didn't get off Death Row because it was proven that the cops had the wrong man. Technicalities spared him."*

John Henry Knapp confessed to the arson-murder of his children and then recanted the confession. He was tried three times. Twice juries hung 7-5 for conviction; in between, he was found guilty and sentenced to death. Eventually the case was settled with a plea bargain. He's on the "Innocence List," too.

A Skewed "Innocence List"

In twelve of the cases on DPIC's list, DNA evidence indicates that the men on Death Row should never have been put there. In another 20 or so, there is other evidence to the same effect. In around 32 cases, then, it has been proven that men on Death Row were innocent of the crime charged. (That's out of more than 7,000 people on Death Row in the modern era.)

No such thing has been proved in the other cases. In some of them, the details are sketchy. Some death sentences were reversed in unpublished opinions. Some cases had to be abandoned because evidence deteriorated with the passage of time. In other cases, people who had participated in murders were removed from Death Row because it was not known whether they had actually pulled the trigger or struck the fatal blow themselves. They were hardly "innocent." There are at least as many Treadaways as Krones on the list. All of them are treated by DPIC, equivalently, as "innocent" and "exonerated."

Richard Dieter, executive director of DPIC, says that former Death Row inmates deserve a presumption of innocence when the charges against them are dismissed. They are indeed entitled to a legal presumption of innocence (in general: John Henry Knapp isn't). But the list leads people to think that innocence has been proven when the most that can be said is that the legal system cannot establish guilt beyond a reasonable doubt. Most of the people who refer to the list clearly

> *"John Henry Knapp confessed to the arson-murder of his children . . . . He's on the 'Innocence List,' too."*

have no idea that many of the "innocents" on it are probably guilty.

There's another problem with the "Innocence List." It's meant to be a critique of the death penalty as it's applied today. But the list includes death sentences that were imposed before today's system emerged. Some on the list got off Death Row because the Supreme Court invalidated the death-penalty statute under which they had been sentenced.

The list is nonetheless widely cited as evidence that the risk of executing the innocent is high. Sen. Leahy wrote [in 2002] that "nearly 100 innocent people have been released from Death Row since 1973." The *New York Times*, the ACLU, and George Will have relied on DPIC's list. It has even been cited, indirectly, at the Supreme Court: The *Los Angeles Times* did a story on Krone as the hundredth exonerated Death Row inmate, and Justice Stephen Breyer referred to the story in his opinion in a death-penalty case.

More Misinformation

Another piece of misinformation is widespread in the death-penalty debate: the claim, from a study led by Columbia University professor James Liebman, that death-penalty cases have a "68 percent error rate." It turns out that the study counts it as an "error" any time a death sentence is reversed at any stage of appellate review—even if the sentence is ultimately upheld. California was found to have an 87 percent "error rate," but half of it could be accounted for by the fact that for several years the chief justice of the state's supreme court was an opponent of the death penalty who kept issuing reversals. In most of the cases in the study, moreover, it was the death sentence that was (sometimes temporarily) overturned, not the murder convictions.

> *"[People] think that innocence has been proven when the most that can be said is that the legal system cannot establish guilt."*

The "over 100" and "68 percent" figures are being used to persuade people that the death penalty is being badly administered and needs to be reformed, if not abolished. The leading reform on offer is Leahy's Innocence Protection Act. In yet another distortion, media coverage of Leahy's bill mostly concerns its provisions to make it easier for Death Row inmates to obtain DNA tests that might prove their innocence. But there isn't much controversy about DNA testing. Most states that have capital punishment have been increasing their use of it. "If Leahy's bill were only about DNA, it would have passed three years ago," says one Senate Republican aide.

The sticking point in the debate is that Leahy's bill would force states to reconfigure their systems for providing Death Row inmates with lawyers. Either states would have to comply with onerous federal mandates, or private organizations that represent such inmates would be given federal money. Opponents of the bill assume that the mandates were designed to be so onerous that states would go for Option Two: taxpayer funding of anti-death-penalty activists.

People facing execution ought to have competent counsel. But there's no crisis calling out for a federal takeover of the area. In most of the 32 cases in which the wrong man faced execution, it wasn't the result of defense lawyers' mistakes. It was the result of gross misconduct by prosecutors and police, or of overreliance on the testimony of jailhouse snitches. Funding 50 miniature versions of the Death Penalty Information Center won't solve those problems. It may, however, lead to some people's release from Death Row—whether or not they're guilty—so that they can be added to the list.

The Mentally Retarded Should Not Be Exempt from the Death Penalty

by Samuel Francis

About the author: *Samuel Francis is a syndicated columnist.*

The Supreme Court is on a rip against the death penalty, ruling [in June 2002] that mentally retarded convicts can't be executed and . . . that only juries, not judges, can decide the facts that justify imposing death. Neither decision appears to be very good law, but it's the former decision that takes the prize for bad logic and dangerous results.

Justice John Paul Stevens wrote the decision in the 6-to-3 ruling in the case of *Atkins vs. Virginia*, arguing that because in the last few years several states have outlawed the execution of mentally retarded convicts, therefore, "It is fair to say that a national consensus has developed against it."

What "National Consensus"?

But in the first place, it's not clear that any such "national consensus" exists. Of the 38 states that allow capital punishment, 18 have laws that bar the execution of retardates. That means that 20 states do not have such laws. In other words, the majority of states that practice capital punishment have little or no problem with executing the mentally retarded. Those that do don't always agree as to who's retarded, how to tell or who should decide. Hence, there is no "national consensus."

In the second place, it's by no means clear what a "national consensus" has to do with whether a practice is constitutional. If there were a "national consensus" that only certain ethnic minority members should be executed, would the Court uphold that? Fifty years ago, when the Warren Court played mumblety-peg with the Constitution, it routinely overrode the existing "national consensus" on a whole series of issues. Many of its decisions were legal garbage, but the whole point of having a Supreme Court composed of unelected judges who hold their seats for life is so they can defy "national consensus" when it violates the Constitution.

But Stevens appealed to the Constitution as well, citing the Eighth Amendment's prohibition of "excessive" bail and fines, and "cruel and unusual punishments." But this principle applies to the retarded only if you assume that their culpability in capital crimes is less than that of mentally normal criminals. Stevens merely asserts that such is the case: "Because of their disabilities in areas of reasoning, judgment and control of their impulses, however, they (the retarded) do not act with the level of moral culpability that characterizes the most serious adult criminal conduct."

In most cases involving retarded defendants, that's probably not true. It may be true in cases in which the defendant is so retarded he probably wasn't able to commit the crime at all, but in the case before the Court, of Daryl Renard Atkins, with an IQ of 59, it clearly was not true. Atkins, with an accomplice, kidnapped a man, robbed him at an ATM machine and then, as Stevens described the crime, "took him to an isolated location where he was shot eight times and killed." Atkins, in other words, was bright enough to know to try to hide his crime. How is he less culpable than any other murderer?

Of course, if the retarded are "less culpable" than normal people, why are they allowed to be free at all? They're still capable of murdering people, robbing them, and causing all sorts of damage and injury. If they're just too dim to avoid doing so, they belong in institutions, not on the streets. Moreover, if mental retardates shouldn't be executed for the capital crimes they commit, why should they be imprisoned? Imprisonment presupposes moral and legal culpability just as much as the death penalty. The logic of the decision points toward the abolition of punishment itself.

The funny part of the ruling in the *Atkins* case is that exempting mental retardates from the death penalty almost necessarily involves using the concept of IQ. For the last few years, that concept has been in the doghouse with the Progressive Element because IQ tests suggest the existence of racial differences. Blacks score about 15 points lower on average than whites, and lots of researchers are convinced the differences are genetically based. To avoid dwelling on the rather unprogressive implications of that fact, some educrats have been abandoning IQ tests as "racist," "white supremacist" and all the rest. Now, when such tests seem able to keep murderers and rapists alive, the progressive types have discovered that IQ is useful after all.

Penal experts estimate that about 10 percent of the 3,600 inmates currently under sentence of death may be mentally retarded, which means that some 360 murderers who are not the sharpest tacks in the carpet may someday be able to pay you or your family or someone else or his family a visit. If and when they do, remember who it was that decided these brainless killers are not really to blame for what they are about to do to you.

Chapter 3

Is Capital Punishment an Effective Deterrent to Crime?

Chapter Preface

Death penalty proponents often contend that executions satisfy the demands of justice and deter potential killers from committing murder. However, while many people may agree that convicted murderers should suffer a punishment that is proportionate to their crime, experts often disagree about the deterrent effect of the death penalty.

Backers of capital punishment often point to crime-rates statistics as proof that executions discourage would-be murderers. Researcher and death-penalty supporter Jay Johansen points out, for example, that the U.S. homicide rate steadily increased between 1965 and 1982, when there were very few executions in the United States. When a surge of executions occurred in 1983, the U.S. murder rate showed its biggest one-year drop. In 1996, when another spike in executions took place, the national homicide rate again fell. Statistics from specific regions of the country offer additional compelling evidence. In Texas in 1980, just before the state reinstated the death penalty, the murder rate was eighteen per 100,000 people. In the year 2000, after nearly twenty years of state sponsored executions, the rate had dropped to nine per 100,000. The city of Houston, Texas, reported 701 murders in 1980; by 1998, that number had dropped to 241. Such a consistent correlation between murder rates and executions cannot be coincidence, Johansen contends: "The obvious conclusion from looking at the statistics . . . is that capital punishment *does* deter murder."

Death penalty critics often question these data, arguing that murder statistics can be affected by multiple variables, including population density, socioeconomic factors, crime-control measures, and arrest and conviction rates. Capital punishment opponent and author Steven E. Landsburg grants that executions do discourage some homicides, but he argues that a high conviction rate is a more consistent and effective deterrent. This is partly because the death penalty is inconsistently applied in the United States, and most murderers realize that they are not likely to face execution. According to Landsburg, potential killers are more likely to avoid murder if they face larger odds of conviction rather than smaller chances of execution. "For the most part," Landsburg maintains, "criminals prefer a small chance of a big punishment to a big chance of a small punishment. . . . So if you want to make crime less attractive to criminals, it's better to double the odds of conviction than to double the severity of the punishment."

Criminal justice experts and policy makers continue to dispute the alleged deterrent effect of capital punishment. As the following chapter reveals, both supporters and critics of the death penalty seem to have compelling evidence to support their arguments, with some claiming that executions deter crime and others asserting that capital punishment actually increases violence.

Capital Punishment Is a Deterrent

by Paul H. Rubin

About the author: *Paul H. Rubin is professor of economics and law in the Department of Economics at Emory University.*

Many arguments can be made for or against the death penalty. Many of them focus on aspects of morality: Is it just for the state to kill someone? Should a murderer suffer a punishment similar to the loss of his victims? Is "an eye for an eye" still appropriate, or is it barbaric?

I will not consider any of these arguments. I will not even argue a position with respect to the death penalty, or capital punishment. Rather, I will analyze the issue as an economist and ask the following questions: What are the consequences of an execution? Will an execution have the effect of deterring other potential murders, or will it merely satisfy some desire for vengeance? That is, I will examine the best evidence available on the question of deterrence. When I have discussed this evidence, readers will be in a position to make their own decisions as to the merits of capital punishment. One cannot make an informed decision without knowing the consequences.

History of Deterrence Research

The question of deterrence has long been at the forefront of the debate on capital punishment. Theoretical arguments exist on both sides. Those arguing against deterrence claim that murderers are not sufficiently rational to calculate probabilities or respond to incentives, or that murders are committed in the heat of passion and murderers do not consider the consequences. Those making the opposite argument claim that humans are generally rational and respond to incentives, and that criminals are not fundamentally different from others in such qualities. Among the major proponents of the latter view is Gary Becker, the Nobel Laureate in economics who, in a famous article published in 1968, argued that criminals respond to changes in conditions in about the same way as everyone else.

Because theory cannot definitively answer the question of the existence of deterrence, analysts have turned to empirical or statistical methods. Among the first to use such analysis on the question of the deterrent effect of capital punishment was Thorsten Sellin. In a 1959 book, Sellin compared states with and without capital punishment and found no significant difference in homicide rates. His methodology is improper, as I show below, but it is still used by some analysts: the *New York Times*, in an article published on September 22, 2000, used exactly this methodology.

Cross-state comparisons present two problems. First, they do not hold enough factors constant in a statistical sense. That is, even states that appear "similar" can differ in many ways that are relevant for determining the homicide rate, and a gross comparison of murder levels by state cannot adjust for these differences. For example, murder rates have been shown to respond to differences in incomes, racial composition, age of the population, and urbanization and population density. The probability of arrest is also a significant factor, and can also vary across states. A simple state-by-state comparison cannot capture these many differences. The only way to adjust for these multiple factors is to use a multivariate statistical tool such as some variant of multiple-regression analysis; simple two-by-two comparisons such as those used by Sellin and the *New York Times* are inadequate. (Sellin was writing before the statistical and computational tools were available to perform the sort of analysis required; the *New York Times* has no such excuse.)

The second reason for the inappropriateness of state-by-state comparisons is that causality can go either way. That is, a state may have capital punishment precisely because it has a higher murder rate and is trying to control this evil. In such a case, observing capital punishment and a high murder rate says nothing about causality, and the deterrence argument is that rates would be even higher if there were no capital punishment.

The first serious attempts to examine these influences in a modern statistically valid model were made by Isaac Ehrlich, a student of Gary Becker's. In two papers published in the 1970s, Ehrlich examined the effect of executions on homicides, one at a national level and one at the level of states. In both he found a statistically significant deterrent effect. However, others

> *"Each execution [leads] to a significant reduction in the number of homicides."*

have reanalyzed his data extensively and have found no such effects. Statisticians and econometricians have had a very active debate over this issue, using Ehrlich's data.

In 1972 the U.S. Supreme Court imposed a moratorium on executions, which was lifted in 1976. From the perspective of this article, the effect of the moratorium was that for four years no data was available to extend the data used by Ehrlich. Moreover, even when the moratorium was lifted, relatively few executions took place because states had to pass new statutes and determine whether these were acceptable to the Court. It was not until 1984 that more than five executions occurred in any given year in the entire United States. To date, no published study has used this data to analyze the question of deterrence.

A Statistical Analysis

Along with two colleagues at Emory University (Hashem Dezhbakhsh and Joanna Mehlhop Shepherd), I have performed a statistical analysis of this data. Our analysis has several advantages over previous analyses. First, we have used county-level data, rather than national or state data. The advantage of county-level data is that populations are more homogeneous within counties, so statistically the results are more accurate. Moreover, there are more than 3,000 counties in the United States, so there is a large amount of data. This large amount facilitates statistical analysis. Second, we use techniques (called "panel data") that were not available when Ehrlich did his research. Moreover, these techniques require large amounts of data, which again are available for the county-level analysis. Thus, we are able to advance the argument significantly because we have more and better data and better statistical techniques than were available to others.

A multiple-regression analysis such as that which we perform essentially estimates homicide rates as a function of demographic and other characteristics of the jurisdiction (here, the county). The analysis then can implicitly calculate the effect of each execution on the number of homicides that would otherwise have occurred.

> *"If we decide not to execute murderers, then we are making a decision that will lead to many additional murders in society."*

In performing this analysis, we had to solve an important problem. We are interested in the effect of an increase in the probability of an execution on homicides. But a probability must be calculated with a denominator. The probability of an execution is the number of executions divided by the number of homicides. But it is necessary to determine the appropriate year for the number of homicides to put in the denominator. It appears that there is now an average lag of six years between commission of a murder and execution. That is, if an execution occurs in 2001, but the crime was committed in 1995, how do we measure the probability? Does the execution in 2001 deter murders in 1995, or in 2007, or for some year in between? To account for this difficulty, we used three measures of the lag structure. We also used two methods of adjusting for missing data. Thus, we ended with six equations measuring the deterrent effect of executions.

In all six cases, we found that each execution led to a significant reduction in the number of homicides. The most conservative estimate (that is, the one with the smallest effect) was that each execution led to an average of eighteen fewer murders. The "95 percent confidence interval" estimate for this value was between eight and twenty-eight fewer homicides. In other words, we can be 95 percent sure that each execution resulted in at least eight fewer homicides, and it is likely that each execution actually deterred more than eight homicides. All other estimates were even larger than this.

Implications

As I mentioned above, the existence of a significant deterrent effect does not prove that capital punishment is good or socially desirable. But it does indicate that if we decide not to execute murderers, then we are making a decision that will lead to many additional murders in society.

Critics of capital punishment raise numerous issues. I will consider one such issue here: the issue of race. Critics claim that African Americans are more likely to be executed than are whites. This may be true. But there are two relevant factors. First, U.S. Department of Justice figures show that African Americans are much more likely to commit homicide than are others. Secondly, and more importantly, African Americans are also more likely to be victims of homicides. For 1999, for example, homicide victimization rates per 100,000 persons were 3.5 for whites and 20.6 for blacks. For that year, there were 7,757 white and 7,134 black homicide victims. Thus, when an execution deters murders, many of these deterred murders would have been of African Americans.

Executions Deter Felony Murders

by William Tucker

About the author: *William Tucker is a New York–based freelance writer and the author of* Excluded Americans: Homelessness and Housing Policies.

The remarkable thing about the death penalty is why anyone would think it *doesn't* deter murder. No one wants to die. Why wouldn't the fear of death make people think twice?

Liberals spend a great deal of time running around this point. The best they can come up with is that murderers are stupid. They don't think. They don't plan. They act on impulse. Murders are "crimes of passion." Executing people is only a "barbaric ritual" that does no good.

Once upon a time there were some grounds for this argument. By the early 1960s, almost 90% of murders were "acquaintance" crimes involving friends or relatives. The most common scenario was an argument that escalated into deadly violence. True, it might involve a romantic rivalry or two casually acquainted people arguing over a card game. But these were "crimes of passion," liberals said. They couldn't be deterred.

And so, beginning with the U.S. Supreme Court's "incorporation" of the 4th and 5th Amendments into state criminal proceedings in the early 1960s and ending with the outright overturn of all state death penalties in 1972, executions ground to a halt.

Executions and Murder Rates

The results can be seen in the accompanying graph. The murder rate had peaked in 1933 during Prohibition violence and executions peaked two years later at 200—about four every week. As gang violence subsided, murders and executions followed each other down at a steady pace until the late 1950s and early 1960s when the murder rate reached its lowest level in history.

Then the upswing started. Executions dropped precipitously after 1962 when the Supreme Court started intervening on the basis of *Mapp v Ohio* (1961),

William Tucker, "Deterring Homicides with the Death Penalty," *Human Events*, April 7, 2003, p. 18.

Gideon v Wainwright (1963) and *Miranda v Arizona* (1966). After 1966, the murder rate soared to unprecedented heights, peaking in 1974, 1980, and again in 1991 before finally dropping again precipitously—when executions were resumed.

What caused this upsurge? There is a fairly simple explanation. Liberals were probably right in arguing in the early 1960s that capital punishment could not deter the 90% of murders that occurred among relatives and acquaintances. What they did not perceive is the murders that *were* being deterred. These were the "stranger" or "felony" murders that have since come to dominate the murder statistics.

The Only Plausible Deterrent

From the criminal's point of view, the logic is fairly simple. When you are committing a felony—either a rape or robbery—there is a certain calculated advantage in *murdering your victim.* The victim, after all, is also the principal witness to the crime. He or she is the person most likely to put you in jail, but screaming or calling for others, by going to the police immediately after you leave, by identifying you, by testifying against you in court. Murdering the victim "leaves no witnesses."

Sometimes this is premeditated. Particularly cold, heartless killers will enter a situation knowing they must kill their victims. John Taylor, now under death sentence in New York for the "Wendy's Massacre," was a former employee who gained entrance to the store to commit an after-hours robbery only because his victims knew him and let him in. Taylor and an accomplice then lined them up and shot them. He went into the store knowing he would *have* to kill each of his victims to avoid identification.[1]

But far more often the killer is an amateur who doesn't realize *until the robbery has begun* that the victim has "had a good look at him" and must be eliminated.

There is no way to contravene this logic of murder except through the death penalty. No amount of pleading or cajoling—no promises that "I won't tell"—will ever convince a robber or rapist that there *isn't* an advantage to escalating the crime to murder. The only plausible deterrent is a *qualitatively* different punishment. If the punishment for robbery is a few years in jail and the punishment for murder is a few more years after that, there is very little if any deterrence. But if the punishment for robbery is jail time and the punishment for murder is *death*, there is reason to think twice.

A Disincentive to Murder

The need to draw a bright line between a felony and felony *murder* was what inspired Enlightenment reformers to argue against capital punishment for crimes *less* than murder. In *The Spirit of the Laws* (1750), Montesquieu wrote:

---

1. This May 2000 massacre in Queens, New York, left five dead and two wounded.

"In China, those who add robbery to murder are cut in pieces: but not so the others; to this difference it is owing that though they rob in that country they never murder. In Russia, where the punishment for robbery and murder are the same, they always murder. The dead, they say, tell no tales."

But eliminating the death penalty creates the exact same dilemma. Without any qualitative differential, there is no disincentive to murder the victim of the crime.

Almost the entire increase in murder from 1966 to the mid-1990s was an increase in *felony* or "stranger" murders—murders committed during the course of another crime. Only when executions resumed in the 1990s did the murder rate drop precipitously to its 1960s level. About 300,000 Americans died unnecessarily in the interim.

A few years ago a New Jersey housewife was kidnapped at a shopping mall by a teenage carjacker. The youth was obviously an amateur and could think of nothing to do but drive the woman around for a few hours. In the process, though, it became obvious that he intended to kill her. The woman spent the better part of an hour pleading for her life. She also had a pocket tape-recorder, which she activated. Over and over she pleads, "Is it worth *my life* for you to have a car?" The logic did not work. He killed her anyway.

But what if the woman had been able to argue, "Is it worth *your* life?" Would that have made a difference?

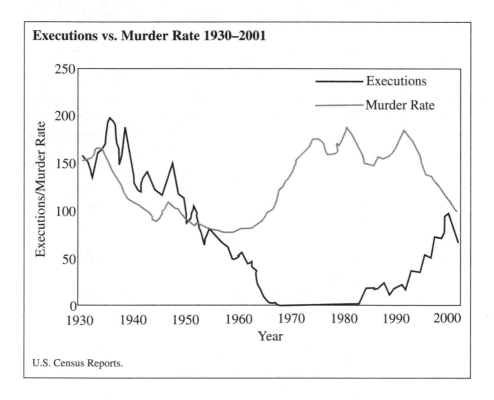

Executions vs. Murder Rate 1930–2001

U.S. Census Reports.

Capital Punishment Protects Innocent Lives

by Jeff Jacoby

About the author: *Jeff Jacoby is a columnist for the* Boston Globe.

Governor Mitt Romney has charged a blue-ribbon commission with drafting a death-penalty law for Massachusetts that can be applied with 100 percent infallibility. The commission will not be able to do so—no legal instrument can be 100 percent infallible—but I don't blame the governor for wanting it to try.

In recent years, anti-death penalty propagandists have succeeded in stoking the fear that capital punishment is being carelessly meted out. But it's a bogus accusation: Of the 875 prisoners executed in the United States in modern times, not one has been retroactively proved innocent. Widely trumpeted claims meant to illustrate the system's sloppiness—that more than 100 innocent men have been freed from Death Row, for example, or that death-penalty cases have a 68 percent error rate—fall apart under scrutiny. In fact, so exacting is the due process in these cases that the death penalty in America is probably the most accurately administered criminal sanction in the world.

The propaganda has taken its toll, however. Romney knows that many people who would otherwise support capital punishment now hesitate for fear it may lead to an awful miscarriage of justice. Hence his call for "a standard of proof that is incontrovertible"—an uncompromising benchmark endorsed by members of the new panel. "In this work," says co-chairman Frederick Bieber, a geneticist at Boston's Brigham and Women's Hospital, "there is no room for error."

That is a worthy goal, but it cannot be an absolute criterion. No worthwhile human endeavor is utterly foolproof. Dr. Bieber's hospital would have to shut down its operating rooms if surgeons had to guarantee their infallibility. Even at hospitals as renowned as the Brigham, patients sometimes die on the operating table because of blunders or inadvertence. Is that an argument for abolishing surgery? Should air travel be banned because innocent passengers may lose their lives in crashes? Should the pharmaceutical industry be shut down because the wrong drug or dosage, mistakenly taken or prescribed, can kill?

The Benefits of Capital Punishment

To make the perfect the enemy of the good is irrational and counterproductive. The benefits of surgery, air travel, and prescription drugs are enormous—far too valuable to give up even though we know that people will die because of the fallibility of doctors and pilots and people who handle medicine. The same is true of capital punishment: The benefits of a legal system in which judges and juries have the option of sentencing the cruelest or coldest murderers to death far outweigh the potential risk of executing an innocent person. And there is this added reassurance: The risk of an erroneous execution is infinitesimal, and getting smaller all the time.

And the benefits? First and foremost, the death penalty makes it possible for justice to be done to those who commit the worst of all crimes. The execution of a murderer sends a powerful moral message: that the innocent life he took was so precious, and the crime he committed so horrific, that he forfeits his own right to remain alive.

When a vicious killer is sent to the electric chair or strapped onto a gurney for a lethal injection, society is condemning his crime with a seriousness and intensity that no other punishment achieves. By contrast, a society that sentences killers to nothing worse than prison—no matter how depraved the killing or how innocent the victim—is a society that doesn't *really* think murder is so terrible.

But there is more to executions than justice for the dead. There is also protection for the living.

Though Romney didn't say so when he introduced his new commission, the real threat to innocent life is not the availability of the death penalty, but the absence of one. For every time a murderer is executed, innocent lives are saved.

The foes of capital punishment have denied for years that putting murderers to death has a deterrent effect on other potential killers. That has always flown in the face of common sense and history—after all, wherever murder is made punishable by death, murder rates generally decline. But it also flies in the face of a lengthening shelf of research that confirms the death penalty's deterrent effect.

A recent study at the University of Colorado, for instance, finds "a statistically significant relationship between executions, pardons, and homicide. Specifically, each additional execution reduces homicides by five to six." A paper by three Emory University economists concludes: "Our results suggest that capital punishment has a strong deterrent effect. . . . In particular, each execution results, on average, in 18 fewer murders—with a margin of error of plus or minus 10."

Comparable results have been reached by scholars at the University of Houston, SUNY [State University of New York] Buffalo, Clemson, and the Federal Communications Commission. All these studies have been published within the past three years. And all of them underscore an inescapable bottom line: The execution of murderers protects innocent life.

The Death Penalty Is the Ultimate Deterrent

by Neil Clark

About the author: *Neil Clark is a teacher and freelance journalist living in Oxford, England.*

No one expects [British prime minister] Tony Blair to seek to reinstate capital punishment during the lifetime of the next parliament. But I should like him to. I am a socialist, and until Mr. Blair jettisoned Clause 4 I was a card-carrying member of the Labour party.[1] According to the childish Left-Right rhetoric of British politics, a socialist is expected to hold a set of 'politically correct' views that includes a 'liberal' approach to punishment and, of course, opposition to the death penalty. Support for capital punishment is supposed to be the preserve of crusty old colonels in the shires or ladies with big hats at the Tory party conference, not that of nationalising, redistributing 'Lefties'. Yet, as a socialist, I believe the case for restoring capital punishment in Britain to be overwhelming, and the opposition to it by many on the 'Left' to be completely illogical.

Opponents of the death penalty argue that it is wrong for the state to take life. This is a line that Tony Blair takes. Yet, to be consistent, holders of this view would also have to be against the state taking life in times of war. As Aldous Huxley once wrote, 'It is impossible to be an 85 per cent pacifist, it is all or nothing.' It is interesting in this context to think back to the 1999 war against Yugoslavia. Then, by and large, the most enthusiastic supporters of the NATO bombing campaign on Belgrade were those politicians and journalists . . . who are fierce in their opposition to any reintroduction of the death penalty in Britain. It seems to me a rather strange morality that justifies the killing of innocent make-up girls and cleaners in a Yugoslav television studio, but not of convicted serial killers at home.

1. Clause 4 is a section of the Labour party's constitution defining its democratic socialist platform, particularly the intent to create "a community in which power, wealth, and opportunity are in the hands of many, not the few."

Neil Clark, "Bring Back the Rope," *The Spectator*, vol. 286, June 9, 2001, p. 12. Copyright © 2001 by *The Spectator*. Reproduced by permission.

The Case for the Death Penalty

The case for the death penalty rests on two tenets: first, that it is just that convicted murderers should pay with their lives; and second, that the death penalty deters.

As for the first point, crucial to the maintenance of any criminal-justice system is that justice should be seen to be done. But in an age when convicted murderers such as Jeremy Bamber[2] can have their own websites, it is of little surprise that public confidence in the whole penal system has broken down.

It is always satisfying when reading crime fiction from the 'Golden Age' that at the end of the novel, the murderer, having been detected by the likes of M. Poirot or Miss Marple, is led off to meet his or her deserved fate on the gallows. Justice was always served. However, if the Queen of Crime [Agatha Christie] were writing today, her convicted murderer would probably be out on appeal after four years and suing the prison authority for

"Every country that has abolished the death penalty has, within five years, seen a dramatic increase in its murder rate."

denying him cable television in his cell. Inadequately protected by the government, police and judiciary, more and more people are seeking to take the law into their own hands. The vigilante state is fast approaching, if it has not arrived already, and cases such as those of the Norfolk farmer Tony Martin[3] will become more and more common.

The second point, that capital punishment acts as a deterrent, has always been disputed by the anti brigade. Yet every country that has abolished the death penalty has, within five years, seen a dramatic increase in its murder rate. The most notable recent example of this phenomenon is South Africa, with Johannesburg being transformed into one of the most dangerous cities in the world. The main reason for this is simple. In the days of the death penalty, criminal gangs would take great care to avoid the risk of violence in their activities, because they knew that, if a killing ensued, they might pay with their lives. Moreover, there is one crime for which the death penalty is arguably the only deterrent, namely the smuggling of hard drugs. With the potential rewards running into millions, and the chances of being caught and punished slim, it is no wonder that, despite 'Drug Czars' and numerous other costly government initiatives, Britain is, in the words of the National Crime Intelligence Service, 'awash with drugs'.

Compare the position of Britain with that of Singapore, a country at which Western liberals love to sneer. All those arriving at Singapore airport are greeted by a large sign stating that anyone convicted of carrying more than a

2. Bamber was sentenced to life in prison in 1986 for murdering five members of his family. 3. Martin served a three-year prison sentence for killing a burglar in self-defense.

small amount of controlled drugs faces the mandatory death sentence. The message could not be plainer. The result is that Singapore is one of the most drug-free nations on earth, and consequently one of the safest. It may be boring for some, but those who get their kicks from watching armed robberies can always go elsewhere.

Miscarriages of Justice Are Rare

Even if we agree that the death penalty acts as a deterrent, what about the possible miscarriages of justice which the anti-hanging liberals love to keep reminding us of? Inevitably, miscarriages of justice did occur when Britain had the death penalty, but their number was tiny and must be set against the considerably larger number of people saved from violent death by the much lower homicide rate. Now, though, there is the very real break-through of DNA-testing, which narrows the odds of wrong conviction to one million to one. That still may not be good enough for [liberal journalists] Paul Foot and Ludovic Kennedy, but it is for me and, I expect, for most other people. The great tragedy about the abolition of the death penalty is that it never was the result of public opinion. In fact, every opinion poll ever taken has shown a clear majority in favour of capital punishment.

To understand why it was abolished, one has to look at changes that took place within the Labour party 50 years ago. From its inception in 1900, the party was primarily working-class. Most of its leaders and key policy-makers were drawn

> *"Death penalty [errors] must be set against the considerably larger number of people saved from violent death by the much lower homicide rate."*

from the working class, and as a result their social values were often more conservative than those of the Tories. The Labour governments of 1924, 1929–31 and 1945–51 all supported the retention of capital punishment. However, from the 1950s things began to change.

A group of middle-class, mainly Oxbridge-educated intellectuals began to gain more and more power within the party. Members of this group . . . were liberals rather than socialists, and their main aim was the social, rather than the economic, transformation of Britain. Out with the death penalty and other such Victorian nonsense, and in with penal reform, easy divorce and the freedom to say 'f——' on television. Although their views had little support among the British working class, this group of 'reformers' managed to take control of the Labour party's social policy and to push through their agenda, starting with the abolition of the death penalty in 1965.

Thirty-five years on, the damaging result of abolition is all too plain to see. Britain has been transformed all right . . . but into a violent and dangerous country. In the year the death penalty was abolished there were 57 murder convictions in Britain; in 1999 there were 241. Britain now has the highest murder rate in Europe. It is time for the people of Britain—the great majority of whom never wanted the death penalty abolished in the first place—to call time on this disastrous liberal penal experiment.

It is also time for the Labour party to acknowledge the mistakes of the past and to ditch its illogical opposition to capital punishment. As Theodore Dalrymple[4] pointed out recently in [the *Spectator*], it is the poor—Labour's natural constituency—whose lives are most severely blighted by violent crime and who have lost most from the reforms of the 1960s. Tony Blair claims to have made New Labour a listening party. He also claims to be 'tough on crime'. Only by bringing back the ultimate deterrent can we start to take these claims seriously, and at the same time to make our ever deadlier streets safe once again.

4. Dalrymple is a physician and psychiatrist who works in a British prison.

Capital Punishment Is Not a Deterrent

by John Bloom

About the author: *John Bloom is a writer for United Press International.*

If I were a death penalty advocate, which I'm not, I would use John Taylor as the poster boy for lethal injection.

Taylor is the guy who masterminded the Wendy's massacre in Queens, [New York, in May 2000]. He tried to execute seven people, but two of them survived and fingered him.

His motive for the crime: money. (He and his accomplice made off with $2,400 in cash.)

His motive for the murders: eliminating witnesses.

He and his mentally retarded assistant duct-taped the mouths of the seven people, put white trash bags over their heads, herded them into a walk-in freezer, lined them up on their knees, and systematically shot them execution-style.

The reason this is the perfect death penalty case, as far as arguing for and against, is that for 50 years now the national debate has centered on one principal issue: Does the death penalty deter crime?

Do Desperate Criminals Consider Consequences?

Since half of the capital crimes that end up going to court are armed robberies gone bad—the stereotypical convenience-store gunman—the whole debate hinges on what we should do when a murder occurs during the commission of a felony. You can argue it either way. Some believe that we'll have fewer armed robberies if potential criminals see the prisons full of drugstore robbers waiting to die.

But the argument is also made that the death penalty doesn't deter crime because the kind of person who wants to hold up a liquor store is not going to be thinking "But what if I kill somebody?" He's already a desperate man, and he's not considering consequences.

But John Taylor ends all ambiguity. He intended to kill those Wendy's employees from the get-go. He didn't think, "If I can get the money and get away clean, I'll let them live." He thought, "The *only* way I can get away clean is to make sure they're all dead." He simply botched the job.

We know this because he was a fired employee of this particular Wendy's, and the only reason they let him inside at closing time was that everyone knew him. Fleeing the scene after a robbery would have gained him nothing. They all knew his name, and the company itself knew where he lived. So the only logical conclusion is that he thought his need for money was worth seven murders.

> *"The kind of person who wants to hold up a liquor store is not going to be thinking 'But what if I kill somebody?'"*

(The other possibility is that he went postal and decided to carry out a massacre as an act of revenge against the company that fired him, and the robbery was just an afterthought. In that case it would be a depraved hate crime that would probably be defended with an insanity defense. Since his public defenders didn't use this, I think we can assume Taylor was not crazed.)

I think the absolute strongest argument for the death penalty comes in cases involving the killing of witnesses. In many crimes, the victim is also the only witness. Most murders by child molesters, for example, are carried out simply to make sure the child doesn't identify the rapist. The idea is that we need the death penalty so that felons will think it's better to let witnesses live than to kill them and get lethally injected later.

If you're thinking about the consequences of your potential crimes when you first case the joint you're going to hold up, your liability runs something like this:

1. Armed robbery: 5 to 15
2. Simple murder: 20 to 40
3. Capital murder: death

The difference between 2 and 3 is what is supposed to keep the witnesses alive. Capital punishment is supposed to encourage the felon to rob but not kill. The idea of getting "stretched" in prison—a sentence often years or more—is frightening to even hardened criminals. And so the question is: are they *more* frightened by the idea of being killed than being stretched?

After all, if you *don't* have capital punishment, then there's very little difference between going down for robbery or going down for murder. If you believe you can get away entirely by killing a witness or two, then your additional risk is *not that great.*

An Undeterred Murderer

And then you have John Taylor. He knew that New York state has capital punishment. It's impossible to live here and *not* know that. He knew he would have to kill the witnesses if he had any chance of avoiding prison. And he chose to do the crime anyway.

This is why I think the death penalty doesn't work. Capital crimes are not committed by people who weigh the consequences of their acts. They don't think, "Well, I'll risk 40 years in prison but I won't risk death." Their whole makeup is focused on the short term. "Tomorrow" is not in their vocabularies.

John Taylor did receive the death penalty, and the verdict was applauded by everyone. But you can't really justify it under any theory of deterrence. He knew he was going to kill. He knew the result of his killing could be his own death. And he was *undeterred*.

In the future, let's retire this word "deterrence" entirely. It's no longer relevant. Let's call it what it is: vengeance. John Taylor must die so that society can feel that a wrong has been righted. But let's not delude ourselves that somehow we've made the streets safer or saved a future life. This is blood for blood. The certainty that he'll die makes us feel better.

Capital Punishment Exacerbates Violence

by Robert Grant

About the author: *Robert Grant is an attorney and former judge living in Augusta, Georgia. He teaches American government in the political science department of Augusta State University. He is also the author of* American Ethics and the Virtuous Citizen: The Right to Life, *from which this essay is adapted.*

To understand the debate over capital punishment, it is necessary to identify the purpose of the criminal justice system. To a majority of Americans it is, essentially, to retaliate and punish those who commit crimes, especially brutal and vicious murders, thus balancing the scales of justice. To others its goal is to reduce violence overall. The question of capital punishment, then, pits two great demands of society against each other: the demand for retribution for violating the most basic duty of the social contract—the duty not to murder another—and the need to eliminate, or at least minimize, society's culture of violence.

A History of Capital Punishment

In the United States, capital punishment was adopted from British common law. Then, from the time of the American Revolution through the Civil War, degrees of murder were developed, dividing the crime into first degree premeditated murder, to which the death penalty applied, and a second degree crime of impulse or passion. This was a compromise between those (mostly Quakers) who wanted to abolish the death penalty entirely and those who wished to keep the law essentially unchanged. From the Civil War until the 1960s many states first abolished and then reinstated capital punishment.

But by the 1960s the role of the federal appellate courts had greatly expanded as they applied the federal Bill of Rights to state criminal proceedings in capital cases, especially the prohibition against cruel and unusual punishment and the requirements for due process and equal protection of the law. This coincided with an increased public demand for an end to capital punishment. As a result,

Robert Grant, "Capital Punishment and Violence," *Humanist*, vol. 64, January/February 2004, p. 25.

capital punishment laws were repealed in several states and no executions were carried out anywhere in the country from 1968 to 1976.

These changes led in June 1972 to the U.S. Supreme Court decision in *Furman v. Georgia*. The Court ruled that the way in which capital punishment statutes were administered was unconstitutional. After reviewing the statistics from the 1920s through the 1960s, the majority concluded: "The death sentence is disproportionately imposed and carried out on the poor, the Negro, and the members of unpopular groups." The conviction and execution of blacks were particularly disparate when the murder victim was white and especially when a white woman was raped. Justice William J. Brennan observed, "When a country of over 200 million people inflicts an unusually severe punishment no more than 50 times a year, the inference is strong that the punishment is not being regularly and fairly applied." The Court also found that excessive punishments are prohibited and concluded that, since life imprisonment is as effective a deterrent as execution, capital punishment was excessive. Justice Thurgood Marshall added, "I cannot believe that at this stage in our history, the American people would ever knowingly support purposeless vengeance."

In response to the decision in *Furman*, the state of Georgia amended its law to provide for capital punishment of certain crimes in a way designed to eliminate excessive penalties as well as discrimination and arbitrariness in deciding who will die. The amended law was then used to convict and sentence to die Troy Gregg for the 1973 murder of two men during his theft of their car. The case, *Gregg v. Georgia*, was appealed to the U.S. Supreme Court, which determined in 1976 that the defendants had been accorded due process of law and that the death penalty in this case didn't constitute cruel and unusual punishment. The Court thus reinstated capital punishment on the ground that the practice wasn't unconstitutional per se.

This decision was reached on the following two bases. First, the Fifth Amendment to the U.S. Constitution expressly recognizes and, to that extent, authorizes the death penalty when it states, "No person shall . . . be deprived of life . . . without due process of law." This is because, by implication, a person may indeed be deprived of life with due process of law. Second, regarding the matter of cruel and unusual punishment, the majority stated that "the petitioners on *Furman* and its companion cases predicated their argument primarily upon the asserted proposition that standards of decency had evolved to the point where capital punishment

> *"Whatever deterrence factor exists for capital punishment . . . exists almost equally for life imprisonment."*

no longer could be tolerated" and that the Eighth Amendment prohibiting cruel and unusual punishment could now be construed "as prohibiting capital punishment." However, "developments during the four years since *Furman* have undercut substantially" that proposition. The majority referred to new death penalty laws that had been enacted in at least thirty-five states in response to *Furman* and to Congress' 1974 passage of a law "providing the death penalty for aircraft piracy that results in death." The majority of justices concluded that all of these "post-*Furman* statutes make clear that capital punishment itself has not been rejected by the elected representatives of the people." Therefore the social evolution in which Justice Marshall had previously placed his belief didn't actually appear evident.

Retribution and Revenge

Today it seems even less evident. Many in U.S. society demand vengeance and retribution for violent criminal conduct. Retributive justice means that the criminal must be made to pay for the crime by a crude mathematics that demands the scales of justice be balanced; this appeals to humanity's basest animal instincts and ancient demands for an eye for an eye, a life for a life. Retributive justice is fueled by hatred and satisfied only with full and complete revenge—the more cruel, the more satisfying. Civil liberties defender and lawyer Clarence Darrow observed that the state "continues to kill its victims, not so much to defend society against them . . . but to appease the mob's emotions of hatred and revenge."

After Oklahoma City bomber Timothy McVeigh was executed amid wide television coverage, over 80 percent of the viewers polled said that he deserved to die; many said his death was too clinical and he should have died more painfully. One man said

> *"Capital punishment actually exacerbates the level and intensity of violence in the community."*

that McVeigh should have been stoned to death. Others were willing to forego his execution because they thought that life behind bars with no possibility of parole would be a greater punishment.

Retributive justice has a bad history, however, as it has historically been used to enforce a class society by oppressing the poor and protecting the rich. It has been used to impose racism by applying the law in an unfairly heavy-handed way upon African-American citizens and in a lenient manner upon white Americans. The U.S. justice system has imprisoned more than two million people; about all are black, although African-Americans constitute only 12 percent of the total population. The prison system has been likened to a twenty-first century form of slavery.

More astonishing, perhaps, is that execution statistics from 1977 through 2002 show that capital punishment isn't so much a national problem as it is a problem local to the South. Nationally, 563 executions occurred during this period and the eleven states of the old Confederacy account for about 87.5 percent of these. Texas is way ahead of the pack, having performed about one-third of all executions. In 2002 Texas alone killed thirty-three death row prisoners. It's no coincidence that the South is also the most violent region of the country.

However as more and more death row prisoners in other states exhaust their appeals, capital punishment will become more of a national problem.

A Deterrent to Murder?

Of those who favor capital punishment, not all would agree that retribution is their motive. Many argue that it is a deterrent to murder. But is it? Think of the troubled boys at Columbine High School who killed a teacher and students first and then committed suicide.[1] Many violent people—particularly violent adolescents—resort to violence toward others only as an alternative to suicide and, in many cases, kill themselves anyway after killing others. Capital punishment wouldn't be a deterrent to them.

If these might be viewed as exceptional circumstances, then a way of

> *"Violence begets more violence."*

covering all circumstances would be to compare statistics between states and nations with and without capital punishment. However, the majority of the justices in *Gregg*, after reviewing the evidence, concluded, "Statistical attempts to evaluate the worth of the death penalty as a deterrent to crimes by potential offenders have occasioned a great deal of debate. The results simply have been inconclusive." This may be because whatever deterrence factor exists for capital punishment probably exists almost equally for life imprisonment.

A far greater deterrent than either, however, would be more efficient police investigation. An average of twenty-two thousand murders and non-negligent manslaughters are committed annually in the United States but only two-thirds, or fifteen thousand, suspects are arrested. And only 45 percent, of about ten thousand, of all accused killers are convicted.

So, in the end, there is only one purpose, one motive, one true reason for demanding death over life imprisonment: revenge. The issue isn't whether the state has the right to execute those who commit premeditated murder; it has. The issue is whether the state ought to execute convicted murders.

Intensifying Violence

The U.S. justice system has reverted to a strictly punitive method in order to prove "tough on crime" and in the hope that stronger punishment will somehow deter future criminal activity. But the reality is that severe punishment isn't working. Kids and petty offenders under the current system become hardened, violent, and persistent criminals. The present punitive and retaliatory justice system is unworthy of the American people's high standard of justice, which values the individual and demands equal justice for all.

Many who seek to eliminate the culture of violence in society assert that capital punishment actually exacerbates the level and intensity of violence in the

1. a reference to the April 1999 school shootings in Littleton, Colorado, which resulted in fifteen deaths

community. They observe that the state is backwardly killing people in order to teach others not to kill. They search for ways to heal the effects of crime upon society, the victim, and the offender. Restorative justice seeks to eliminate violence from the community and heal the harm done to the extent possible.

Violence is a highly contagious social disease that causes emotional, psychological, and physical damage and turns a peaceful person into a hostile one. The essence of violence is hatred, anger, rage, and desire for revenge caused by an act of wrongful violence internalized by the victim. When one allows oneself to be filled with these emotions in response to a violent attack, it allows the attacker to do more than just cause physical injuries. The attacker then does emotional and psychological damage as well. She or he has destroyed the victim's sense of inner tranquility and stability—a destruction that remains long after the physical injuries have healed. When anger, rage, hatred, and vengeance fill that space, the victim is turned from a peaceful to a violent person. This violence is the self-inflicted destruction of one's inner peace.

And violence begets more violence. It is a contagion spreading hatred, anger, rage, and desire for revenge to others out of empathy for the victim. Moreover, a violent victim may seek revenge against the original perpetrator and can be tempted to take out that anger on family members and friends when emotional triggers enflame the violent condition. Violent people don't have ample social skills to resolve differences peacefully and thus the contagion spreads. Each time a person commits a violent act with the intent to injure or kill, the attacker not only causes physical, emotional, and psychological injury to the victim but becomes a more violent person as well. Every act of violence makes the perpetrator more violent—whether the person is someone assaulting an innocent shopkeeper, acting in self-defense, performing a state execution, or soldiering in war. The contagious nature of violence infects the morally righteous police officer as well as the brutal lawbreaker. In his study of young murderers, Cornell University human development professor James Garbarino observes:

> Epidemics tend to start among the most vulnerable segments of the population and then work their way outwards, like ripples in a pond. These vulnerable populations don't cause the epidemic. Rather, their disadvantaged position makes them a good host for the infection. . . . The same epidemic model describes what is happening with boys who kill.

Horrifically, this is a social disorder that can turn innocent people against each other.

How to Respond to Violence

A productive way to react to an act of violence is to have the courage to resist the normal impulse for revenge and punishment, to refrain from allowing anger, hatred, rage, and vengeance to destroy one's inner peace. Civil rights activist Martin Luther King Jr. observed: "Returning violence for violence only multiplies violence, adding deeper darkness to a night already devoid of stars. Darkness cannot drive out darkness, only light can do that. Hate cannot drive out hate; only love can do that."

On the day of McVeigh's execution, a pastor at a memorial service for some of the victims' families asked, "Is there another way we can respond to this violence without doing violence ourselves?" Restorative justice doesn't promote anger, hatred, rage, or revenge by society or by the victim but offers a nonviolent response to the violence done. The focus of restorative justice isn't the punishment of the offender; it is the separation of the violent person from peaceful society for the protection of law-abiding citizens. With a peaceful attitude and conscious decision to choose a nonviolent and nonvengeful response, the cycle of violence can be broken and the contagion stopped. It is all a matter of attitude and the realization that violence should be countered in a mature and rational manner in order to protect society without doing damage to its citizens.

So we need to approach the problem of capital punishment not as a legal matter determining the rights and duties of the parties but as if we were treating a disease—the disease of violence. The past one hundred years have comprised the most violent century in human history. That violence is reflected in our television programs, movies, video games, literature, political attitudes, militaristic paranoia, the alarming abuse toward children, pervasive domestic violence, hostility toward the genuinely poor and helpless, the persistence of racism and intolerance, the way we treat petty juvenile offenders, and the mistreatment of prisoners. When we impose severe and excessive punishment, when we seek an eye for an eye, a tooth for a tooth, a life for a life, when we seek revenge on lawbreakers by some clumsy arithmetic we call justice, we become violent law abiders. We become what we say we abhor—more like criminals—more violent people. And the contagion spreads.

Every time we send a criminal to jail, especially a juvenile offender, it is a failure of society; every time that we execute a murderer, it is another failure of society. Where were the caring family members, helpful friends, concerned teachers, and supportive social workers when that criminal was a child being abused and neglected? Who loved that child? Who educated that child so that he or she could succeed in this world? Who demeaned that child because his or her skin color or religion or ethnicity was different from the majority in the community? Who did violence to that child by relegating him or her to poverty and then hating that child because he or she was poor? Generally speaking, children who are loved and cared for don't become criminals. Family and community violence toward children, including top-down governmental violence, turns some of them into criminals. Ethical communities don't need a police officer on every street corner because ethical communities care for all their children. Criminals aren't born; they are made.

> *"A productive way to react to an act of violence is to have the courage to resist the normal impulse for revenge."*

And once made, society gives little thought to rehabilitating the offender, since the purpose of retributive justice is to punish. Or they view punishment as itself rehabilitative. Americans pretend that state-inflicted cruelty will somehow teach a violent felon not to be cruel and violent; and then 97 percent of these "rehabilitated" violent criminals are released into civil society. The theory seems to be that punishment teaches one how to become a good and respected member of the community. Yet the current punishments only succeed in destroying an offender's self-esteem by imprisoning that person and separating him or her from family and friends, then dehumanizing the prisoner by referring to him or her by a number instead of a name. Prisoners also become victims of the internal violence of prison life and, when not building up resentments, become schooled by other inmates in the techniques of crime—aware that society's rejection will continue once they are released.

> *"If we don't find a way to break the cycle of violence we will never be able to end the culture of violence that infects the United States."*

Restorative Justice

In order to foster a less violent society, the treatment of the offender should be as humane and non-violent as forcible incarceration can allow. Rehabilitation of the offender ought to be a necessary condition of parole. Life imprisonment without the possibility of parole ought to be the alternative to capital punishment.

Restorative justice seeks to eliminate the culture of violence in U.S. society and replace it with a culture of caring. It's a matter of attitude. We must not allow our hearts to be filled with hatred, anger, rage, and the desire for revenge. It's hard to put aside such feelings when a child or loved one is murdered, especially if the killing is particularly brutal of cruel. This is why violence is so hard to subdue. Look at the difficulties in restoring peace in countries like Northern Ireland, Israel, Bosnia, and India and Pakistan which have engaged in civil wars. Similarly, if we don't find a way to break the cycle of violence we will never be able to end the culture of violence that infects the United States.

Restorative justice doesn't ask that we "turn the other cheek." Restorative justice doesn't seek mercy of forgiveness for those who, by the calculus of duties and rights, deserve to die. Rather, it asks us to protect ourselves from the disease of violence by not killing the despised one. Someone must go first to stop the cycle of violence; the obvious candidate is the state. The words of John Donne from his poem "No Man Is an Island" seem particularly appropriate when we execute a condemned prisoner: "Ask not for whom the bell tolls; it tolls for thee!"

The Theory That Capital Punishment Deters Crime Is Flawed

by Ernest Partridge

About the author: *Ernest Partridge is a research associate in the philosophy department at the University of California in Riverside.*

On Friday, March 9, 2001, Lionel Tate, a Black fourteen-year-old Florida boy was sentenced to life in prison without parole—for a crime he committed when he was twelve. This life sentence rests upon the assumption that, at twelve, Lionel Tate was fully responsible for the killing of Tiffany Eunick, age six. In addition, the sentence appears to presume that at no time in the long life remaining to him can this child be rehabilitated. He freely chose to do what he did, we are told, and now "He must pay for it."

The same defenders of the criminal justice status quo assure us that sentences such as these deter similar crimes. This opinion is shared by defenders of capital punishment. While insisting that the death penalty deters murder, they would have us believe at the same time that convicted killers are beyond redemption—that all attempts to rehabilitate them will fail.

Few proponents of this theory of justice seem to be aware that it rests upon two fundamentally contradictory views of human nature: it is both deterministic (in holding that punishment can cause others to be deterred from crime) and indeterministic (in proclaiming that incarceration cannot cause the culprit to be rehabilitated). This incoherent view of human nature reflects a larger inconsistency that is manifested in the extant politics and corporate practices of our day. One face of this contradiction, which we will call "the operative theory" is presupposed in marketing strategies and political campaigns. The other face, "the public theory," is encountered in political rhetoric and corporate public relations campaigns.

Ernest Partridge, "The Two Faces of Justice," *Free Inquiry*, vol. 21, Summer 2001, p. 43. Copyright © 2001 by the Council for Democratic and Secular Humanism, Inc. Reproduced by permission.

Chapter 3

The Operative Theory

By this account, human motives can be identified, mapped, and measured, and, when applied to a marketing or a political campaign, this knowledge can be put to effective use. (Lately the strategies and tactics of advertisers and politicians have become virtually identical, as the same "experts" manage both marketing and political campaigns). If public tastes and opinions do not incline toward the company's product or the party's candidate, then these tastes can be "manufactured" to order.

Evidence? Consider annual expenditures for advertising—more than $30 billion just for television ads. Business enterprises will not casually throw that kind of cash at the television industry without a firm and proven expectation that such investments will produce the intended results, namely sales. As Vance Packard pointed out a generation ago, and Bill Moyers a decade ago, all the accumulated skills and knowledge of behavioral science are put to use to the task of utilizing, and perchance creating, public motives and tastes to profitable ends. No laboratory of applied psychology is more lavishly funded than that of the market researcher. From Dr. Ernest Dichter's application of Freudian "depth psychology" in the 1930s to GOP pollster Frank Luntz's "focus group" micro-analyses in the 2000 presidential campaign, "the consumer and citizen mind" is examined, cross-examined, and meticulously inventoried, and this information is then applied to the greater benefit of the candidate or the bottom line.

In the jargon of philosophy, the operative theory of marketing and politics is deterministic: that is, it holds that human behavior ("output") is the result of prior experiences ("input"), and that if the inputs are carefully designed and skillfully manipulated, then public motives, tastes, and behavior can be "usefully directed" and even manufactured. Of course, public relations is not an exact science; however, it is a highly empirical and experimental science. Numerous strategies and devices are tried until the public "hot button" is located, whereupon it is "pushed" as long as it "works out." ("Let's run it up the flagpole and see if anyone salutes.") But while there is much trial and error in marketing and political strategies, implicit throughout is the assumption that public behavior is the result of external causes. What then remains is the task of finding and applying the most "efficacious" causes.

> "While insisting that the death penalty deters murder, [capital punishment supporters] would have us believe . . . that convicted killers are beyond redemption."

The Public Theory

Corporate spokesmen and their political fellow-travelers (the so-called conservatives) have prepared a contrary theory for public consumption. According to this account, each human personality appears *ex nihilo*, independent, autonomous, and undetermined. Being "unformed" by outside causes, each individual is fully and completely responsible for his or her behavior. "But why does poverty correlate with crime?" No explanation is offered or even felt to be necessary. To cite a typical example, when a conservative lawyer was recently asked on a television talk show why the Columbine High School killers did what they did,[1] her reply was, "Those boys were just evil, that's all." Why they were "evil" was regarded as a pointless question.

Behavior isn't "caused," this theory asserts, it is simply freely "chosen," and that is all there is to it. "Don't ask me, or 'society,' or (heaven forbid!) the government to do anything about it. It's just not my concern." Clearly, according to this public theory, the only appropriate response to those who commit crimes is "lock 'em up." If the culprits are given less than a life sentence, then we can only hope for the best when they are released. No point in attempting rehabilitation or teaching a useful skill to prepare them for life after release.

As with behavior, so too with public taste and preferences. Tobacco companies tell us that "We are only giving the public what it wants." Likewise, from the media we hear, "Don't complain to us about the sex, violence, and vulgarity in the movies, on television, or in rock lyrics. We're only giving the public what it wants." Those "wants," we are told, which free enterprising entrepreneurs are so generously satisfying, also appear *ex nihilo*—uncaused and freely chosen by each

> *"This theory of justice . . . rests upon two fundamentally contradictory views of human nature."*

consumer-citizen. "What the public wants" is thus unexplained and unexplainable, and thus out of reach of "cultivation." It follows that there is no need to squander tax money on art and music education, or on noncommercial public broadcasting.

According to the public theory, marketing has no side effects or unintended consequences. Sex-saturated ads and media are totally disconnected from the incidence of teen pregnancy and single-parent families. "Just do it!" say the ads. "Just say no!" reply the Christian conservatives. But if the teens "do it" anyway, don't blame the promoters. The kids are "just sinful." A child's encounter with tens of thousands of depictions of violent murders on television, we are expected to believe, has nothing to do with whatever violent behavior he or she might exhibit. "Guns (and the gun culture) don't kill people, (autonomous) people kill people."

In sum, the public theory insists that "private enterprise" bears no responsibility whatever for social problems. "The social responsibility of business," Milton Friedman once wrote, "is to increase its profits." All social problems, according

1. On April 20, 1999, two student gunmen shot and killed thirteen people at Columbine High School in Littleton, Colorado. They then killed themselves.

to this theory issue from the uncaused and freely chosen behavior of "simply evil" individuals.

The Contradiction

It is abundantly clear that these two "theories" are radically contradictory. If business executives genuinely believed the nondetermenist theory that they present to the public, they would not invest a thin dime in their advertising campaigns. On the other hand, if they were to extend the determinist operative theory beyond their corporate conduct, they would be burdened with a responsibility for the harmful "side effects" of their marketing schemes—effects upon public health, taste, and morality. Instead, they move back and forth between these contradictory determinist and indeterminist theories, as the requirements of public relations and the bottom line demand—all with the ease with which one sheds one's raincoat and puts on one's sunglasses as the weather changes.

In the same way, when conservatives claim (contra the evidence) that capital punishment deters murder, they are determinist. But when they refuse to attempt to rehabilitate incarcerated prisoners, preferring "retribution" and "punishment," they are indeterminists again. According to this latter view, because convicted murderers are "beyond redemption," the only suitable response to their crimes is to "do away with them."

There is a third alternative to these contradictory theories—what philosophers call "compatibilism." By this account, human beings are significantly influenced by the circumstances of their birth and upbringing, and thus criminals are more likely to emerge from conditions of poverty and abuse. However, unless severely traumatized by such misfortunes, most individuals can be educated to a condition of moral responsibility—informed as to the consequences of their acts, recognizing the humanity and dignity of others, and capable of acting according to moral principles—whereupon each attains the freedom to conduct his or her own life.

This is the humane theory and practice of penology found in most enlightened nations. Sadly the United States of America has yet to achieve this stage of civilization.

Chapter 4

Should Capital Punishment Be Reformed?

Chapter Preface

Statistics and public opinion polls reflect conflicting views on the death penalty. For example, while most Americans claim that they support capital punishment, a majority also supports a temporary moratorium on executions until fairness can be assured in death penalty trials. Moreover, a majority of states have passed laws making the sentence of life without parole available as an alternative. When life without parole is offered as an option, juries return fewer execution verdicts.

This information raises the hopes of capital punishment opponents, who often argue that first-degree murderers should receive life sentences rather than death sentences. Death penalty critics believe that juries' preference for the sentence of life without parole reveals the popular desire to avoid the possibility of executing innocent people. In states that do not offer life without parole, however, juries are forced to choose between the following two options: a long prison sentence with the possibility of parole, and execution. In such cases, juries often return a sentence of death because they fear that the murderer will someday be released. Life without parole seems to be the "wave of the future," explains Richard Dieter, director of the Death Penalty Information Center: "There will be greater use of life without parole as people gain confidence that it means what it says. I think what people want is safety. And they want punishment. Life without parole gives them that."

Supporters of capital punishment, on the other hand, contend that the sentence of life without parole guarantees neither safety nor punishment. These proponents point out, for one thing, that a dangerous murderer serving a life sentence can escape from prison and kill again. Some also fear that state sentencing laws could change and possibly allow the release of convicts who had originally been sentenced to life. Furthermore, as syndicated columnist Don Feder maintains, life without parole is an inadequate punishment for the crime of deliberate murder: "Lifers aren't exactly living the life of Reilly. Still, they live. Even in the harshest of [prisons], there are opportunities to laugh, form friendships, read, be entertained, learn, communicate, even love—emotions and experiences forever denied to [murder victims]." To protect the public and to ensure that murderers face a punishment befitting their crime, most capital-punishment supporters promote the retention of the death penalty rather than life without parole.

Death-penalty alternatives and reforms continue to provoke debate among lawmakers, criminal justice experts, murder victims' relatives, and the general public. The authors in the following chapter discuss the option of life imprisonment as well as the significance of post-conviction DNA evidence and the possibility of televised executions.

Capital Punishment Should Be Abolished

by the *Progressive*

About the author: *The* Progressive *is a monthly journal of left-wing political opinion.*

Anyone who pays attention to the death penalty can feel it. A sea change is under way. Support for the death penalty has fallen to its lowest point in years. It now [in 2001] stands at 63 percent, down from 77 percent [in 1996], according to the latest available poll. However, that drops to 46 percent when life in prison is offered as an option. [In] September [2000], a bipartisan study showed that 64 percent would favor a moratorium on further executions until "issues of fairness can be resolved."

But the numbers tell only so much. The cultural shift on the death penalty is going on in kitchens and neighborhoods and factories and offices and press rooms across the country, where people are talking about it as they have not since 1976, the year the Supreme Court lifted its ban on executions. Many are looking at capital punishment with newfound horror and sudden doubts.

Conservative Doubters

Among the doubters, some surprises:

Pat Robertson, the rightwing Christian conservative and former Presidential candidate, has called for a federal moratorium on the death penalty. Robertson's reason? He says that capital punishment is discriminatory, unfairly affecting minorities and those who are too poor to pay for good lawyers.

George Will, the conservative columnist for *Newsweek* and the *Washington Post*, warns that "careless or corrupt administration of capital punishment" appears to be "intolerably common."

Even President George W. Bush seems to have had second—or first—thoughts on the subject. On June 11 [2001], Bush said, "We should never execute anybody who is mentally retarded." As numerous papers reported, the statement led to some confusion about what Bush really believed. As governor of Texas, he opposed bills that would have stopped executions of mentally retarded people, and at least a few of the 152 people whose deaths he oversaw had very low IQs.

An Embarrassment Abroad

While the American public examines its conscience, the U.S. capital punishment system is an enormous embarrassment overseas.

Until recently, U.S. executions got much more attention abroad than they did here. "An average person in France," reported the *New York Times*, "could not help but be familiar with the case of Betty Lou Beets," who was executed in Texas in February of [2000] for killing her fifth husband. "Her story, with particular attention to her assertion that she was abused by her father and husbands, has been on the front page of many newspapers."

The same was true, said the *Times*, of Odell Barnes. French editorialists had penned columns questioning whether Barnes was innocent, and the mayor of Paris even traveled to Texas to meet him. Barnes was executed in March of [2000].

The moral isolation of the United States has grown more glaring almost by the day. In April [2001], the United Nations Human Rights Commission called for a global moratorium "with a view to completely abolishing the death penalty." The proposal was put forward by the European Union. The vote was 27 to 18, with the United States, along with Japan, China, Indonesia; and Saudi Arabia, voting against.

Then, in late June [2001], the Council of Europe, the continent's forty-three-nation human rights group, voted to remove Japan and the United States as observers unless they call a moratorium on executions "without delay" and begin a formal repeal of the death penalty.

"The debate at the Council of Europe is further evidence that the credibility of the U.S. on human rights issues has reached a new low point," said Ajamu Baraka, acting director of Amnesty International USA's Program to Abolish the Death Penalty. "The U.S.'s reputation continues to be tarnished by its defiant and puzzling commitment to a punishment that has no deterrent effect and that the majority of the world's nations has abandoned as barbaric and outdated."

> *"The U.S.'s reputation continues to be tarnished by its defiant and puzzling commitment to a punishment [that is] . . . barbaric and outdated."*

A few days later, the World Court ruled that the United States had violated the Vienna Convention in a death penalty case involving Karl and Walter LaGrand, both German nationals who were executed in 1999. Neither of the LaGrands was informed of his right to seek assistance from the German consul upon arrest.

More than ninety foreign citizens from thirty-three nations are reportedly under death sentences in the United States, according to Amnesty International. In most of these cases, says Amnesty, local authorities failed to inform the prisoners upon detention of their right to consular notification and assistance—"in glaring violation of the Vienna Convention." In the past ten years, at least fourteen foreign nationals who were not informed of their consular rights have been executed here in the United States.

In mid-June [2001], Frank Keating, the governor of Oklahoma, granted a thirty-day reprieve to a Mexican national named Gerardo Valdez. Valdez, like the LaGrands, was not told of his right to contact his consulate upon arrest. Keating later criticized the legal standard for capital punishment in Oklahoma as "too low."

Reason for Skepticism

It is becoming increasingly evident that those who are leery of the death penalty have reason for skepticism. The last-minute news that the Federal Bureau of Investigation had withheld thousands of pages of documents from Timothy McVeigh's[1] attorneys spoiled what should have been the strongest possible argument for capital punishment. This bungling drew attention to the fact that prosecutors often withhold documents, and that in cases with less media scrutiny than *The United States vs. McVeigh*, such a violation might never be discovered. "If the FBI could fail to turn over documents in a case this important, think what happens in the thousands of lesser cases where the death penalty is also meted out," said Kenneth Roth, executive director of Human Rights Watch.

The error rate in capital cases is astounding. In June [2001], a Columbia University study revealed that "two out of three [death penalty] convictions were overturned on appeal, mostly because of serious errors by incompetent defense lawyers or overzealous police officers and prosecutors who withheld evidence."

But access to appeals can vary drastically by region. "In Alabama and Georgia . . . these is no guarantee of a lawyer after the direct appeal of a conviction, and prisoners have only inconsistent access to a legal process that frequently overturns death sentences," the *New York Times* reported on June 16, [2001]. Even more disturbing, "Thirty prisoners on Alabama's death row have no lawyers to pursue appeals, by far the largest such group in any state."

No Closure After the Execution

Much of the media attention surrounding the McVeigh execution looked at the reactions of the family members of McVeigh's victims, many of whom decided not to watch the execution. Others, however, did watch—some of them in

---

1. McVeigh was convicted for the 1995 bombing of the Oklahoma City federal building. He was executed in May 2001.

the hope of closure, others in the desire to see McVeigh suffer for his crime. Paul Howell, whose daughter Karen died in the blast, said he wished that the survivors could have stoned McVeigh to death. "I kind of thought what they ought to do, bring him down here and get all the family members, survivors, together and start just throwing small rocks and just keep getting bigger and bigger until somebody does kill him with it," he said prior to the execution.

> *"The error rate in capital cases is astounding."*

But some who hoped for vengeance reported feeling unsatisfied after the execution.

This is common. "More often than not, families of murder victims do not experience the relief they expected to feel at the execution, says Lula Redmond, a Florida therapist who works with such families," *U.S. News & World Report* said in a June 1997 article. "'Taking a life doesn't fill that void, but it's generally not until after the execution [that the families] realize this,'" Redmond said.

Helen Prejean—the author of *Dead Man Walking*, which was turned into a movie starring Susan Sarandon and Sean Penn—stresses how illusory the relief is. She tells of a father who insisted on seeing the execution of the man who murdered his daughter. Once it was over, he said: "The S.O.B. died too quick. I hope he burns in hell." Prejean notes, "He could have watched him die a thousand, thousand times," and that still would not have healed his loss.

The Federal Death Penalty

Eight days after McVeigh's execution, the federal government was at it again. The government had gone nearly four decades without any executions, but then in June it put two people to death. The second victim of federally sanctioned murder was Juan Raul Garza.

Garza's fate raises further questions about the U.S. death penalty. His lawyers, in an attempt to stay his execution, pointed out that eighteen of the twenty men on federal death row at the time were black or Hispanic.

Janet Reno had expressed doubts about the fairness of the federal death penalty during her tenure as U.S. Attorney General. [In] September [2001], she said she was disturbed by a Department of Justice report that mentioned the large numbers of minorities on federal death row. She ordered an investigation "to determine if bias does, in fact, play any role in the federal death penalty system."

On June 6, [2001], however, current Attorney General John Ashcroft brushed aside Reno's concerns with a new report claiming the federal death penalty is applied fairly, though he acknowledged that a more systematic study was necessary.

Ashcroft's haste to execute before the lengthier study was done is inexcusable. And his own report is shoddy. It fails to grasp the basic question of whether minorities are more likely to be charged with federal capital offenses than whites are. "The Ashcroft report purports to study this issue without looking at the much larger universe of cases in which federal charges could have been filed but were not. . . . For all we know, there were so many white defendants with cases just as suitable for federal capital prosecution as the minority defendants who were charged, or more so," wrote Samuel R. Gross in an op-ed for the Progressive Media Project. Gross is a professor of law at the University of Michigan and co-author of *Death and Discrimination: Racial Disparities in Capital Sentencing.* He criticized Ashcroft's assertion that the racial imbalance occurred because federal courts target crimes associated with drugs and that "organized drug trafficking is largely carried out by gangs whose membership is drawn from minority groups." Gross said, "This explanation has a depressingly familiar ring" of racial profiling about it.

In federal capital cases, blacks and whites are often treated differently. As the *Chicago Tribune* recently reported, "White defendants are more likely than black defendants to work out plea bargains saving them from the death penalty in federal cases, according to an analysis of 146 cases prosecuted since Congress reinstated federal capital punishment in 1988."

Evidence of Racial Bias

And evidence that courts punish people more harshly for murders of whites than of blacks is also stark. A study of the death penalty in North Carolina released this year found that the likelihood of landing on death row was much higher if the victim was white and the perpetrator was nonwhite.

Jack Boger, a professor at the University of North Carolina School of Law, examined 3,990 homicide cases. He found that 11.6 percent of nonwhite defendants charged with murdering white victims were sentenced to death versus 6.1 percent of whites who murdered whites and 4.7 percent of nonwhites whose victims were nonwhite.

"The death penalty is biased against the poor and against racial minorities. It is arbitrary. It is capricious. It is cruel. It should be banned."

These results are nothing new. A 1998 study released by the Death Penalty Information Center in Washington, D.C., found that blacks in capital cases in Philadelphia were almost four times as likely to be sentenced to death as whites in similar cases. It also said there is a "disturbing and consistent" pattern of imposing the death penalty much more often when the victims are white.

This bias is not lost on Prejean. "When people of color are killed, when poor people are killed, when 'the nobodies' of this society are killed, there is no big quest to pursue the ultimate punishment to avenge their deaths," she says.

What About Deterrence?

Then there is the bogus claim of deterrence.

During the Presidential campaign [in 2000], Bush said that the only reason he was in favor of the death penalty was because it is a deterrent. But it isn't. The most striking recent evidence to emerge on this front comes from a September 2000 article by Raymond Bonner and Ford Fessenden in the *New York Times*. The piece showed that the twelve states that have not enacted the death penalty since it became legal in 1976 have not had higher rates of murder than those states with the death penalty. More revealing yet, the study also found that "homicide rates had risen and fallen along roughly symmetrical paths in the states with and without the death penalty."

The death penalty is biased against the poor and against racial minorities. It is arbitrary. It is capricious. It is cruel. It should be banned.

Even in especially heinous cases, such as that of Timothy McVeigh, where the guilt is beyond question, capital punishment is an abomination and an absurdity. If it's wrong for the murderer to kill, it's wrong for the state to kill the murderer.

Capital Punishment Should Be Reformed

by Scott Turow

About the author: *Scott Turow is a lawyer and a novelist.*

Capital punishment has been one of the most notorious train wrecks of American politics. The Supreme Court declared it unconstitutional in 1972, but the resulting public furor led the court to reverse itself in 1976. Although polls continue to show majority support for capital punishment, opposition is fierce, especially from religious leaders and humanitarian organizations who denounce it as a moral affront.

Meanwhile, the operation of the capital punishment system remains under attack. According to the Death Penalty Information Center, the 100th innocent person was released earlier this year [2002] from death row, raising questions about how many innocents have already been executed, while the surviving family members of murder victims often find the wait from trial to execution, averaging 11.5 years in 2000, an insulting protraction of their grieving.

These patterns came under intense scrutiny in Illinois in March 2000 after the 13th exoneration of a death row inmate in that state. Gov. George Ryan declared a moratorium on further executions and appointed a commission to determine what reforms, if any, would ensure that the capital punishment system was just and accurate. I served as one of the 14 members of the commission, which delivered its report [in April 2002]. I believe some aspects of our experience may help make the national debate less heated and more focused.

Unanimous Recommendations

Our report contained 85 specific recommendations directed to every stage of the criminal process, from police investigation through clemency proceedings. Included were proposals for a statewide panel to review local prosecutors' decisions to seek the death penalty; banning capital punishment for the mentally retarded; significantly reducing the number of factual circumstances rendering a murderer eligible for capital punishment; controlling the use of jailhouse informants at trial; and allowing trial judges to reverse a jury's decision to impose death. (An idea distinct from [the 2002] Supreme Court argument about whether only a jury may find death justified in the first place).

Before the arguments about the wisdom of specific recommendations gather steam in Illinois and elsewhere, I wanted to focus on one important aspect of the report that may be overlooked. More than 85% of the recommendations we made were unanimous.

This was no small achievement, given the diversity of opinion in the group. The governor appointed, among others, a former U.S. senator, the general counsel to the Chicago Police Department, the current head of the Illinois State Attorneys organization, the public defender in Chicago, a past president of the local bar association and the son of a murder victim. Among us, there were fierce opponents of capital punishment and stout defenders, but we worked for two years in a spirit of amity and conciliation.

Looking over the recommendations, there were three assumptions that limited the contentiousness of our deliberations and might, for that reason, be guideposts in the death-penalty debate. First, respect for the political process. Second, respect for the legitimate needs of the surviving loved ones of murder victims. And third, recognition that the system requires reform.

A Political Question

Because nine of the 14 members of the commission were present or former prosecutors, abolitionists criticized the choices, assuming there was a pro-death-penalty majority. At the end of two years, after our recommendations were formulated, we called the question of whether the death penalty should be repealed. By then, at least, a majority of us favored abolition.

But repeal was not one of our recommendations. That is because it remains clear that the majority of Illinois citizens and legislators favor capital punishment. As a body, we accepted that the Supreme Court's decisions make capital punishment a political question, meaning it is properly left to the citizenry. By denouncing capital punishment as barbaric, opponents have en-

> *"The system requires reform."*

gaged in a frontal attack on the moral character of those who favor it. Not surprisingly, this end less game of yes-you-are, no-I'm-not has bogged down public discussion.

Accepting the political nature of the question means the argument should be refocused as one about policy, not morality, requiring detailed information about how the system operates and not just a gut-check. As a nation we need to decide if the costs of capital punishment—the staggering financial toll of litigation, the consumption of limited court resources, the disparities in the system's results, and the enduring risk of executing the innocent—are worth the powerful denunciation of ultimate evil that capital punishment is meant to trumpet.

Survivors' Needs

Second, we remained conscious throughout of the proper role of the surviving loved ones of murder victims. In the last decades of the 20th century, capital jurisprudence went through a sea change in its attitudes toward survivors. As late as 1987, the Supreme Court found it unconstitutional to offer evidence in a capital sentencing of the impact of a murder on survivors, deeming it irrelevant to the only proper issue, the blame-worthiness of the defendant. Yet the rising tide of the victims' rights movement changed that. In most jurisdictions, loved ones are entitled to be heard during the death-penalty hearing, and prosecutors frequently pay close attention to their desires. Often one defendant lives and another dies for virtually identical crimes simply because of the wishes of survivors.

"The Supreme Court's decisions make capital punishment a political question, meaning it is properly left to the citizenry."

We met often with surviving family members in hopes of determining their views of the death penalty and what they wanted from the process, including their search for emotional closure. We found that survivors need enhanced support services and reliable communication about developments in a case. Compassionate services, rather than a determinative role in the penalty process, may be a better answer for survivors as well as for the system.

The Need for Reform

Finally, whether we supported or opposed the death penalty, we were all able to agree that the capital punishment system as it stood was in need of dramatic reform. Gov. Ryan, a long-time death penalty proponent, set a courageous example by taking the politically dangerous step of halting executions in the face of mounting evidence of mistakes.

Too often, those who favor capital punishment in principle have wedded themselves to present practices. In Illinois, 65% of death penalty cases have been reversed, either because of errors in sentencing, or less often, in determining guilt. Dueling studies published [in 2001] put the national rate at somewhere between 43% and 68%. While those numbers reflect commendable scrutiny by reviewing courts, they also bespeak a system which, facing the inflammatory nature of most capital murders, fails with dismaying frequency to produce legally acceptable results. As Tom Sullivan, a co-chair of our Commission, said in handing our report to the governor, "repair or repeal" of the capital punishment system are the only principled choices. It is time we arrived at national resolve about that.

Capital Punishment Should Be Temporarily Suspended

by Russ Feingold

About the author: *Russ Feingold is the Democratic senator from Wisconsin.*

Editors Note: The following viewpoint was originally given as testimony before the U.S. Senate on April 10, 2002, in support of the National Death Penalty Moratorium Act. As of this writing, the act had not passed

[In April 2002], Mr. Ray Krone walked out of an Arizona state prison a free man. In doing so, he became the 100th innocent person to be released from death row in the modern death penalty–era that is, since the Supreme Court found the death penalty unconstitutional in 1972.

At about 5 P.M. on [that] Monday, Krone "traded his orange prison jumpsuit for blue jeans and a T-shirt," then walked away from a prison in Yuma, AZ, according to the *Arizona Republic*. Krone had spent the last 10 years of his life in prison for a crime it is now almost certain he did not commit.

In 1992, Krone was sentenced to death for the gruesome sexual assault and murder of Kim Acona, a cocktail waitress at a Phoenix lounge. After his conviction was overturned on a technicality, Krone received a retrial but was convicted again in 1996 and, this time, sentenced to life in prison.

The key to his release was DNA testing that pointed not to Krone, but to Kenneth Phillips. It just so happens that Phillips is serving time in another Arizona prison for an unrelated sex crime. Prosecutors are now deciding whether to charge Phillips.

"There's tears in my eyes," Krone said upon his release. "Your heart's beating. You can't hardly talk."

At a press conference announcing that the prosecutor and Phoenix Police chief would seek Krone's release, the prosecutor said, "[Krone] deserves an apology from us, that's for sure." He continued, "A mistake was made here. . . .

Russ Feingold, testimony before the United States Senate, Washington, DC, April 10, 2002.

```text

what do you say to him? An injustice was done and we will try to do better. And we're sorry."

## More than an Apology

But, there is more that the American people can say to Krone. We can do more than just talk or apologize. An apology is the first step. But we can also act. We can act to ensure that not another innocent person faces execution. We can do so by conducting a thorough review of the death penalty system. And while this review is taking place, we can and should suspend executions.

Congress has the opportunity to do just that. We can act by passing my bill, the National Death Penalty Moratorium Act. Together we can say enough is enough. Together we can say that one mistake too many has been made. Together we can say let us pause and have an independent, top-to-bottom review of the administration of the ultimate punishment our society can exact, the death penalty. This review should include the death penalty systems of Arizona and all states that authorize the use of the death penalty, as well as the use of the death penalty by our Federal Government.

An innocent man, who at one time faced certain death at the hands of his government, today walks free. If we can call that luck, how many others in Mr. Krone's shoes have not been and will not be so lucky?

How many innocent Americans today sit in their prison cells wrongly accused, counting down the days until there are no more?

## A Broken System

There have now been [at least] 100 exonerations and 766 executions since the early 1970s. In other words, for every seven to eight death row inmates executed by the States or Federal government, one has been found innocent and released from death row. Now, this does not bode well for the fairness and effectiveness of a government program.

Some have said that exonerations are proof that the system is working. But how can they be proof that the system is working when, in at least some cases, it is not the lawyers or judges, but newspaper reporters and college students—people clearly outside the justice system—who have done the work of uncovering evidence of innocence? That is not proof the system is working. Quite the opposite. When the justice system must rely on outside actors, it is further, disturbing evidence that the system is broken.

> *"Let us pause and have an independent, top-to-bottom review of the administration of the ultimate punishment our society can exact."*

I also fear that 100 exonerations is probably a conservative estimate. How many innocent people were not freed before being executed? How many mistakes did we miss? How many times were we too late to correct mistakes? I
```

don't think anyone really has an answer to these questions. And that is precisely why we should have a pause and review. Before sending yet another person to the execution chamber, we should be sure that the system is fair, just and error-free.

Grave Concerns

The risk of errors is troubling to an increasing number of Americans. From Supreme Court Justice Sandra Day O'Connor, to Republican Illinois Governor George Ryan, to even Reverend Pat Robertson, a growing number of Americans are expressing grave concerns about the fairness of the administration of the death penalty.

And it is not just a question of access to modern DNA testing. A number of factors have resulted in unfair or even wrongful convictions. Incompetent counsel. Too many times, sleeping lawyers, drunk lawyers, or lawyers who are later suspended or disbarred are the lawyers representing people facing the death penalty. Sometimes there is prosecutorial or police misconduct—like failing to share evidence that might be helpful to the defendant's case or coerced confessions. These problems also plague the administration of the death penalty. We have also seen that testimony from jailhouse informants produce a high risk of unreliable convictions.

> *"How many innocent Americans today sit in their prison cells wrongly accused, counting down the days until there are no more?"*

Now, Governor Ryan took a very important first step in 2000 when he had the courage to recognize these flaws, declared a moratorium on executions, and created a blue ribbon panel to review the fairness of the Illinois death penalty system. . . .

If we are prepared to admit, as Illinois has, that there may be flaws with the death penalty system, it is then really unconscionable that we should continue with executions without a thorough, nationwide review.

Ray Krone's exoneration provides us all with another opportunity to take a moment and ask ourselves "what if?" What if we hadn't caught this mistake? What if an innocent man ate his final meal, took his last breath, said goodbye to his family and was put to death, alone, silenced by a failing system? The most important of these "what ifs," however, is this: What if we don't ask ourselves these questions? What if we could have saved a life and we didn't? What if we acknowledged that the system is unfair, and yet we didn't do anything about it at all?

The National Death Penalty Moratorium Act

One risk, one error, one mistake, is one too many. But 100 mistakes, proven mistakes, qualifies as a crisis. And a crisis calls for action.

My distinguished colleague and chairman of the Judiciary Committee, Senator [Patrick] Leahy, has introduced the Innocence Protection Act. This bill would reduce the risk of executing the innocent by allowing for post-conviction DNA testing and establishing certain minimum competency standards for defense counsel. And I support this bill and hope the Senate acts on it without delay.[1]

> *"Before sending yet another person to the execution chamber, we should be sure that the system is fair, just and error-free."*

But I submit that Congress can and must do more. For, if we recognize that the system is broken, that innocent people have been freed based on DNA testing, then it is only logical and right that we suspend executions while these reforms can be implemented and while all steps are taken to conduct a top-to-bottom review of the death penalty system.

My bill would do just that. The National Death Penalty Moratorium Act would create a National Commission on the Death Penalty to review the fairness of the administration of the death penalty at the State and Federal levels. The bill would also suspend executions of Federal inmates and urges the States to do the same, while the commission does its work. . . .

The expansion of the death penalty and increase in death penalty prosecutions during the last two decades have had literally life-or-death consequences. The people of Illinois have learned a serious lesson that the administration of the death penalty is plagued with errors. And as the events in Arizona just showed us, the people of Illinois are certainly not alone. But Illinois and Arizona account for only 19 of the 100 exonerations nationwide. The remaining 81 mistakes have occurred in other death penalty States. These 100 mistakes tell us, loudly and clearly, that it is past time for our Nation to have a thoughtful debate on capital punishment.

A commission, and pause in executions while the Commission does its work, is the only right and just response.

And, so, I urge my colleagues to join me in supporting the National Death Penalty Moratorium Act.

1. As of this writing, the bill had not passed.

Capital Punishment Should Be Retained

by Ernest van den Haag

About the author: *Before his death in 2002, Ernest van den Haag was a psychoanalyst and a professor of jurisprudence and public policy.*

The case of Timothy McVeigh[1] reminds us that the endless dispute about the death penalty is mainly religious in origin, even if many of the arguments employed are secular. The religious belief is that only God can legitimately end a human life; no crime can justify the death penalty for anyone, regardless of how great and certain his guilt is, or how powerful a deterrent his execution would be. Theologians disagree on the death penalty—it is warranted by Biblical passages and was traditionally favored by churches—but it is currently opposed by a majority of religious leaders.

The secular objections to the death penalty hold that its rational purposes, such as deterrence, should be achieved by alternative means, since we can never be entirely certain that all those convicted of capital crimes are actually guilty. The possibility—in the long run, the likelihood—that some convicts are not guilty is currently the most persuasive objection to capital punishment.

No Satisfactory Alternatives

Why execute anyone? Why not avoid the risk of miscarriages of justice by abolishing capital punishment altogether? Simply because there are no fully satisfactory alternatives. Life imprisonment is not necessarily lifelong; life imprisonment without parole still allows governors to pardon prisoners. The finality of death is both the weakness and the strength of capital punishment. We are not ready to do without it, yet hesitate to use it: There are many convicts on death row, but only a few are actually executed. Between 1973 and 1995, 5,760 death sentences were imposed; as of 1995, only 313 had been executed, and

1. McVeigh was convicted for the 1995 bombing of the federal building in Oklahoma City. He was executed in 2001.

Ernest van den Haag, "The Ultimate Penalty . . . and a Just One: The Basics of Capital Punishment," *National Review*, vol. 53, June 11, 2001. Copyright © 2001 by National Review, Inc., 215 Lexington Ave., New York, NY 10016. Reproduced by permission.

only some 400 have been executed since. Gary Graham, executed in June 2000, spent 19 years on death row exhausting his appeals, which were reviewed by more than 30 different judges. His case is far from exceptional.

Abolitionists often argue as though no one would die were it not for capital punishment. Yet we are not spared death in any case; a death sentence may shorten the life span, but—unlike imprisonment—it does not introduce an avoidable event, but merely hastens an unavoidable one.

Even if—without executions—society would be fully and permanently protected from murder, many people would feel that the survival of murderers is morally unjust, that the death penalty for murder is deserved, that it is a categorical imperative as [philosopher] Immanuel Kant thought. There is no way of proving or disproving such a moral idea, but there is little question that it is widely shared.

The Issue of Deterrence

The issue of deterrence is raised by the abolitionists, who often point out that the number of homicides does not decrease as the frequency of executions increases; from this they conclude that executions do not deter crime. But deterrence depends on the credibility of the threat of execution, and this credibility does not depend on the number of executions. To be sure, a threat never carried out will become incredible; to deter, it must be carried out often enough to remain credible. This does not mean it has to be carried out

> *"A death sentence may shorten the life span, but . . . it does not introduce an avoidable event, but merely hastens an unavoidable one."*

in all cases; but the threat of execution is currently so minuscule, compared with the homicide rate, as to be altogether ineffective.

It is often argued that criminals do not calculate, and that threats are therefore ineffective. Undoubtedly that is the case for some of them, but it is unlikely that all criminals are so different from the rest of the population that they do not respond to threats at all. If there are no executions over a long period, the deterrent effect of capital punishment may well be reduced to zero; but as long as the threat of execution is not entirely empty, there will be some deterrent effect. How great a deterrent it is will depend on such factors as the certainty of the punishment and the time that elapses between death sentences and executions; currently the deterrent effect is undermined by the uncertainty, infrequency, and delays involved in execution. (Indeed, a calculating criminal might look at the extreme rarity of the death penalty and thereby be encouraged in his murderous course.)

The existence of capital punishment is a disincentive, as threats of punishment always are. But the evidence is insufficient to prove that capital punishment deters murder more than do other punishments. Even if it did, however, capital punishment would be shown to be useful, but not morally justified. Deterring the crimes, not yet committed, of others does not morally justify execution of any convict (except to utilitarians, who think usefulness is a moral justification). If deserved, capital punishment should be imposed. If not, it should not be. Deterrence, however useful, cannot morally justify any punishment.

Inequities Do Not Justify Abolition

Some of the most popular objections to capital punishment do not actually deal with the punishment itself, but with its distribution. The issues that are raised are not unimportant, but they do not belong in a discussion of the legitimacy of capital punishment itself. Racial discrimination, for example, would disappear as an issue if the population were racially homogenous. Analogously, the argument that wealthy defendants can avail themselves of legal defenses not available to the poor depends on an unequal distribution of wealth; this argument is relevant to a discussion of social inequality, but is extraneous to an attempt to determine the rightness of the death penalty.

Although we have made great progress, we cannot ignore the remaining inequalities in the criminal-justice system. But there is no good reason to confuse such inequalities with an inherent inequity in the administration of justice. There is nothing in the nature of capital punishment that demands an unfair administration.

Issues of deterrence are peripheral to the moral argument at stake here, and the race and wealth issues are more peripheral still. The core of the matter is this: Murderers volunteer for the risk of capital punishment, and the punishment they volunteered to risk should be imposed if, in the view of the courts, they are guilty and deserve it.

Life Imprisonment Is Preferable to the Death Penalty

by Citizens United for Alternatives to the Death Penalty

About the author: *Citizens United for Alternatives to the Death Penalty is an organization that is working to abolish executions in the United States through public education and grassroots activism.*

Citizens United for Alternatives to the Death Penalty (CUADP) recognizes and upholds the responsibility of society to protect everyone from people who are dangerous, in particular, those who are convicted murderers.

CUADP also understands the legitimate response of human nature to seek vengeance in the form of harsh punishment for persons who have committed violent crimes. CUADP believes that as a society we are obligated to do better than to respond with a gut primal response, regardless of how natural that response may feel.

CUADP is concerned that our justice system is currently a retributive justice system which only heightens the pain and deepens the wounds of the families of victims of murder, the families of perpetrators, and the perpetrators themselves. CUADP also recognizes the strong ability of human nature to change and heal.

CUADP is concerned about well-documented and indisputably persistent problems in the application of the death penalty and in the criminal justice system as a whole in the United States of America.

Bad Public Policy

CUADP calls attention to politicians who perpetuate a myth through their advocacy of the death penalty to demonstrate a "tough on crime" position on matters of public policy. To suggest that the death penalty is a deterrent to violent criminals and is a vehicle to somehow grant relief to the suffering of victims families is to deceive the constituents they serve.

CUADP calls on all citizens to urge their elected representatives to work towards violence prevention programs which identify and help "at-risk" youth and adults.

CUADP calls on all citizens to look beyond emotions and to learn the facts about how our system actually functions before deciding for themselves where they stand on the question of empowering the government to kill in their name.

Morally, socially and economically, the death penalty is a bad public policy. There is a better way.

A Viable Alternative

Citizens United for Alternatives to the Death Penalty advocates the following as a viable alternative to the death penalty:

- Persons convicted of capital murder should serve a *minimum* of 25 years in prison before the possibility of consideration for parole. Please note: consideration for parole in no way suggests an inmate will receive parole. Parole boards

> *"Morally, socially and economically, the death penalty is a bad public policy. There is a better way."*

must abide by strict but fair standards in deciding who should receive parole. The abolition of parole endangers prison workers.
- *In certain cases, imprisonment should be for life, With no possibility of parole—ever.*
- While in prison, prisoners should work in jobs which are not slave-like and allow for some dignity and purpose of life for the inmate. *Such work situations create safer conditions for guards and others who work in prisons.*
- A portion of the prisoners' earnings should go to pay for their incarceration, and a portion should go into a fund for the victims of violent crime and their survivors. This would allow for a restitution fund for social, psychological and religious help for victims and survivor families. Such funds could also provide financial help for families which have lost a wage earner to murder.

CUADP supports the concept of restorative justice, including the bringing together of perpetrators and victims' family members by qualified professionals working with both, to help facilitate the process of reconciliation.

States Offering Life Without Parole

The following is a list of states which [as of 2004] have the death penalty and which also offer life without parole as a sentencing option. Currently there are *NO* states with an integrated restorative justice program which would allow convicted murderers to pay for their own incarceration or even to make restitutions directly to the survivors of their victims.

Alabama, Arizona, Arkansas, California, Colorado, Connecticut, Delaware, Federal Government, Florida, Georgia, Idaho, Illinois, Indiana, Kentucky, Louisiana, Maryland, Mississippi, Missouri, Montana, Nebraska, Nevada, New Hampshire, New York, North Carolina, Ohio, Oklahoma, Oregon, Pennsylvania, South Carolina, South Dakota, Tennessee, US Military, Utah, Virginia, Washington, Wyoming.

Total: 34 states.

[As of 2004] states with the death penalty but no provision for life without parole are Kansas, New Jersey, New Mexico & Texas.

Total: 4 states.

The people want alternatives. "Tough on crime" prosecutors do not.

To Wit: "You're not going to find 12 people back-to-back on the same jury that are going to kill somebody when the alternative is throwing away the key," [according to Harris County, Texas, District Attorney Johnny Holmes].

The Death Penalty Is Preferable to Life Imprisonment

by Gregory Kane

About the author: *Gregory Kane is a columnist for the* Baltimore Sun.

Frederick Anthony Romano remembers the night. More than 15 years later, he remembers it as if it happened within the last week.

It was Sunday night, Nov. 1, 1987. Seventeen-year-old Romano had gone to bed. His mother, Betty Romano, was in the house with him and his father, Frederick Joseph Romano. Soon the father received a call from his son-in-law Keith Garvin, a Navy petty officer who had returned to his base in Oceana, [Virginia]. Garvin had called his wife, Dawn Garvin, to let her know he had arrived back safely. But there was no answer.

After two calls to his daughter's house, Frederick J. Romano headed to the newlywed couple's White Marsh apartment. He found his daughter beaten, tortured, mutilated and dead.

Frederick A. Romano remembers his mother's panic-filled voice as she talked to his father, of himself grabbing the phone only to hear his father tell him that his older sister had been hurt.

"But he knew she was dead," Frederick A. Romano said. . . . Yes, Frederick A. Romano—who prefers to be called just "Fred"—remembers it all. He remembers the man who murdered his sister and two other women—Patricia Antoinette Hirt and Lori Elizabeth Ward—and how he has waited for 15 years for one Steven Howard Oken to, in the younger Romano's words, "meet his maker."

The Pain of Victims' Relatives

"It's caused a lot of emotional problems for me and my mom and dad," Fred said. "They're on so many drugs to keep themselves calm, it's unbelievable."

That is a suffering death penalty opponents can't or won't understand. The pain of homicide victims' relatives never ends. It chips away at their souls and psyches year after depressing year. So what's the appropriate punishment for that?

Death penalty opponents would have us believe that squirreling Oken away in a cell—where Frederick A. and Frederick J. Romano, Betty Romano and Keith Garvin would be among the taxpayers footing the bill for his housing and meals—is punishment enough. If the correctional system offered any college courses, the Romanos and Garvin would pay part of the cost if Oken wanted to take them. Dawn Garvin never got to finish her education at Harford Community College.

> *"The pain of homicide victims' relatives never ends. . . . So what's the appropriate punishment for that?"*

Justice but No Closure

Capital punishment foes figure that's justice. Here's what death penalty advocates feel is justice. Execute Oken the week of March 17, [2003], as a Baltimore County judge ordered. . . . After Oken is dead, death penalty advocates can then defy death penalty opponents to show us why and in what ways Oken's execution was not justice.

That's what it's about for Fred Romano. He doesn't buy into the closure argument some death penalty advocates make. (It's just as well. Death penalty opponents, ever noble with grief not their own, dismiss the notion of closure, too.)

"It won't bring closure," Fred Romano said. "Dawn will never be back. I'm not looking for closure. That's a bad misconception on the part of some people. I want Oken to die for the murder of Dawn, Patricia Hurt and Lori Ward."

Not About Revenge

This isn't even about revenge, another rallying cry of the anti-capital punishment crowd, who chide death penalty advocates for seeking vengeance.

"It's justice," Fred Romano said. "It's not revenge."

His wife, Vicki Romano, agreed, then elaborated.

"Revenge would be going out and killing one of [the murderer's] family members," Vicki Romano said. "The death penalty isn't revenge. It's the law."

Fred Romano believes the man who's supposed to uphold that law, Maryland Attorney General J. Joseph Curran, has inserted himself squarely in the path of Oken's execution. [Early in 2003], Curran called for abolishing Maryland's death penalty. . . .

Fred Romano called Curran after the announcement, to give the attorney general a piece of his mind. Curran, to his credit, called Fred Romano back and heard him out.

Curran, Fred Romano said, asked him if he had a problem with a sentence of life without parole as opposed to the death penalty. His response was what you might expect from a guy who organized the Maryland Coalition for State Executions [in 2002] and who's had the group's Web site (www.mc4se.org) up for [several] months.

"My problem with it is that 10 years from now some other idiot will come along and say life without parole is too harsh," Fred Romano said. "Then they'll pass a bill granting them parole and then we'll have a bunch of murderers walking the streets."

In Maryland's bleeding-heart liberal legislature, that's exactly what would happen.

Postconviction DNA Testing Should Be Encouraged

by Tim O'Brien

About the author: *Tim O'Brien covered Supreme Court issues for ABC News from 1977 to 1999. He has also worked as a professor of law at Hofstra University.*

My editors and I thought it was a good story: the black, one-eyed, homosexual rapist who claimed it was a case of mistaken identity. P.S.: He also walked with a limp.

The U.S. Supreme Court had agreed to review the case in its 1988 term, because it had raised an important constitutional question: Do the police have any obligation to preserve potentially exculpatory evidence?

The Case of Larry Youngblood

The defendant, Larry Youngblood, had been convicted of abducting a 10-year-old boy from a church carnival and repeatedly sodomizing him. Youngblood had argued that if the police had preserved semen samples taken from the boy's clothing, DNA tests would have shown they had arrested the wrong man.

Never mind that the tests in question weren't ordinarily available at the time of the trial (although they are now routine). Never mind that Youngblood fit the description provided by the victim, or that the traumatized child also identified Youngblood in court as the perpetrator. Never mind that the evidence appeared so overwhelming that it took the jury only 40 minutes to convict Youngblood and send him on his way to a 10-year prison term.

The legal issue the case raised was significant; it was to resonate years later in the O.J. Simpson case[1] and doubtless many other lesser cases. In my heart, I

---

1. In 1995 former football star O.J. Simpson was found not guilty of murdering his ex-wife and her friend. Controversies over evidence had been a significant factor in the murder trial.

questioned the judgment of the public defenders who would bring such an important issue to the Supreme Court with such an obviously guilty defendant. If, as Oliver Wendell Holmes put it, hard cases make bad law, then what do bad cases make?

But public defenders Dan Davis and Carol Wittels seemed less concerned with the precedent the court might set than with winning freedom for their client. Could they possibly believe he was really innocent? Yes, without a doubt, they both said. Defense lawyers can believe, or appear to believe, anything.

> *"DNA testing, by providing statistical proof of innocence (or guilt), may be the only way to effectively offset invidious biases."*

Supreme Court justices are supposed to decide cases on the basis of the law, but like all humans, they too can be influenced by the facts. And the facts in this case couldn't have been worse for Youngblood. Moreover, he lived alone, had a history of mental illness and had had previous run-ins with the law.

As expected, the Supreme Court upheld Youngblood's conviction, deciding his fate with exceptional speed, just as the jury had two years earlier. Only three justices dissented, with the late Harry Blackmun writing that "the Constitution requires a fair trial, not merely a 'good faith' try at a fair trial."

Mistaken Identity

A good story? We didn't know the half of it. [In August 2000] Youngblood's conviction was vacated—thrown out by the Pima County Superior Court in Tucson. While the small amount of semen that was preserved was insufficient for reliable testing at the time of the appeal, new testing procedures that only recently became available were conducted by the Tucson police. They showed conclusively what attorneys Wittels and Davis knew all along: The police really did have the wrong man. It was a case of mistaken identity.

Youngblood may have been less a victim of bad facts than of societal biases that can seep into and poison the criminal justice process. Could his race have been a factor? His multiple disabilities, mental and physical? His perceived sexual orientation? The fact that he had been accused of a horrendous offense that cried out for retribution?

There is no scientific way to quantify the effects of these illicit considerations in Youngblood's case, nor anyone else's for that matter. And the Supreme Court, in another case, has ruled that even a statistical probability of bias is insufficient to set aside a conviction, even a death sentence. DNA testing, by providing statistical proof of innocence (or guilt), may be the only way to effectively offset invidious biases.

Yet at every turn prosecutors are resisting the use of DNA tests whenever it might mean reopening an old case. There are now hundreds of inmates on death row who claim DNA tests would show they were not guilty of the crimes for which they were convicted. Most, perhaps even all, are mistaken. But in light of what happened to Larry Youngblood, the complaints that such tests are too expensive and time-consuming or that a jury's verdict must be accorded finality ring hollow indeed. The Tucson police have graciously conceded that it was "unfortunate" Youngblood spent so much time incarcerated for a crime he didn't commit, but they say they did what they thought was right at the time. Youngblood is angry to have been robbed of "the best part of my life," and he wants to sue the police. All agree it should not have happened.

To prevent it from happening again, courts must be receptive to any credible claim that new tests might prove the actual innocence of one who has already been convicted. Had Larry Youngblood been charged with first degree murder, he'd probably be dead now.

Postconviction DNA Testing Should Not Be Encouraged

by Peter Roff

About the author: *Peter Roff is a political analyst for United Press International.*

To deprive an individual of their liberty—even for a short time—is to limit their most basic freedom. It is a serious matter and should be done with the utmost care. The Anglo-American system of jurisprudence gives every benefit of every doubt to the accused. At trial, the state must prove guilt beyond a reasonable doubt while the accused is presumed to be innocent.

What Justice Oliver Wendell Holmes said in defense of the Fourth Amendment is generally true where the free exercise of liberty is at issue: "It is less evil that some criminals should escape than that the government should play an ignoble part (in gathering evidence)."

This does not, however, require evidence be re-examined years after the fact because the science changes.

Prisons Full of Innocent People?

Technology may have advanced to the point where certain types of evidence may conclusively identify a guilty party. This is just part of the entire equation, admittedly an important part. Yet the idea that many of the inmates on death row or serving long sentences could be freed by new DNA evidence has been ingrained in the American mind by Hollywood. While dramatic, it is hardly true and runs counter to the argument, most often heard from inmates and their lawyers that the prisons are full of innocent people, wrongfully convicted.

While the presence of DNA at a crime scene can be used to establish guilt in a court of law, the converse is not automatically true. The absence of a particular individual's DNA at a crime scene is not alone proof of their innocence. Prosecutors and legislators arguing against the unlimited opportunity for taxpayer-funded DNA tests in pursuit of the exoneration of convicted felons are correct in their objections.

It is the entire body of evidence that must be considered, not just the results of lab tests performed on old clothing.

Doubtful Evidence

The rights of the accused are protected in the courtroom, often at the expense of the victims'. Physical evidence, eyewitness testimony and evidence often circumstantial in nature but attesting to means, motive and opportunity are considered during trial under accepted rules of evidence. Can that chain of evidence still be as reliable 10, 15 or 20 years after the fact? It is doubtful.

Can the state, fairly and years later, represent the interests of the victim and society as a whole if the judicial system lets doubt—which increases over time—adhere to the benefit of the accused, especially when DNA tests often produce more doubt than proof?

In the same way repeated death penalty appeals slowed the wheels of justice for many years these DNA requests will tax the already overburdened legal system, depriving the victims and the wrongfully accused of their day in court in a timely manner.

The requests for these tests amount more to lawyerly shams rather [than to] efforts to overcome justice denied. The state is right to limit them.

Executions Should Be Televised

by George J. Bryjak

About the author: *George J. Bryjak is a professor of sociology at the University of San Diego.*

Attorney General John Ashcroft announced that the May 16, [2001], execution of Timothy McVeigh would be televised via a live, encrypted, closed-circuit telecast and made available to the survivors of the Oklahoma City bombing and relatives of those killed. In light of this decision, we might ask ourselves why all state executions are not televised.

Although the number of Americans who advocate the death penalty has declined from 80 percent in 1994 to 67 percent in October 2000, this latter number still demonstrates strong support for capital punishment. Two of the reasons most often cited by death penalty proponents are retribution—"an eye for an eye, a tooth for a tooth"—and deterrence for would-be killers.

Prime-Time Viewing

If as a nation we execute people in large measure because of our belief in the death penalty's deterrent capacity, then we should maximize that capacity by making state-sanctioned deaths public spectacles. Since 74 percent of all known homicide offenders between 1976 and 1999 were under 35 years of age (including 10.7 percent under 18) watching executions on television should be a mandatory component of the school curriculum beginning at an age when children can be tried and sentenced as adults (if not sooner). Minimally, young males could be compelled to witness these executions. (Females comprise only 10 percent of those arrested for murder.)

Surely we cannot oppose children witnessing executions for fear of damaging their psychosocial development. By the time the typical American child graduates from high school, he or she will have watched thousands of killings via the media, many of them graphically and gruesomely portrayed.

If we honestly believe in the deterrent value of capital punishment, executions should be given the widest public audience. These state-sanctioned events could be scheduled for prime-time television viewing; the first Tuesday of the month designated "execution day." Why not execute mass murderers, serial killers and other heinous offenders during a halftime extravaganza at the Super Bowl when half the nation is watching?

Although some studies have concluded that criminal homicides decline after well-publicized executions, most have found no effect, while still others have discovered that homicides actually increase after executions. This latter phenomenon is

> *"Why not execute mass murderers, serial killers and other heinous offenders during a halftime extravaganza at the Super Bowl?"*

called the "brutalization effect": Well-publicized executions desensitize people to the immorality of killing, thereby increasing the likelihood that some individuals will make the decision to kill.

In a major death penalty study published [in 2000], Columbia University law professor James S. Liebman found that the 39 states with capital punishment account for about 80 percent of the nation's homicides and 76 percent of the population. Although this is negative evidence for the deterrence perspective, it could be argued that the number of homicides in these states would have been lower if the executions had been televised. The entire deterrence thesis rests on the premise that people will desist from criminal activity if they are made aware of the high certainty and severity of punishment for a given offense.

Asking Tough Questions

There are additional advantages to having public-viewed executions. After a year or so of such fare, we may begin asking ourselves some tough questions. For example, why are a disproportionate number of those persons slated to die in some locales African-American? A 1998 study found that black defendants in Philadelphia were almost four times more likely than other defendants convicted of committing identical crimes to receive the death penalty. In 1994, Supreme Court Justice Harry Blackmun said, "Even under the most sophisticated death penalty statutes, race continues to play a major role in determining who shall live and who shall die."

Watching executions may give us pause to reexamine patterns of race-of-victim and race-of-defendant discrimination in sentencing. Of the 172 people executed [between] 1976 [and 2000], for interracial murders, 11 were white offenders convicted of killing black victims, and 161 were black defendants convicted of killing white victims. More than 80 percent of capital cases involve white victims even though only 50 percent of murder victims are white. Why is the taking of the life of a white person more deserving of the death penalty than the slaying of a nonwhite person?

Perhaps when we look into the terror-filled eyes of those who are about to die proclaiming their innocence, we may wonder how many of them are telling the truth. After examining almost 5,500 death penalty cases from 1973 to 1995, Liebman concluded, "American capital sentences are persistently and systematically fraught with serious error." He found these cases replete with mistakes including "egregiously incompetent defense lawyers," prosecutorial misconduct (notably the suppression of exculpatory evidence) and faulty jury instructions.

A thoroughly researched series of articles by the *Chicago Tribune* concluded that almost half of the 285 death penalty cases in Illinois involved defense attorneys who were later suspended or disbarred; jailhouse snitches attempting to shorten their sentences by testifying against the accused; questionable "hair analysis"; and black defendants convicted by all-white juries.

With the expenditure of relatively small amounts of investigative resources between 1976 and 2000, 87 death row inmates have been cleared of wrongdoing and released from prison. How many innocent people "living the ultimate nightmare" will not be as fortunate?

Justice System Travesties

Perhaps a steady diet of television executions will familiarize us with some of the travesties of the justice system. In January [2001] 14 judges of the U.S. Fifth Circuit Court of Appeals met to reconsider a ruling issued in October [2000] by a three-judge panel of the court that held that the state of Texas can execute a man convicted of murder even though his attorney slept through substantial portions of the trial. . . .

Mohandas Gandhi opposed capital punishment, stating that only God has the right to take a life and since human beings can never fully understand the motives and thinking of another person, we are not capable of making life-ending decisions. I am against capital punishment for these reasons as well as the injustices rife in the implementation of this penalty.

However, I realize that because of strong public support, the death penalty is likely to be part of the American criminal justice system for the indefinite future. This being the case, we should follow the example of Saudi Arabia and maximize the potential deterrent effect of this penalty by making state-sanctioned executions

> *"Watching executions may give us pause to reexamine patterns of . . . discrimination in sentencing."*

public spectacles. If we are going to kill people for killing people, let us make the most of it.

As a nation we have the collective heart (retribution) and mind (deterrence) to execute individuals. What we lack is the stomach to do so publicly. Michael Kroll is correct when he states that capital punishment is "America's own schizophrenia. . . . We believe in the death penalty, but shrink from it when applied."

Executions Should Not Be Televised

by Sally Peters

About the author: *Sally Peters is a freelance writer.*

The notion that witnessing executions brings "closure" to victims' families is false, experts say. The evidence, in fact, shows that doing so can cause witnesses additional stress.

When 232 family members assembled on June 11 [2001] to watch the closed circuit televised execution of Timothy McVeigh, whose 1995 bombing of the Alfred P. Murrah federal building in Oklahoma City claimed 168 lives, most of them undoubtedly hoped that witnessing the event would end their grief. Not so, said Dr. David Spiegel, a psychiatrist at Stanford (Calif.) University. "Nothing we know clinically shows that witnessing executions ends grieving."

The theory that execution provides "closure" is a "naive, unfounded, pop psychology idea" perpetuated by politicians and the media, he said.

True closure after the death of a loved one is achieved only through extensive "grief work" with family members. This lengthy process requires families to acknowledge, bear, and put their loss into perspective.

Eventually family members will be able to take pleasure in the time they had with their loved ones. "[But] it's not easy," Dr. Spiegel said.

The Effects of Witnessing Executions

Witnessing executions not only fails to provide closure, it also may cause symptoms of acute stress—even in observers who are not related to the victims.

A 1994 study coauthored by Dr. Spiegel polled 18 media eyewitnesses to the California execution of convicted murderer Robert Alton Harris, who died in the San Quentin gas chamber. The journalists, who stood within 15–20 feet of the chamber, had an unobstructed view of the execution.

When they began the study, researchers knew that being a target of violence was psychologically traumatic, but few, if any, studies had been done on the effects of witnessing violence. They postulated that the journalists who witnessed the execution would experience dissociative and anxiety symptoms.

Roughly 1 month after the Harris execution, researchers sent questionnaires to the 18 media eyewitnesses. Fifteen, of whom nine were men, responded. The questionnaire asked them to rate their experiences during and shortly after the execution on 17 items, including psychic numbing, stupor, and depersonalization as a means to assess for dissociative

> *"Witnessing executions not only fails to provide closure, it may also cause symptoms of acute stress—even in observers . . . not related to the victim."*

symptoms. Anxiety also was assessed—based on signs of intrusion, avoidance, and increased arousal—using the respondents rating of 13 additional items on the questionnaire.

All of the media eyewitnesses who completed the questionnaire were further invited to participate in a follow-up telephone interview with one of the psychiatrists on the research team. Twelve of the fifteen journalists who completed questionnaires participated in the telephone interview.

Although researchers did not find evidence that witnessing that execution caused long-term negative effects in the journalists, the short-term effects were "considerable."

The occurrence of dissociative symptoms was strongly correlated with experiencing symptoms of anxiety:

- 47% felt the intrusive effects of witnessing the event, noting that they experienced a narrowed focus of attention.
- 53% struggled to avoid thoughts or feelings about the execution.
- 53% described their increased arousal as shortness of breath, and muscle tension, aches, and soreness.

Researchers also noted that the incidence of dissociation in the journalists, as detailed below, was similar to that experienced in people who have endured a natural disaster:

- 53% experienced a distancing from their emotions.
- 33% felt confused and disoriented.
- 53% described their surroundings as surreal or dreamlike.
- 40% described a sense of self-depersonalization.
- 60% said they felt estranged or detached from other people.
- 27% complained of trouble remembering daily activities.
- 3% had flashbacks of the event.

In the follow-up telephone interviews, one journalist reported experiencing emotionalism and crying for weeks at a time; and two said they had discussed the experience with a counselor. None of them felt they would volunteer to cover such an assignment again.

Long-Term Consequences

Four years after this study was conducted, a similar study, also coauthored by Dr. Spiegel, found that witnessing violence can have long-term effects. Researchers polled 36 employees who witnessed a shooting in a California office building where a gunman fired upon 14 people, 8 fatally. Thirty-three percent of the employees met the criteria for a diagnosis of acute stress disorder 8 days after the shooting.

When researchers polled the employees again 7–10 months later, 32 of them responded. The follow-up poll showed that the early symptoms of acute stress disorder were an "excellent" predictor of later development of posttraumatic stress disorder.

"We underestimate the profound negative effect [witnessing executions] has on people," Dr. Spiegel said.

Organizations to Contact

The editors have compiled the following list of organizations concerned with the issues debated in this book. The descriptions are derived from materials provided by the organizations. All have publications or information available for interested readers. The list was compiled on the date of publication of the present volume; the information provided here may change. Be aware that many organizations take several weeks or longer to respond to inquiries, so allow as much time as possible.

American Civil Liberties Union (ACLU)
125 Broad St., 18th Fl., New York, NY 10004
(212) 549-2500 • fax: (212) 549-2646
Web site: www.aclu.org

The ACLU believes that capital punishment violates the Constitution's ban on cruel and unusual punishment as well as the requirements of due process and equal protection under the law. It publishes and distributes numerous books, pamphlets, and position papers, including "A Question of Innocence," "Juveniles and the Death Penalty," and "Race and the Death Penalty."

Amnesty International USA (AI)
322 Eighth Ave., New York, NY 10001
(212) 807-8400 • fax: (212) 627-1451
Web site: www.amnesty-usa.org

Amnesty International is an independent worldwide movement working impartially for the release of all prisoners of conscience, fair and prompt trials for political prisoners, and an end to torture and executions. AI's Program to Abolish the Death Penalty (PADP) coordinates efforts to build coalitions with grassroots activists and social justice organizations working toward the elimination of the death penalty worldwide. AI's Web site includes links to news releases, fact sheets, and reports, including "The Exclusion of Child Offenders from the Death Penalty Under General International Law."

Canadian Coalition Against the Death Penalty (CCADP)
PO Box 38104, 550 Eglinton Ave. W, Toronto, ON M5N 3A8 Canada
(416) 693-9112 • fax: (416) 686-1630
e-mail: info@ccadp.org • Web site: www.ccadp.org

CCADP is a not-for-profit international human rights organization dedicated to educating the public on alternatives to the death penalty worldwide and to providing emotional and practical support to death row inmates, their families, and the families of murder victims. The coalition publishes pamphlets and periodic press releases, and its Web site includes a student resource center providing research information on capital punishment.

Criminal Justice Legal Foundation (CJLF)
PO Box 1199, Sacramento, CA 95816
(916) 446-0345
e-mail: cjlf@cjlf.org • Web site: www.cjlf.org

Established in 1982 as a nonprofit public interest law organization, the CJLF seeks to restore a balance between the rights of crime victims and the criminally accused. The foundation supports the death penalty and works to reduce the length, complexity, and expense of appeals as well as to improve law enforcement's ability to identify and prosecute criminals. Its Web site offers reports on pending cases and links to studies and articles about capital punishment.

Death Penalty Focus
870 Market St., Suite 859, San Francisco, CA 94102
(415) 243-0143 • fax: (415) 243-0994
e-mail: info@deathpenalty.org • Web site: www.deathpenalty.org

Founded in 1988, Death Penalty Focus is a nonprofit organization dedicated to the abolition of capital punishment through grassroots organization, research, and the dissemination of information about the death penalty and its alternatives. It publishes an information bulletin, *The Catalyst*, as well as a quarterly newsletter, *The Sentry*.

Death Penalty Information Center (DPIC)
1320 Eighteenth St. NW, 5th Fl., Washington, DC 20036
(202) 293-6970 • fax: (202) 822-4787
e-mail: dpic@deathpenaltyinfo.org • Web site: www.deathpenaltyinfo.org

DPIC conducts research into public opinion on the death penalty. The center believes capital punishment is discriminatory and excessively costly and that it may result in the execution of innocent persons. It publishes numerous reports, such as *Innocence and the Death Penalty: Assessing the Danger of Mistaken Executions, With Justice for Few: The Growing Crisis in Death Penalty Representation*, and *International Perspectives on the Death Penalty: A Costly Isolation for the U.S.* The DPIC Web site features a searchable database for executions, recent news releases, and video clips.

Justice Fellowship (JF)
1856 Old Reston Ave., Reston, VA 20190
(800) 217-2743 • fax: (703) 904-7307
e-mail: mail@justicefellowship.org • Web site: www.justicefellowship.org

Justice Fellowship is an online community of Christians working to reform the criminal justice system so that it reflects biblically based principles of restorative justice. Founded in 1983 as a subsidiary of Prison Fellowship Ministries, JF seeks to recognize the needs of crime victims and their families and hold offenders accountable to society. It does not take a position on the death penalty, but it publishes the pamphlet *Capital Punishment: A Call to Dialogue*.

Justice for All (JFA)
(713) 935-9300
e-mail: info@jfa.net • Web site: www.jfa.net

Justice for All is a not-for-profit criminal justice reform organization that supports the death penalty. Its activities include circulating online petitions to keep violent offenders from being paroled early and publishing the monthly newsletter *The Voice of Justice*. JFA also manages the Web sites www.murdervictims.com and www.prodeathpenalty.com.

Lamp of Hope Project
PO Box 305, League City, TX 77574-0305
e-mail: ksebung@lampofhope.org • Web site: www.lampofhope.org

The project was established and is run primarily by Texas death row inmates. Its goals include educating the public about the death penalty and its alternatives, supporting victims' families by promoting healing and reconciliation, and breaking the cycle of violence by supporting prisoners' families. Lamp of Hope publishes and distributes the periodical *Death Row Journal.*

Lincoln Institute for Research and Education
1001 Connecticut Ave. NW, Washington, DC 20036
(202) 223-5112

The institute is a conservative think tank that studies public policy issues affecting the lives of black Americans, including the issue of the death penalty, which it favors. It publishes the quarterly *Lincoln Review.*

National Coalition to Abolish the Death Penalty (NCADP)
920 Pennsylvania Ave. SE, Washington, DC 20003
(202) 543-9577 • fax: (202) 543-7798
e-mail: kjones@ncadp.org • Web site: www.ncadp.org

The National Coalition to Abolish the Death Penalty is a collection of more than 115 groups working together to stop executions in the United States. The organization compiles statistics on the death penalty and publishes information packets, pamphlets, and research materials. Its Web site includes press releases, news archives, legislative action links, and execution alerts.

National Criminal Justice Reference Service (NCJRS)
U.S. Department of Justice
PO Box 6000, Rockville, MD 20849-6000
(301) 519-5500 • (800) 851-3420 • fax: (301) 519-5212
e-mail: askncjrs@ncjrs.org • Web site: www.ncjrs.org

Sponsored by the U.S. Departments of Justice and Homeland Security, the federally funded National Criminal Justice Reference Service is one of the most extensive sources of information on crime and justice in the world. For a nominal fee, this clearinghouse provides topical searches and reading lists on many areas of criminal justice, including the death penalty. It publishes an annual report on capital punishment.

Bibliography

Books

James R. Acker, Robert M. Bohm, and Charles S. Lanier, eds.	*America's Experiment with Capital Punishment: Reflections on the Past, Present, and Future of the Ultimate Penal Sanction*, 2nd ed. Durham, NC: Carolina Academic Press, 2003.
Laura Argys and Naci Mocan	*Who Shall Live and Who Shall Die?: An Analysis of Prisoners on Death Row in the United States.* Cambridge, MA: National Bureau of Economic Research, 2003.
Stuart Banner	*The Death Penalty: An American History.* Cambridge, MA: Harvard University Press, 2002.
Hugo Adam Bedau and Paul G. Cassell, eds.	*Debating the Death Penalty: Should America Have Capital Punishment?: The Experts on Both Sides Make Their Best Case.* New York: Oxford University Press, 2004.
Walter Berns	*For Capital Punishment.* Lanham, MD: University Press of America, 2000.
Antoinette Bosco	*Choosing Mercy: A Mother of Murder Victims Pleads to End the Death Penalty.* Maryknoll, NY: Orbis Books, 2001.
James E. Coleman Jr., ed.	*The ABA's Proposed Moratorium on the Death Penalty.* Durham, NC: Duke University School of Law, 1998.
L. Kay Gillespie	*Executions and the Execution Process: Questions and Answers.* Boston: Allyn and Bacon, 2002.
Mike Gray	*The Death Game: Capital Punishment and the Luck of the Draw.* Monroe, ME: Common Courage Press, 2003.
Harry Henderson	*Capital Punishment.* New York: Facts On File, 2000.
Jesse L. Jackson Sr., Jesse L. Jackson Jr., and Bruce Shapiro	*Legal Lynching: The Death Penalty and America's Future.* New York: New Press, 2001.
Robert Jay Lifton and Greg Mitchell	*Who Owns Death? Capital Punishment, the American Conscience, and the End of Executions.* New York: Morrow, 2000.
Ann Chih Lin, ed.	*Capital Punishment.* Washington, DC: CQ Press, 2002.

Bibliography

Dan Malone and
Howard Swindle

America's Condemned: Death Row Inmates in Their Own Words. Kansas City, MO: Andrews McMeel, 1999.

Naci H. Mocan and
R. Kaj Gittings

Pardons, Executions, and Homicide. Cambridge, MA: National Bureau of Economic Research, 2001.

Lane Nelson and
Burk Foster, eds.

Death Watch: A Death Penalty Anthology. Upper Saddle River, NJ: Prentice Hall, 2001.

Louis P. Pojman and
Jeffrey Reiman

The Death Penalty: For and Against. Lanham, MD: Rowman & Littlefield, 1998.

Austin Sarat

When the State Kills: Capital Punishment and the American Condition. Princeton, NJ: Princeton University Press, 2001.

Ivan Solotaroff

The Last Face You'll Ever See: The Private Life of the American Death Penalty. New York: Harper-Collins, 2001.

Tom Streissguth

The Death Penalty: Debating Capital Punishment. Berkeley Heights, NJ: Enslow, 2002.

Scott Turow

Ultimate Punishment: A Lawyer's Reflections on Dealing with the Death Penalty. New York: Farrar, Straus, and Giroux, 2003.

Ted R. Weiland

Capital Punishment: Deterrent or Catalyst. Eugene, OR: Far Horizons Press, 2000.

Periodicals

John L. Allen Jr.

"U.S. Allies See Death Penalty as Fascist Relic," *National Catholic Reporter*, January 19, 2001.

Bruce Anderson

"A Hanging Matter," *Spectator*, November 22, 2003.

George M. Anderson

"Healing the Wounds of Murder: Among the Victims Are Family Members of Both the Murdered and the Murderer," *America*, July 30, 2002.

Peter L. Berger

"Beyond the 'Humanly Tolerable,'" *National Review*, July 17, 2000.

Alan Berlow

"The Broken Machinery of Death," *American Prospect*, July 30, 2001.

John D. Bessler

"America's Death Penalty: Just Another Form of Violence," *Phi Kappa Phi Forum*, Winter 2002.

Philip Brasfield

"The End of Innocence," *Other Side*, December 2000.

Antony J. Blinken

"Listen to the People: Capital Punishment Is More Popular in Europe than Its Politicians Admit," *Time International*, May 21, 2001.

Carl M. Cannon

"The Problem with the Chair—A Conservative Case Against Capital Punishment," *National Review*, June 19, 2000.

Catherine Cowan

"States Revisit the Death Penalty," *State Government News*, May 2001.

John Dart	"Executing Justice," *Christian Century*, February 13, 2002.
Gregg Easterbrook	"The Myth of Fingerprints: DNA and the End of Innocence," *New Republic*, July 31, 2000.
Don Feder	"It's Hard to Pardon the Excuses Given by Death-Penalty Opponents," *Insight on the News*, July 16, 2001.
Samuel Francis	"Processions of the Damned," *Chronicles*, September 2000.
Linda Greenhouse	"Citing 'National Consensus,' Justices Bar Death Penalty for Retarded Defendants," *New York Times*, June 21, 2002.
Jonathan I. Groner	"Lethal Injection: A Stain on the Face of Medicine," *British Medical Journal*, November 2, 2002.
Cragg Hines	"There Should Be No Deadline for Justice," *Houston Chronicle*, October 2, 2003.
Jeffrey L. Johnson and Colleen F. Johnson	"Poverty and the Death Penalty," *Journal of Economic Issues*, June 2001.
Frank Keating	"Why I Support Capital Punishment," *Human Events*, May 19, 2000.
Alice Kim	"Death Penalty Exposed," *International Socialist Review*, March/April 2003.
Eugene H. Methvin	"Death Penalty Is Fairer than Ever," *Wall Street Journal*, May 10, 2000.
Deborah Potter	"Witnessing the Final Act," *American Journalism Review*, July 2001.
Sally Satel	"It's Crazy to Execute the Insane," *Wall Street Journal*, March 14, 2002.
Bruce Shapiro	"Rethinking the Death Penalty: Politicians and Courts Are Taking Their Cues from the Growing Public Opposition," *Nation*, July 22, 2002.
Kathy Swedlow	"Forced Medication of Legally Incompetent Prisoners: A Primer," *Human Rights*, Spring 2003.
William Tucker	"The Chair Deters," *National Review*, July 17, 2000.
William Tucker	"Why the Death Penalty Works," *American Spectator*, October 1, 2000.
James Q. Wilson	"What Death Penalty Errors?" *New York Times*, July 10, 2000.
Lewis Yablonsky	"A Road into Minds of Murderers," *Los Angeles Times*, January 14, 2003.
Gabino Zavala and Michael Kennedy	"Death Penalty Diminishes Us as a Society," *Los Angeles Times*, October 27, 2000.

Index

punishment, justifications for, 21–22

racism
  in criminal justice system, 121
  in death penalty cases, 19, 64–65, 69, 106,
    135–36
  is not true, 88
  influences administration of death
    penalty, 72–76
    con, 92–94
  jury selection and, 74–76
Radelet, Michael, 73
Rector, Ricky, 65
Redmond, Lula, 135
Reed, Colleen, 91
reforms, 10–12, 71, 77–82, 138–40
Reno, Janet, 135
restorative justice, 124–25
retribution, 21–28, 46–48, 121–22
retributive justice, 121–22, 125
revenge, 42–43, 121–22, 152–53
  desire for, 14–15
  vs. retribution, 22–25
Robertson, Pat, 132
Rodriguez, Reynaldo, 43
Roe v. Wade, 31
Roff, Peter, 157
Romano, Frederick A., 151–53
Romney, Mitt, 110, 111
Ross, Michael B., 83
Roth, Kenneth, 134
Rubin, Paul H., 103
Ryan, George, 11, 52, 67, 138, 140, 143

Scalia, Antonin, 29
Sellin, Thorsten, 104
September 11, 2001, 45, 51–52
Sharp, Dudley, 16, 63
Sheets, Jeremy, 96
Shepherd, Joanna Mehlhop, 105
Singapore, 113–14
Smith, Clarence, 87
Smith, Frank Lee, 43–44
social protection, 46–47
South, execution rate in the, 121–22
Spiegel, David, 162–64
states rights, 81
Stevens, John Paul, 99–100
Stewart, Potter, 64

Supreme Court rulings, on death penalty, 10,
  29–30, 74–75, 87, 99–100, 107–108, 120
survivors
  attitudes toward, 140
  closure for, 134–35, 162
  pain of, 151–52

Tate, Lionel, 126
Taylor, John, 108, 116–18
terrorist attacks, death penalty and, 45, 51–53
terrorists
  pre-emptive execution of, 44–45
  see also McVeigh, Timothy
Texas, 38–39, 121
Thernstrom, Abigail, 93–94
Thernstrom, Stephan, 93–94
Thompson, William, 90–91
Treadaway, Jonathan, 96
Tremoglie, Michael, 86
Tucker, Karla Faye, 38
Tucker, William, 107
Turow, Scott, 138

United States, moral isolation of, 133–34
U.S. Constitution, as living document, 29–31

Valdez, Gerardo, 134
van den Haag, Ernest, 145
Venable, James, 65
vengeance. *See* revenge
victims
  race of, 73
  as witnesses to crime, 116–17
  see also survivors
violence, 119–25
  in American society, 55–56
  death penalty as form of, 52–53, 55–56
  productive response to, 123–25
  punitive punishments intensify, 122–23

Washington, Earl, Jr., 11, 82
Weeks, Varnell, 84
Wells, Ida B., 72
Wilbanks, William, 93
Williamson, Ronald Keith, 65
Will, George, 97, 132
Wolfgang, Marvin E., 46

Youngblood, Larry, 154–56

PN   Miles-Brown, J.
2053
.M54   Directing drama.

DATE			

89011647

DIRECTING DRAMA

JOHN MILES-BROWN

Directing Drama

ILLUSTRATED WITH PLATES, DIAGRAMS
AND CHARTS

PETER OWEN · LONDON

ISBN 0 7206 0557 1

PETER OWEN LIMITED
73 Kenway Road London SW5 0RE

First published 1980
© 1980 John Miles-Brown

Printed in Great Britain by
Bristol Typesetting Co Ltd
Barton Manor St Philips Bristol 2

To Barbara

ACKNOWLEDGEMENTS

Thanks are due to the following for their kind permission to quote from published works and articles:

Tania Alexander, executor of Moura Budberg's estate, and Davis-Poynter Ltd for Moura Budberg's translation of *Three Sisters* by Anton Chekhov; A. D. Peters & Co. Ltd for *An Inspector Calls* by J. B. Priestley; The Bodley Head Ltd for *Building a Character* by Konstantin Stanislavski; Jerzy Grotowski and Odin Teatrets Forlag for *Towards a Poor Theatre* by Jerzy Grotowski (© 1968 Jerzy Grotowski and Odin Teatrets Forlag); Penguin Books Ltd for Una Ellis-Fermor's translation of *Hedda Gabler* by Henrik Ibsen, and for John Wood's translation of *The Imaginary Invalid* by Molière; Eyre Methuen Ltd for *Loot* by Joe Orton; the executor of Luigi Pirandello's estate for *The Rules of the Game*, translated by Robert Rietty; and *Theatre Quarterly* for the quotation by Paul Scofield in Chapter 9.

CONTENTS

ILLUSTRATIONS

Plates

Plates are reproduced by courtesy of the following: 1, 2, Bernard Watson; 3, 5, TABS (Rank-Strand Electric); 4, The Festival Theatre, Chichester; 6, The Crucible Theatre, Sheffield; 7, The Royal Exchange Theatre, Manchester; 8, The Victoria Theatre, Stoke-on-Trent; 9, Camera Press Ltd; 10, John Vere Brown; 11, David Farrell and the Royal Shakespeare Company; 12, 13, Zoe Dominic.

Figures in the Text

Figures are reproduced by courtesy of the following: pages 43, 46, TABS (Rank-Strand Electric); 44, Theatre Projects Consultants Ltd; 48, Architects, Denys Lasdun & Partners; 49, 51, Jerzy Grotowski and Odin Teatrets Forlag (© 1968), drawings by Jerzy Gurawski.

Introduction

Theatre is an ephemeral art. The text of a play remains in print, but the performance, in terms of live theatre, lives only in the memory of the audience and is finally extinguished. Criticism, film or video tape of a stage play can impart a flavour of what it might have been like to be present at a certain performance, but it cannot recapture the immediacy and the feedback between cast and audience, what Bernard Levin calls 'the electricity of the theatre', that makes each enactment unique. When the performance is over we are left with only the memory of a complex series of thoughts and images that may have moved us to laughter, tears, anger, disgust, uplifted us, made us think, subjected us to a variety of thrills, or allowed us to escape into the staged world of the dramatist.

The making of theatre is the work of the director and each director, inevitably, to a greater or lesser extent, imprints upon the finished production his personal style – for he has translated the text from page to stage, using his chosen cast, production team and technical facilities to present his particular interpretation of the play.

In recent years we have become accustomed to what is called 'director's theatre', where gifted directors with strong personal styles make their treatment of the play the outstanding feature of the production. The director virtually becomes the star, a function formerly monopolized by the leading player, and his treatment sometimes makes more impact than the work of the cast. There has, however, recently been a reaction to this trend; indeed, Peter Hall has suggested that it is perhaps time the actor returned to a more dominant role in the theatre. The Actor's Company, founded by Ian McKellan in 1972, has this view in mind and chooses the

11

director it feels is most suitable for the company, which is the reverse of the usual procedure.

Nevertheless, it is the director, as artistic overseer, who is finally responsible for creating the dramatic image that burns on in the memory, sometimes for years, when most of the minor details of a production are forgotten. These persistent images usually contain the essence of the interpretation of the play. Let me give some examples. There was that moment in Peter Brook's 1949 production of *The Dark of the Moon*, when William Sylvester as the Witch Boy returned to his kindred spirits. He was sitting on the ground centre stage, tense and still in the moonlight, aware of the pull of the witch world calling him back to freedom. In a long silence we were aware of the intensity of his inner conflict, then, triggered by a sound of the night, we saw him released from human bondage. He suddenly relaxed – seemed to lose weight, spun like a top, froze suddenly then leaped to his feet and was in that instant transformed to a creature of another world, a wild thing – evil. It was splendid acting, but the total impact was engineered by the impeccable sense of atmosphere, movement and timing set by the director.

Another occasion was at the end of Act IV in Laurence Olivier's production of Chekhov's *Three Sisters* at the Old Vic in 1969, when the sound of the military band escorting the departing regiment, which has made itself part of the texture of the lives of the sisters, grows faint in the distance. Chebutikin, the failing Army doctor, sits with the paper and hums softly to himself, 'Tara-ra-Boom-di-ay. . . . *(Reads the paper.)* It's all the same, all the same. Nothing matters.'

The whole delicate arrangement of timing, stillness, lighting and sound levels captured the mood of that final moment when the three sisters standing together face the prospect of a life the suffering and purpose of which they do not understand. From this ostensibly gloomy prospect was distilled an image of great dramatic power and beauty.

Finally, I remember a moment during the Moscow Art Theatre's performance of *The Cherry Orchard*, at Sadler's Wells Theatre in 1958. In Act II, during the conversation at sunset by an old shrine, there is a pause, and, according to the script, 'a distant sound coming as out of the sky, like the sound of a string snapping, slowly and sadly dying away.' Of all the various productions that

I have seen of *The Cherry Orchard* this was the most moving. The entire theatre was stilled by a quiet, but unearthly, sound that seemed to herald irrevocable change. The masterly handling of this brief moment reflected the quality of direction of the whole play.

There is no one 'correct' way to direct a play. A study of the methods of the outstanding directors of the past and the present reveals very clearly that each director has his own personal approach which arises from his view of the function of theatre in society, the particular play in production, the technical facilities at his command, his individual aptitude as the interpreter of a text, his manner of working with a cast and gauging the reactions of the audience for whom the play will be staged. Directors evolve their methods of work over a period of years and also modify their approaches from play to play. Directing is learned by directing plays and there is no substitute for that practical experience. Experience as an actor or stage manager or working in the production team, as well as having an insatiable appetite for theatre, seems to be the usual way in which a director develops his sense of dramatic imagery and gains an understanding of the practicalities of theatre.

This book attempts to show methods of approach to the job of directing drama and the various factors that must be considered from the time of choosing the play to the opening performance. Whether working on a professional or amateur basis the director has to strive constantly for the highest standard possible within the prevailing conditions. It is this constant striving for perfection – perhaps, in the end, unattainable – and the realization of a particular interpretation, in an art form where compromise is inevitable, that creates the challenge and compulsion of directing.

1 *Some Directors Past and Present*

Surprisingly, it was only about one hundred years ago that theatre programmes indicated that one person (then called the producer) was responsible for directing the production. He might also have been the leading actor, stage manager or the author, so his work was not exclusively that of directing and therefore it would not be easy for him to have had the single-minded concentration, interpretation and objectivity that we expect from today's directors. Today the producer is the person with financial and managerial responsibilities. The director is responsible for all artistic aspects of the staging of productions.

The present-day function of the director has, of course, been influenced by and evolved from the work of a succession of dynamic men of the theatre during the past century, who have brought new vision to the task of staging drama. Directors, designers and theoreticians have constantly experimented with new forms of drama, theatre shapes, styles, techniques and methods of interpretation, in the quest for the ideal synthesis of text, actor, setting, and audience that makes theatre.

One of the first of these was a German, the Duke of Saxe-Meiningen, who had married an actress, Ellen Franz. From 1874 until 1890 he ran his own company, with Ludwig Chronegk as his stage manager and later as producer. The aim was an integrated company paying great attention to accuracy of detail in settings and costumes, which were designed by the Duke himself. All aspects of the production were subject to his firm discipline (Stanislavski regarded him as justifiably despotic) in which actors, costumes, realistic settings, sound effects and stage movement were blended in intensive rehearsals into a unity of pictorial and dramatic effect. The European tours of this co-ordinated and disciplined company had great influence on the theatre. They played at Drury Lane in 1891.

The French director, actor and manager, André Antoine was influenced both by the work of the Meiningen Players and by Emile Zola's doctrine of naturalism. He founded the Théâtre Libre in Paris in 1887, and presented the work of Ibsen, Strindberg, Brieux and Hauptmann among others. He regarded the influence on performance of a facsimile stage as highly important, as this 'real' setting would determine the movement and influence characterization; the environment becoming a dramatic element in its own right. Later he founded the Théâtre Antoine, presenting the plays of the younger dramatists, thus foreshadowing the work of George Devine at London's Royal Court Theatre in Sloane Square.

The Meiningen Players' attention to details and veracity also influenced Konstantin Stanislavski, co-founder of the Moscow Art Theatre with Vladimir Nemirovich-Danchenko in 1898. Although Stanislavski died in 1938 his work as actor, director, teacher and writer provides us to this day with a method for training the actor and guiding the work of the director. His famous 'System' is still the basis of most drama training, although it may not be necessarily referred to as the 'Stanislavski System'. In America, 'the Method' propounded by Lee Strasberg and Elia Kazan at the Actors' Studio, New York, is an adaptation of the Stanislavski System and has produced some remarkable actors.

Stanislavski was responsible with Nemirovich-Danchenko for the famous Chekhovian productions at the Moscow Art Theatre, which are, of course, theatre history. In his early days Stanislavski devoted great attention to external naturalistic details, such as properties, furniture, costumes, sound effects and lighting. He would work out extraordinarily detailed production notes with plans and sketches to realize his visualization on the stage. Everything was exactly delineated; movement, business, voice, mannerisms, and so on. In later productions, however, he revealed that he regarded external truth as insufficient and worked for an inner truth in the actor's performance – psychological realism. The quest for these two forms of truth, internal and external, led him over the years to formulate his System, which is not, it must be firmly stated, a rigid process, but a method of approach, aspects of which good actors have always used instinctively.

Stanislavski was one of the first to suggest that the duty of the director was to seek in the work of the dramatist a 'ruling idea', or super-objective, which would be the main factor guiding the interpretation of a play. Gradually he placed less emphasis on external naturalism and more on the development of the actor's character. His three books, *An Actor Prepares, Building a Character* and *Creating a Role,* are a trilogy planned to show the training of an actor. The first deals mainly with the psychology of the actor, the second and third books have more emphasis on technique. His autobiography *My Life in Art* was published in Russia in 1924, while *Stanislavski Produces Othello* (1948) and *Stanislavski Directs* (1954) concern his work as a director.

Adolph Appia, a Swiss designer and theorist, urged in his book *Die Musik und die Inscenierung* (1895) that the director should become a despotic drillmaster synthesizing the elements of scenic production and dominating the actor. He compared him to the leader of an orchestra. He advocated symbolic and anti-realistic staging, suggesting the atmosphere of the location rather than faithful naturalism. He also worked out a system of stage lighting to create atmospheric effects. His ideas were intended to be applied to operatic and Shakespearian productions rather than plays written in the naturalistic style.

Edward Gordon Craig, the son of Ellen Terry, was a director, designer and theorist. His influential book, *On the Art of the Theatre* (1911), proposed the idea of the director being the supreme power, an alchemist of the theatre, using the actor as a kind of marionette. Rather like Adolph Appia he stressed the importance of creating a setting that would be non-representational, an environment that would reflect the style, accommodate all the scenes of a play and by means of colour in lighting affect changes of mood and atmosphere. This type of setting for an all-purpose acting environment is frequently utilized by designers today – especially in productions of classical drama.

Another director who moved away from naturalistic representation was Jacques Copeau. In 1913 he devised for his theatre company, the Vieux-Colombier, a permanent acting environment with a variety of levels, entrances, steps and a central raised platform. Scenery was reduced to a minimum. This method of staging was designed to accommodate a style of acting in which the movement and the diction of the actors would reflect the dramatic rhythms of the play with the precision of a musician playing notes of music. He regarded the dramatists' text and the direction of it as two stages of a single operation and felt that the director as a specialist had a duty to be completely faithful to the text. To strengthen the actor-audience relationship he removed the proscenium arch and footlights, creating an open-staging form.

An Austrian actor, director and manager, Max Reinhardt, was renowned for his highly spectacular productions with masterly crowd movement. He was a creator of grandiose effects, using all the theatrical means that he could command. For his production of *The Miracle* at Olympia in 1911, the interior was transformed to look like a cathedral. His productions used the widest range of techniques. Reinhardt felt that each play demanded its own style and mode of staging in order to bring it fully alive. He prepared his productions in his *Regiebuch* (director's text) in meticulous detail with diagrams and elaborate notes for all concerned, so that the completed *Regiebuch* was a master-plan covering every aspect of the production: rehearsals, staging, costumes, characterization, lighting, music, and even at times audience disposition. For Reinhardt the text was not of prime importance, as for Jacques Copeau, but just one of many factors he could use to create a theatrical experience. The actors were treated in much the same way as he manipulated the text and technical facilities, so that voice, gesture and movement were all subservient to the masterplan. However, it should be remembered that he was also a skilful director of intimate chamber dramas in the 300-seater Kammerspiele and the Kleines Theatre, which demanded great subtlety of treatment. He was, incidentally, the first to run a school to train directors.

A contemporary of Stanislavski, Vsevolod Meyerhold, was a member of the Moscow Art Theatre from 1898 until 1902. A Russian actor, director and theoretician noted for his experimental work, he sought upon the stage 'a symbolic expression of life'. He relied heavily upon improvisation, rather than having the play meticulously documented in his director's copy, as, say, Stanislavski did in his earlier productions. Meyerhold moulded both the text and the actors to create a vigorous theatrical event. He wanted his actors to move in a stylistic and acrobatic manner and have considerable mimetic skills, with lightning reflexes and absolute control. To this end he developed in his Theatre Workshop a method of movement training for actors which he called 'bio-mechanics'. The actor was basically a super-marionette as advocated by Edward Gordon Craig.

Bertolt Brecht (1898-1956), was a German poet, dramatist, director, theoretician and Marxist. His theatre company, the Berliner Ensemble, was, and still is, devoted to the presentation of his own plays, for each of which he prepared a *Modellbuch* (an elaborate version of the director's copy of the play) complete with a record of all moves, timing and photographs of productions. His theories of drama, about which he wrote copiously and revised from time to time, are reflected in his production techniques. The Alienation Theory (*Verfremdungseffekt*) was a way of making the audience constantly aware that they were sitting in a theatre watching a play about which they were required to think, rather than be carried away on a wave of emotion or sympathy for a particular character. The actor 'demonstrates' his role rather than immerses himself in it, as Stanislavski wished, so that the audience will not wax sympathetic and lose their ability to criticize the situation. Actors may wear masks, or step in and out of character to become a narrator for a moment. Placards carried by the cast may announce the title, time and location of a scene; slides and film clips may be projected; the mechanical apparatus of staging may be in full view; there may be a small band on stage to accompany a burst of song from the actors, who are not to be mellifluous singers, but can put a song across with a gutsy rawness that inclines one to listen to the words rather than wallow in the sound. Brecht's form of theatre, which he called Epic Theatre, is a series of self-contained scenes designed to appeal to reason, not that emotion or empathy could be entirely excluded, for the poetic element in Brecht's dramatic writing does not always keep an audience 'alienated' in the way he wanted. The Berliner Ensemble visited London in 1956, shortly after his death, and his methods of staging were perhaps more influential than his political form of theatre. Brechtian staging methods are now fairly commonplace and have been used notably by Robert Bolt in *A Man for All Seasons,* John Osborne in *Luther* and in musicals such as *Godspell* and *Cabaret.*

Antonin Artaud (1896-1948) was a French playwright, director (he founded the Théâtre Alfred Jarry with Roger Vitrac) and theorist. His book *The Theatre and Its Double* (1938) has, belatedly, in the last twenty years, inspired many directors to attempt to put his theories into practice. Artaud wanted the theatre to move away from psychological realism to the realms of myth and magic. It was to be a theatre of spectacle, using emotive effects, spectacular lighting, beautiful costumes, rhythmical movements, masks, giant effigies, strange music and sounds, cries and groans. Dialogue was to be minimal and delivered in an incantatory manner. He wanted the theatre to be a place where the audience would be subjected to a visual and auditory experience that would liberate forces in the subconscious and by so doing have a cathartic effect.

Peter Brook and Charles Marowitz together presented a Theatre of Cruelty season, using Artaud's methods, at the LAMDA Theatre in London in 1964. Those who attended the performances, drawn from a variety of material, will not easily forget the impact of Artaud's play *Spurt of Blood,* although it lasted only three minutes. The audience were seated in the acting area and the action took place on and around the steeply raked auditorium, so all the action was directed down at the audience – the victims, as it were. Bizarre characters shouted, groaned, cried out, ran, contorted, conflicted in an agony of spirit and then with an almighty shriek a huge hand about twelve-foot-long thrust out above the heads of the audience with blood-red streamers that spanned the theatre vibrating from the fingers. The image was indelible. Elements of Artaud's Theatre of Cruelty ('cruelty', by the way, may be construed as akin to ecstasy combined with the terror and awe of primitive ritual, and in his letters answering objections to the term, published with his book, he explains that he used the word 'cruelty' in the sense of an appetite for life – a cosmic rigor) are to be found in many exotic theatrical productions today, where spectacle is supplied by scenic effects, flashing lights, bizarre costumes, masks, pyrotechnics with explosions, flashes, smoke, incense and audience bombardment by quadrophonic sound.

Lindsay Kemp's production of Oscar Wilde's *Salome* was a very clear example of this – where the performers spoke the little dialogue there was in an incantatory manner as well as using the other techniques mentioned above. We were drawn into an exotic and bizarre world of mime, dance, throbbing music, incense, multi-coloured lighting and fantastic costuming where the impact was sensory and emotional rather than cerebral and approached what is called Théâtre Total, a technique used at times by the French director Jean-Louis Barrault.

Jerome Savory's Grand Magic Circus Theatre Company uses rather similar techniques. When this French company brought *Robinson Crusoe* to the Roundhouse they used elements of Defoe's story to stage a rumbustious spectacle, in-the-round, in which almost every possible tactic was employed to enliven their interpretation, the loneliness of man. The audience were packed in tightly, some sat on chairs, some on the floor and many were standing. From the start, the performance literally exploded in and around and over the audience with deafening music, garish lighting, acrobatics, tightrope walking, fire eaters, audience confrontation, strippers, song, dance, shouted dialogue and unlimited vitality.

In 1953, Joan Littlewood took over the Theatre Royal, Stratford East, and forged a brand of theatre the basis of which was a company improvising around a text. The final results, which were invariably dynamic, often incorporated song, dance and Brechtian techniques such as simple functional settings and actors stepping in and out of character. She excelled in presenting the meatier aspects of life in a broad and flamboyant style that made one come out of the theatre, if not necessarily uplifted, enriched and enthused. Her greatest achievement to date, is, I believe, *Oh What a Lovely War,* in which with Charles Chilton and the company she devised a show depicting the patriotism, courage and futility of World War I. It is a musical on the lines of a pierrot show using Brechtian techniques, including a lighted indicator totting up the mounting casualties as the show proceeds. The context of a musical threw into relief the waste, madness and heartbreak of war.

Jerzy Grotowski, a Polish director, has his own theatre laboratory in Wroclaw. It is subsidized by the state and has the status of Institute for Research into Acting. He works with a small group of actors and the results of his work are occasionally shown to audiences of often not more than forty people. Performances are based on Polish and other classics 'whose function is close to the myth in the collective consciousness'. The performances have about them an intensity and anguished concentration. The acting area is one of extreme simplicity – in fact he calls his type of theatre a 'poor' theatre. The use of voice and movement by the actor are considered all important and portray moods and emotions that have the style of what might, at times, be described as a religious frenzy. The actors produce vocal tones and movement patterns that are quite removed from those experienced in conventional theatre and perform as though they are in a trance. In his book *Towards a Poor Theatre,* Grotowski acknowledges that this is a theatre for an elite. The film *Theatre Laboratorium* issued by Contemporary Films shows vocal and movement training and performance.

Another influence on contemporary British theatre has been the removal of censorship in 1968. Under the office of the Lord Chamberlain plays could be banned, subject to the removal of references or actions that could give offence. Usually these were of a religious, sexual or violent nature. If you look at the rear of many play texts printed just before the removal of censorship you may see a list of words and actions that must be omitted in performance. However, immediately censorship was removed some directors felt that they had to get in on the act and nude scenes seemed to be almost obligatory for a short time, not because the text demanded it, but to produce a fashionable *frisson.* Now that the novelty has worn off, violence, sexual acts and four-letter words (the most common of which was launched into the ether by Ken Tynan, the then dramaturge of the National Theatre, during a BBC Television broadcast) are usually to be found only in productions where they are thought to be essential to character or theme. Impact is not necessarily enhanced by saying, showing or doing what has previously been taboo. One has to leave something for the imagination of the audience to work on and, as in a radio play, imagination can sometimes beggar an attempt at scenic reality.

These then are some of the influences that have shaped the approach to directing today. In his work the director has behind him the theories, experiments and practice of the Meiningen Players, André Antoine, Stanislavski, Adolph Appia, Edward Gordon Craig, Jacques Copeau, Max Reinhardt, Vsevolod Meyerhold, Bertolt Brecht, Antonin Artaud, Joan Littlewood, Charles Marowitz, and Peter Brook, who like Jerzy Grotowski and Artaud before him is seeking a language that will transcend the barrier of national languages. In Brook's production of *Orghast* at the Persepolis Festival in 1971 Ted Hughes devised a text for him that attempted to do this. Brook is one of the most brilliant present-day directors. As Ken Tynan says, he has an uncanny way of skilfully manoeuvring actors, in an almost hypnotic manner, into carrying out his intentions.

In this brief survey of the diverse approaches of some directors during the past century, what emerges, apart from the individuality of style and varied aims and methods, is the single-mindedness, indefatigability and in some cases fanaticism they have brought to the quest for the unattainable – the amalgam of play, cast, setting and audience that is perfection.

Let us now take a look at some of the qualities that the contemporary director may need. Perhaps the first essential is to have a fairly broadly based understanding of human behaviour and relationships and an awareness of the complexities of life, because drama normally deals with people at a point of crisis. This means that you need to have an interest in psychology and what it is that makes people behave as they do. Then you need a well-developed sense of visual and aural imagery, so that when you read a script you can, in your mind's eye, see and hear the play as a staged performance. You need a sound knowledge of present-day theatre techniques, so that you know that your ideas are capable of being developed by your cast and are realizable in practical terms by your designer and stage management. Similarly an understanding of the history of drama, staging, costume and social customs and an appreciation of music are necessary. It is essential to be able to establish an easy working relationship with people and to inspire your cast to be truly creative, experiment and extend themselves to the limit. You have, by one means or another, to create the atmosphere and conditions in which this can take place. A sense of humour is vital, as is a sympathetic insight into the psychology of the actor, but at the same time you need discipline and control. It may seem strange to talk of discipline in the theatre, but it is an attitude towards the work and is an internal thing in actor and director, not superimposed. As a director you will find that your role will, at times, range from the artistic and organizational to being a drama instructor, diplomatic listener or oracle.

You need to be able to analyse a play to:

    a. Find its theme or, as Stanislavski referred to it, the ruling idea or super-objective.

    b. Observe its intricacies of plot, sub-plot and sub-text.

    c. Locate its dramatic climaxes.

d. Understand the style of the play and the characters and their relationships.

e. Visualize how it can be most effectively staged and moved, with sets, costuming, décor, lighting, sound effects and music.

You also need to have an understanding of the actor's technique. Most directors have at some time been actors and this experience gives them an insight into the various ways actors work.

A useful exercise is to see different productions of the same play and observe the way each director has handled it. You will find that one of the problems in analysing productions is that the better the direction the more difficult it is to be absolutely certain of the exact degree of responsibility of each contributor, for a first-class production is shaped with such harmony that the individual elements, clearly visible in a poor production, fuse into the unity of the dramatic experience.

2 *The Drama Company: Areas of Responsibility*

The director must be familiar with the structure of the organization that backs up his work of interpreting and staging a play. The performance on the stage is supported by specialized teams that may be divided into two main functions: *artistic,* under the guidance of the director, and *administrative,* under the General Manager or Administrator.

A drama company is usually governed by a Board of Management, which normally appoints an Artistic Director to assume responsibility for the actual functioning of the company, choice of plays for presentation and maintenance of standards. In an amateur company the chairman of the Theatre Management Committee or Drama Society may also be the artistic director.

The artistic director and his administrator must work together to ensure smooth functioning of the organization and to check that the cost of mounting productions and running expenses do not outstrip income.

DRAMA COMPANY ORGANIZATION

The Producer

The Producer is the board of management, drama society or individual with the financial and promotional responsibility.

Artistic Functions

Artistic Director

The Artistic Director controls production policy, directs major productions and may have one or more

24

Associate Directors.

Designer

The Designer works closely with the artistic director designing productions, supervising construction and painting. He may have one or more Design Assistants. The designer may also design the costumes, if not, he will nevertheless be in close consultation with the Costume Designer, as the costumes are an integral part of the overall design.

The Acting Company

The actors are either cast for specific roles in a certain production or 'play as cast' in a permanent company.

The Production Manager

The Production Manager is responsible for costing productions and supervising and co-ordinating the work of all the departments backstage.

The Stage Manager

The Stage Manager is responsible for all the physical aspects of staging a production. He makes up the prompt copy of the play, showing actors' entrances, exits and moves, as decided in rehearsals by the director, together with all cues for curtains, lighting, effects, music, flies, warning bells, etc. He orders costumes, wigs and furniture. To his Deputy Stage Manager and Assistant Stage Managers he delegates such jobs as properties, prompting and the dozens of tasks a production entails. An efficient and imaginative stage manager, who works without fuss and organizes his team in a businesslike way is an inestimable asset to any director.

The Lighting Designer

The Lighting Designer is a specialist and in consultation with the director designs the complete lighting set-up. The Lighting Technicians rig and operate the lighting. In a small company one person may take responsibility for all lighting work. Some directors prefer to design their own lighting.

The Sound Technician

The Sound Technician records and plays back all music and effects on tape. In a small company an assistant stage manager may do this work.

The Master Carpenter

The Master Carpenter, with his assistants, constructs the setting from the designer's scale drawings. He also, with the stage manager, supervises the erection of the completed setting.

The Wardrobe Mistress

The Wardrobe Mistress has charge of all costumes on hire, as well as those made for individual productions. At the dress parade and at the dress rehearsals she and her staff note any repairs and alterations that have to be made and keep costumes in good condition during the run.

Administrative Functions

The Administrator

The Administrator has responsibility for budgets, control of expenditure, payment of accounts, the legal aspects of drama presentation, including theatre regulations, and all business matters.

The Public Relations Officer

The Public Relations Officer arranges for printing and display of posters, handbills and hanging cards. He designs the layout of programmes and arranges printing. He contacts the press, radio and television with advance information about anything newsworthy and puts advertisements in the press. He runs the mailing list and generally stimulates interest in the theatre and its presentations.

The House Manager

The House Manager is in charge of the reception areas, bars, buffets and cleaning staff. He may have responsibility for checking ticket money with the Box Office Manager and money from sale of refreshments. An important part of his job is to welcome the audience and ensure that the auditorium is in readiness with usherettes in attendance with programmes.

The Box Office Manager

This is a job needing patience and tact. The box office is the first contact the members of the audience have with a production – apart from publicity. It therefore is essential that there is a sense of welcome. Curtness at the box office can dull the edge of an evening's entertainment, while a friendly reception can at least predispose the audience to start the evening in a receptive frame of mind.

These are the people who create the environment within which you, as director, present your production to the audience. You are dependent on them and you need their full support, therefore the establishment of a pleasant working relationship with all concerned is essential.

The range of artistic and administrative tasks outlined above represents the basic set-up for most theatre companies. However, it is wise to remember that the conditions under which the director works vary enormously. In an established company there will, of course, be a resident production staff, headed by the production manager, to carry out all your staging requirements, but in very small companies such as fringe, itinerant groups and some amateur companies, there may perforce be some doubling up of jobs. The producer may also be the director and the cast may have some responsibility for stage management, wardrobe, lighting and décor; or in an *ad hoc* situation you, as director, may have to form a production team from scratch.

3 *The Script*

Before proceeding further it is necessary to consider the raw material that the director shapes into a stage presentation – the script. Weeks of work will be invested in the production by you, your cast, the production team and business management – so, firstly, it is essential to make a choice that can be cast and staged satisfactorily and will appeal to the appetite of your particular audience, and secondly, and this is most important, it must excite your creative instinct strongly enough to impel you to direct it.

This means that you will be looking at plays from a particular point of view – the director's point of view and with the above criteria in mind. On the other hand, of course, you may have been invited to direct one particular production and therefore you may proceed immediately to the stage of thinking about the text for production purposes.

As you study the text there are certain points you must clarify for yourself, so that when you come to your pre-rehearsal preparations you will be sure of your line of approach for the whole production. This analytical stage usually means that you will be reading the play through as many times as are necessary to gain a thorough grasp of the play, with, hopefully, a breathing space between each reading to mull over the impressions you have received.

The first reading will be, perhaps, just to enjoy the play and to observe the main action, leading characters and general style. In subsequent readings, in which it may be useful to make notes of things that strike you as important, there will be various points that you will want to resolve for yourself. They are:

THE THEME

What is the theme of the play as a whole? What does the play say? What is it about?

As director, you must know towards what conclusion you are to steer the production, otherwise it will drift and be an incomplete, and therefore unsatisfying, experience for the audience. Stanislavski talked about the 'through line of action' of the play, which gives continuity and guides the actors from the beginning and leads to the super-objective or main theme. Stanislavski regarded the 'through line of action' as being constituted from the small units of the play, each having an objective or theme and combining to lead on to the super-objective, that is the main theme or, as he sometimes called it, the ruling idea of the play. Harold Clurman calls it the spine of the play, a term he took from Richard Boleslavsky, in which the smaller units of the play may be compared to the vertebrae, which together form the spine. So, call it the theme, message, super-objective, ruling idea, or spine of the play, as you will. These terms convey the author's conscious or, sometimes, unconscious meaning. You may find that some plays do not have any clearly definable theme – they may work in terms of theatre by creating moods, atmosphere and situations or revealing characters. The realization of these can therefore be your theme. In a light comedy, for example, the success of the whole play may depend upon revealing the verbal wit, the foibles of contrasting characters, the twists of the plot, the exuberance of the situations and getting the audience to relax, laugh and thoroughly enjoy themselves.

STYLE

What style or dramatic convention does the author use to put across the content of his play? Formerly it was thought desirable to have plays neatly classified into types of drama that conformed to certain literary requirements, such as comedy, farce, tragedy, melodrama or other conventions. In the present day the range of drama has widened to include all aspects of human life and many plays do not fit snugly into a classification or indeed may embrace two, three or more styles. For example, Joan Littlewood's

Oh What a Lovely War has elements of a comedy, a documentary, a musical, a political play, a tragedy – you may discover other styles in it. One of the greatest and most influential plays of recent times, Samuel Beckett's *Waiting for Godot* is at one and the same time comic, tragic and philosophical. A play does not necessarily conform to what were regarded in the past as set conventional patterns. Today an author may simply describe his play as 'a play', or say nothing, leaving it to the director, cast and audience to decide its genre. However most plays do veer nearer one mode than another. For those not already familiar with the range of dramatic conventions it might be helpful to point out the characteristics of certain styles.

Naturalism is a style of presentation in which the dialogue, situations, acting, production and settings attempt to show, as Zola put it, 'a slice of life'. The audience watches the action through the 'fourth wall' of the setting, represented by the open proscenium arch, with the actors ostensibly unaware of them, although, of course, voice, speech and movement are meticulously rehearsed to be heard and seen in all parts of the auditorium. The content of plays presented in a naturalistic manner can, of course, range from comedy to tragedy.

In *comedy* the humour arises, in part, from characterization revealing the foibles of human nature. Comedy usually demands a deeper sense of characterization than is normally found in farce, but the success of comedy, as with farce, depends very much upon subtlety of timing. (Examples are *The Government Inspector* by Nicholai V. Gogol; *Enter a Free Man* by Tom Stoppard; *The Philanthropist* by Christopher Hampton.)

The *comedy of manners* satirizes manners and social behaviour. The style is usually brittle and the dialogue has a scintillating quality. Comedy of manners makes considerable demands on the actor's technique. (*The Relapse* by Sir John Vanbrugh; *The Importance of Being Earnest* by Oscar Wilde; *Hay Fever* by Noel Coward.)

Many musicals could be regarded as *romantic comedies,* where in a mood of fantasy, love and adventure may be combined with song and dance routines. Some of Shakespeare's plays have the qualities of the romantic comedy. (*Twelfth Night* by William Shakespeare; *The Enchanted* by Jean Giradoux; *Ring Round the Moon* by Jean Anouilh.)

In *farce* we watch stereotyped people caught up in the mechanics of a fast-moving plot that has been carefully constructed to manoeuvre the characters into situations that are for them embarrassing, but for the audience hilarious. As the farcical plot is a contrived situation, the action has to be fast-moving, well timed and acted with considerable technical skill to prevent the audience dwelling on any improbabilities. Maintaining a façade of calm and respectability amid calamitous occurrences, often of a sexual nature, is the mode of farce. (*Hotel Paradiso* by George Feydeau and Maurice Desvalliers; *The Magistrate* by Arthur Wing Pinero; *Loot* by Joe Orton.)

Greek classical tragedy deals with the decline of a noble character from fortune to misfortune culminating in death. The progression to the downfall of the protagonist is occasioned by an error of action which leads inexorably to destruction. The language is elevated, being in verse, and the chorus, who establish a link with the audience as they comment on the action, sing and dance.

The performances of the four plays, three tragic and the fourth a bawdy satyr play, on the same day in the Theatre of Dionysus, below the Acropolis in Athens, were in the 'Golden Age' a matter of religious and civic observance. The catastrophe of the downfall of the protagonist should have the effect of *catharsis,* inducing, by a savouring of pity and terror, a cleansing of the emotions.

Although the original notations of music and choreography are lost, each year in the summer, you may see, in the Theatre of Herodes Atticus, next to the ruins of the Theatre of Dionysus, performances of the Greek classics, tragedy and comedy, which give an insight into the handling of the plays and the engineering of stage devices, such as the *deus ex machina.* (Examples of tragedies are *Agamemnon* by Aeschylus; *Oedipus Rex* by Sophocles; *The Bacchae* by Euripides.)

In *Shakespearian tragedy* the protagonists are of noble stature (Hamlet, a prince; Othello, a noble Moor, general of the Doge's forces; Lear, an aged king; and Macbeth, a general in the king's army) marked by the Shakespearian tragic flaw of character that brings them to eventual destruction. As Hamlet says in Act I, Scene iv,

> So oft it chances in particular men,
> That, for some vicious mole of nature in them,

As, in their birth, wherein they are not guilty,
Since nature cannot choose his origin,
By the o'ergrowth of some complexion,
Oft breaking down the pales and forts of reason,
Or by some habit, that too much o'er-leavens
The form of plausive manners; that these men,
Carrying, I say, the stamp of one defect,
Being nature's livery, or fortune's star,
Their virtues else, be they as pure as grace,
As infinite as man may undergo,
Shall in the general censure take corruption
From that particular fault: the dram of evil
Doth all the noble substance of a doubt
To his own scandal.

The complexity of the characters, subtlety of themes and quality of language give a finely textured drama that probes the nature of humanity.

The protagonists of *modern tragedy* (some would question if tragedy in terms of drama is possible in these times) have not the distancing effect of time or high estate that gives the aura of legend and nobility to Greek and Shakespearian tragedy. Three modern plays regarded as being in the tragic style are: *Death of a Salesman* by Arthur Miller; *The Shadow of a Gunman* by Sean O'Casey; *Huis Clos* by Jean-Paul Sartre.

Melodrama nowadays infers a sensational type of drama portraying strong emotions and employing music, lighting, and stage devices to heighten the effect. The situations are relatively unsubtle, without the texture of plot found in more realistic plays. The characters also tend to be stock types representing a set point of view, again without the characterization in depth found in realistic drama. In Victorian times melodrama was common theatrical fare. (*The Bells* by Leopold Lewis; *Sweeney Todd* by George Dibdin Pitt; *The Silver King* by Henry Arthur Jones.)

Expressionism is a form of theatre which attempts to show inner psychological conflicts rather than represent outward appearances naturalistically. Characterizations and settings tend to be symbolic, with extravagant playing and striking décor making a strong visual impression in order to put across the dramatic point forcefully. Frequently there is a mood of great stress and

B

sometimes a nightmarish quality. (*The Ghost Sonata* by August Strindberg; *R.U.R.* by Karel Capek; *The Adding Machine* by Elmer Rice.)

The *Theatre of the Absurd* was not an organized movement, but rather the manner in which some dramatists in the 1950s expressed their views of the world. In 1942 Albert Camus, in his essay 'The Myth of Sisyphus', used the term 'absurd' to describe the purposelessness of an existence out of harmony with its surroundings. Similarly the drama of the Theatre of the Absurd reflects shock at the absence of stable systems, beliefs and values. If the world is irrational then the Absurd dramatists reflect it. The form and content break away from the style of the well-made play, with its clear-cut theme, plot, characters and conclusion based upon set values. In its place we find ourselves confronted by irrational situations often presented in the form of poetic images, with the mocking of convention and language. The plays often free-wheel into a world that is a mixture of Monty Python, the Marx Brothers, Lewis Carroll, nightmare and Franz Kafka. The best of them have a firm philosophical undertone and apart from, intentionally, disturbing the conventional they are frequently hilarious and macabre while at the same time establishing their own stageworthiness. (*Waiting for Godot* by Samuel Beckett; *The Chairs* by Eugene Ionesco; *Professor Taranne* by Arthur Adamov.)

Epic theatre is a style of theatre evolved in the 1920s by Erwin Piscator and Bertolt Brecht. The plays are written in short self-contained scenes and the object is to present social and political issues in such a way that the audience, instead of becoming emotionally involved with the fate of the characters, can sit back and arrive at a judgement of the case as presented. This is achieved by what Brecht called the Alienation Effect (*Verfremdungseffekt*) in which the audience is constantly reminded it is in a theatre watching a performance. The actors demonstrate their roles rather than fully embody the character, as in normal naturalistic acting. The action is interrupted by the projection of slides, film clips, actors holding placards and songs sung in such a way that makes you notice their content rather than the beauty of the singer's voice. The singers are usually accompanied by a small band situated on stage with the actors, not hidden in an orchestra pit. Actors step in and out of character as they address the audience or become narrators. Settings are usually simple and the trappings of theatrical machinery such as lighting, scenic devices and ropes, which are normally hidden by the drapes or flats of the proscenium arch stage, are revealed to constantly remind the spectator that he is in a theatre watching a play. Brecht wanted the removal of theatrical illusion to keep the audience alert and critical, but nevertheless strove to keep his form of theatre as entertaining as possible. The use of Brecht's methods of staging is now fairly widespread.

These then are some of the more common styles of drama. There are various permutations and combinations; to attempt to list a full range would be pedantic. Each text has its own distinctive style and set of values and every production of the same text is subject to the interpretation given to it by its director and cast. Furthermore, the interpretation given by a director to a text can give an emphasis that appears to change its style.

THE CHARACTERS

In your preliminary study you must satisfy yourself of the following:

a. Who is the main character?

b. What is his driving force or objective? (What makes him tick?) You can probably answer this by asking, What does he want?

c. What are the relationships and attitudes between the main character and the other characters?

d. Who are the other characters? What are their objectives and their relationships with each other?

You need to be able to see each character as a person with a background, a present state of mind and some sort of objective which motivates the line of action of the character through the course of the play. Further, you must observe if and how the characters are changed during the action of the play. Every character, if it is a fully written character, no matter how small the part may be, has some sort of objective or urge that makes him a credible stage presence.

THE PLOT

The plot is the arrangement of the situations in the play by means of which the dramatist has manoeuvred mutually reacting characters to reveal the action, tensions and final resolution. There may be one or more sub-plots which link, in greater or lesser degree, with the main plot. An example of excessive attention to plotting can be found in the well-made plays of Eugène Scribe (1791–1861) and Victorien Sardou (1831–1908) in which the plot, engineered with mechanical precision, made everything appear over-contrived. The famous farces of Labiche, Feydeau, Pinero and Ben Travers rely upon the highly ingenious manipulation of situations to give the momentum for arousal of the 'constant laughter' of well written, well directed and well acted farce. It is important therefore for you to have a clear image of the structure of the play so that you can see how the plot enables the characters to reveal themselves and the theme to emerge. In thinking about the plot, observe how it operates. Is it sequential – unfolding from A-Z, in a straightforward style? Does it use the flashback technique? Does it use the 'onion skin' technique in which bits of information are fed to the audience until eventually the complete set-up is revealed? Is it in short self-contained scenes, as in Brecht's Epic theatre? Observing the structure of the play should also help when you are preparing your rehearsal call sheet, so that you can plan to rehearse scenes and characters in the most convenient order.

Some plays, of course, have the minimum of what you could call a formal line of plot. The characters talk, tensions build, characters react, we receive a sequence of impressions, souls are bared, moods are created, but no marked sequence of events occurs and the characters remain much as when we first met them, as in Harold Pinter's *No Man's Land* for example. The power of the drama lies largely in savouring moods, images, timing, the language and tensions.

DIALOGUE

Dialogue in drama has a very precise function. As you read the play through, the dialogue should be giving you the information you need to direct the play. The language, as a whole, should reflect the style (convention) of the play to inform you whether the mood is, say, one of comedy, tragedy, melodrama or absurd; whether the treatment is naturalistic, with colloquial or regional dialogue, or moving away from naturalism into the realms of romanticism or fantasy or a classical style, where the use of verse form, with rhythm and imagery, reinforces the content and imparts a universality not easily conveyed in vernacular styles.

The dialogue should reveal the individuality of the characters and show the way they think and react towards other characters. As the dialogue carries the action forward it should (apart from stage directions) indicate time, place, occasion, mood, and variations of tempo, and should reflect the climactic moments of the play. The dialogue may also possibly range back to before the time of the present action to fill you in with details necessary for the understanding of the events of the play.

SUBTEXT

The words spoken may also cover the meaning of any unspoken subtext, where what is said hides or is different from what is really in the minds of the characters. When looking at a text it is important to probe, to attempt to discover implications beneath the surface meaning of the dialogue. Is the dialogue meant to be taken literally, or is there a wealth of meaning and feeling behind the words spoken that can be indicated by subtle use of voice, timing, gesture or business that will give the dialogue a richer texture and reveal the character in greater depth?

Inflexions, timing, gesture and movement can completely change the meaning of a printed sentence. 'No,' can be inflected, timed and acted to mean 'Yes', or vice versa. As a director you must be sensitive to the possibilities of interpretation.

In this extract from Act II of J. B. Priestley's play *An Inspector Calls,* the Inspector is questioning Mrs Birling about the death of a girl. He is showing Mrs Birling a photograph of her.

INSPECTOR [*taking back the photograph*]: You recognize her?
MRS BIRLING: No. Why should I?

This could be played as a completely honest denial, but if it was it would nullify the character of Mrs Birling, who has in fact recognized the girl immediately. Therefore, although she says, 'No. Why should I?', her voice and timing and possibly some subtle gesture should reveal to the audience that behind the words of her denial there is a wealth of feeling: a mixture of pride, apprehension, an intense dislike of the girl and disapproval of the Inspector.

In Chekhov's *The Cherry Orchard* in Act IV, almost at the end of the play, Lopahin, the self-made man and purchaser of the estate, has agreed to meet Varia to propose to her before she leaves for good. Varia comes into the room and pretends to search for something in the pile of luggage. Their mutual embarrassment makes them talk of anything but the purpose for which they have come together. After a short series of hesitant speeches somebody outside calls to Lopahin. He instinctively seizes this as an excuse to avoid forcing himself to propose to Varia and quickly leaves the room. Varia, left alone on the stage, weeps. Not one word of Chekhov's dialogue mentions the thoughts that are in both their minds. It is the subtle revelation of these unspoken thoughts that can make this one of the most memorable scenes in the play.

In Edward Albee's *A Delicate Balance*, towards the end of Act I, Harry and his wife Edna arrive unannounced at the home of their old friends Tobias and Agnes. Their arrival might at first appear to be a social call, but they are deeply frightened – of what they cannot say – and they need the comfort of their old friends. Under the text, behind the things said and done lies this fear and the stresses it places on relationships. It permeates the whole play. What cannot be stated in words must be substantiated by a mental imagery that gives the sense of fear Harry and Edna carry with them a credibility. This is the problem the actor and director have to solve together – the fear may be of the void of death, the emptiness of a life-style, a final realization of dispensability, a need for physical contact or a lack of sustaining faith.

CUTTING THE TEXT

Cutting dialogue, especially with authors whose pens run away with them, is, on occasions, necessary. It must, however, be done with great care to maintain the completeness of the action and the fullness of character. There are many plays that are most difficult to cut without causing complications. Some of Ibsen's plays, for example, are so textured that a line of dialogue may contain important information not just from actor to actor, but also for the audience about past events, the characters themselves, the locale or the dramatic situation. Generally Ibsen writes so 'tightly' there is no redundant dialogue at all; even what appear to be generalized pleasantries are an essential part of the text conveying information.

4 *The Audience*

The Drama's laws the drama's patrons give
For we that live to please, must please to live.
DR SAMUEL JOHNSON

The audience is an essential component in making theatre. Each production is undertaken as an offering to a particular type of audience. Without the presence of an audience the purpose of a production is lost; for the purpose is the reaction of the audience to the play and cast and the reaction of that cast to the response of the audience. Theatre is a creative interchange that is clearly observable in the laughter, silent absorption or applause from the audience; also the quality of the performance itself is influenced by the degree of appreciation and attention of the audience. The audience and cast are evaluating one another during the progress of the play. The audience are responding to the play and the playing; the cast are responding to the audience's response to their playing. Responses flow backwards and forwards all the time. Casts, during and after a performance, comment on the quality of an audience. One almost tangible quality of an audience is how much it can give in the way of rapt attention or quality of laughter and this can guide the playing. A danger in this last point is that some casts may be less sensitive to the full attention of an audience than to the more limited aim of obtaining their laughter and in a basically serious play may be tempted to 'play for laughs' rather than as rehearsed. One has to envisage something like an electrical circuit, in which actor responds to actor *through* the audience and it is this inclusion of the audience in the flow of thought and action that makes possible a fully satisfying theatrical experience.

Audiences have different appetites; they attend certain plays and theatres to savour a certain type of theatrical fare – it may

40

be to be morally uplifted, reassured, thrilled, to savour romance, be shocked, titillated, sexually aroused, to gain psychological and philosophical insights, to escape from dull routine or even just to be a member of an audience and savour and share the process of making theatre. If you ask people why they attend the theatre you may be given a mixture of the above reasons, or indeed some may not be able to pinpoint the particular satisfaction they obtain. The director must, during the time of preparation and rehearsal, plan everything as he would wish his future audience to see and hear it. The director *is* the audience until the first performance. Therefore it is imperative to consider the audience at all planning stages and rehearsals.

It is interesting to compare audiences one sees at theatres with a reputation for drama of a certain calibre with others offering different fare. The National Theatre's and Royal Shakespeare Company's audiences are usually a different mixture from those attending, say, a Haymarket or Drury Lane musical. Again smaller companies operating in pubs, clubs and cellars will attract a different type of audience from those for the frothy comedies of Shaftesbury Avenue. A regional repertory company may, on the other hand, because the choice is limited to one or possibly two theatres, have an audience representative of a wider range of the population, often with an apparent preponderance of older people. It is sobering to realize that it has been calculated that not much more than 2 per cent of the population are regular theatre-goers.

Remember that a parochial audience is unlikely to wax enthusiastic over a very sophisticated or *avant-garde* play and that an unsubtle play presented to audiences used to more demanding fare is not likely to get a good reception. There is a place and an audience for all types of drama from the lightest comedies to the most intellectually demanding of plays. The experience of release in laughter from a very simple comedy, for example, may not be shared by the academically minded, but it fulfils a valuable social function that is not to be scorned. It is a way of viewing life that is as valid for its particular audience as the savouring of the metaphysical anguish of Beckett is for his audience. Audiences shop around for theatrical fare which they feel they might enjoy at that moment. Therefore in choosing a play, the type of audience you are likely to attract in the region of your theatre must be given consideration. The co-operation of the audience is imperative for the making of successful theatre. They must feel that the content and style of your presentation gives satisfaction, so that they can return to the stage the quality of appreciation that is necessary for the full experience of theatre. Appreciation is inevitably modified by cultural background, temperament and the average age of the audience. Audiences do have to be encouraged to appreciate drama that is new to them or alien to their expectations.

As a director you will want to present a complete range of drama. Drama deals with all aspects of life, some of which may not appeal to people with limited views. When Ibsen's *Ghosts* was first performed in London in 1891, the critics and audiences were unaccustomed to the frankness and allusions of the play and seemed quite unaware of its spiritual qualities. William Archer, the translator, critic and dramatist, collected some of the outraged comments which he published in the *Pall Mall Gazette* on 8 April, 1891. Here are a few of the press reactions: 'Noisome corruption' – *The Stage*; 'Gross, almost putrid indecorum' – *The Daily Telegraph*; 'A repulsive and degrading work' – *The Queen;* 'Just a wicked nightmare' – *The Gentlewoman*; 'Garbage and offal' – *Truth.*

Yet on seeing a production of *Ghosts* today one is impressed by the honesty of Ibsen's theme and the sober strength of his play. Conversely, plays that were very successful in their day may later appear naïve or dull and require very skilful direction to make them interesting to a contemporary audience. As a director you should be aware that even what you regard as your finest offerings will not necessarily meet with the appreciation that you feel is your due. A dramatic criticism that is full of unstinting praise is very rare indeed and even the most favourable have their reservations. Press criticism does not always accord with audience reactions – so tumultuous applause from the audience does not mean that all critics will like the play and production. Alternatively, a play that gets a tepid reception from an audience may receive favourable reviews. Again, productions that have been panned by the critics sometimes enjoy long runs. So, be warned, you won't please all of your audience all of the time, for as Jean Giradoux said, 'The audience hears and composes as it pleases, following its own imagination and feelings.'

5 *Theatres and Stages*

A theatre is a place where a theatrical experience is created by the interaction of actors and audience. It may be in the open air, as with the ancient Greeks or the contemporary Regent's Park Open-Air Theatre, or a purpose-built or adapted structure, but in all cases the most important factor is the manner in which the actors and audience can communicate. That is, firstly, the audience hearing, seeing and being physically near enough to the action to feel fully involved with the business of the stage and, secondly, the actors being able to project voice and speech and reveal the action in terms of movement to the audience and at the same time be sensitive to the response of that audience.

It follows that the size, shape and relationship of the acting area and auditorium are very important indeed. Each theatre has its own characteristics, which predispose it to be more suitable for some types of performances than others. A subtle naturalistic drama would be too intimate and be almost lost in a large theatre that might satisfactorily accommodate a musical. Members of the audience furthest from the actors might miss the nuances received by those sitting near the stage, but if you enlarged the scale of playing to project to distant members of the audience those near the actors would probably be put off by the exaggerated use of voice and movement. It is necessary, therefore, to think in terms of the scale or amplitude of what has to be fed to the audience. If you stand on the stage of a theatre and look out into the auditorium you should become aware of the way in which your production must be tailored to the characteristics of the stage and auditorium. The size and shape of the theatre need to be considered carefully when planning a production.

Perhaps one of the most interesting features of contemporary theatre design has been the realization of the need for the theatre building to bring the actor and his audience into the most favourable physical relationship, not only in order to facilitate the interchange between the acting area and the auditorium, but for the audience to be able to generate an identity and awareness as an audience that transcends the individuals composing it. The experience of being an audience is perhaps most manifest at a football game or boxing match, where the audience surrounds the action and comments audibly on the proceedings. In drama this awareness of being an audience is clearly felt in the Odeon of Herodes Atticus in Athens, which holds 6,000, or at Epidaurus, which can seat 14,000 people, where the audiences sweep in a huge semi-circle round the acting areas and spectators are aware of each other, not just because they can see and pick up reactions from one another, but because they are almost in contact, side by side, on the stone seating. The shapes of the tiered auditoria also focus the attention of the audiences sharply down on the acting area.

As plays are usually written with a particular form of staging in the mind of the author, normally that form of presentation best serves the play. Perhaps I should hastily add that most plays are adaptable and many plays that were conceived for, say, the proscenium arch stage work satisfactorily in other forms of theatre, such as in-the-round or on thrust or open stages, but there is usually one shape of theatre building that suits a play best. A farce, for example, written with a proscenium arch stage in mind and needing six doors, from which the cast make quick entrances and often even quicker exits, might be impossible to stage in-the-round where scenery of that nature has no place, because the use of doors is essential for the proper functioning of the play. Some recently constructed theatres have been designed to be flexible, so that the staging area and auditorium are easily changed to give proscenium arch, thrust, in-the-round, traverse or other forms of staging.

For example, the Octagon Theatre, Bolton, can be used as an open end stage, thrust, or in-the-round. The Questors Theatre, Ealing, adapts to proscenium arch, thrust, or in-the-round. The LAMDA Theatre can be adapted for proscenium arch, open stage, thrust, in-the-round or, as in the Theatre of Cruelty season, the whole auditorium can be used for staging, with the audience

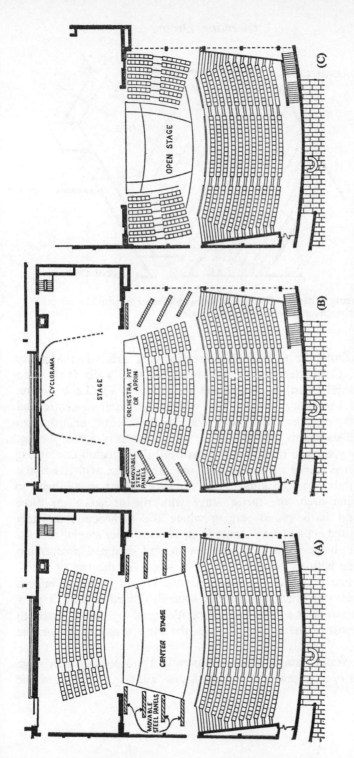

The Leob Centre, Harvard University, adapted to (a) centre stage, (b) proscenium arch stage, (c) thrust stage.

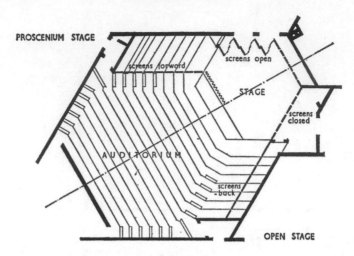

The Mercury Theatre, Colchester. Movable screens provide adaptability
for either open or proscenium arch staging.

viewing from the normal floor-level staging area. The Mercury
Theatre, Colchester, adapts by adjustable side walls from open
(with partial thrust) to proscenium arch staging. The Leob Centre,
Harvard University, adapts from proscenium arch to centre and
thrust staging. The Bristol Old Vic Studio Theatre adapts from
open end staging to either thrust or various forms of centre staging.

A few years ago there was a great deal of discussion concerning
the relative merits of the proscenium arch stage, with its house
curtain (tabs) and the audience all viewing the action through the
proscenium arch, the thrust stage with the audience on three
sides, and in-the-round staging where the audience completely
encircles the acting area – apart from various other staging shapes.
Basically, however, it is agreed that a well designed proscenium
arch stage with fly tower offers more scope for the use of scenic
devices and thus gives the audience the benefit of scenic effects,
which may be flown in and out speedily, together with a view
of the flow of the dramatic action designed by the director to
enable most of the audience to see the same visual image on the
stage.

The open end stage, which is basically a proscenium arch stage
with the proscenium arch removed, also allows the use of scenic

devices and gives a unified view of the flow of dramatic action. However, any method of staging in which the audience partially or completely surrounds the action prevents the use of scenery the height of which would mask the actors from any part of the audience. In thrust staging, therefore, scenery has to be in the nature of a background to the action and furniture and props set to cause the minimum of visual obstruction. No conventional scenery can be used with in-the-round staging, although I have seen ingenious skeletal frameworks in use that cause the minimum of obstruction. The visual impact usually has to be made by floor décor, suspended items that do not interfere with lantern angles, low furniture and costumes of a quality to bear the scrutiny of an audience in close proximity.

Perhaps the best known British theatres in-the-round are the Theatre in the Round at Scarborough, the Victoria Theatre, Stoke-on-Trent, designed by the late Stephen Joseph, and of course the Royal Exchange Theatre, Manchester. This is a theatre module built inside the Royal Exchange hall. It has three tiers of seating encircling the acting area. It can be converted into a modified thrust stage or a three-quarters round stage. These three theatres are professional, but in-the-round staging is a form frequently used in schools and colleges and has the great advantage of enabling the encircling audience to be very near the acting area, and – important these days – it is an inexpensive method of staging, as everything has to be kept as basic as possible. Also, the proximity of the cast and audience creates an atmosphere of involvement with the action and does not put the demands of projection techniques, that are second nature to the professional, on young amateur actors. However, in in-the-round and thrust forms the actor inevitably has his back to a proportion of the audience and as, apart from voice, the main instruments of communication are the face and eyes, the director of an in-the-round or thrust stage performance has to be extra skilful in his use of movement and grouping to ensure that the encircling audience is getting value for money, without it appearing that the actors are moving too obviously to feed out points and reactions in all directions. Also, both in-the-round and thrust forms need special care in lighting to ensure that lantern angles do not illuminate or dazzle any member of audience.

The majority of professional theatres operate on a proscenium

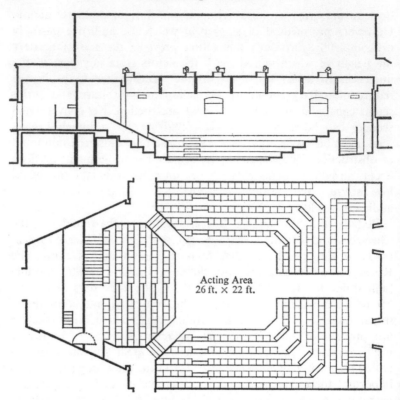

The Victoria Theatre, Stoke-on-Trent. Theatre-in-the-round.

arch stage equipped with a fly tower; some also have revolving stages, traps giving access from below stage, and means of adjusting the height of the acting area and extending the stage out towards the audience over the area of the orchestra pit or front stalls. In some cases the width and height of the proscenium arch can be adjusted for special productions.

Some theatres built in recent years utilize the form of the thrust stage, with the audience on three sides of the acting area. The best known of these are the Festival Theatre, Chichester; the Festival Theatre, Stratford, Ontario; the Tyrone Guthrie Theatre, Minneapolis; the Playhouse, Leeds and the Crucible Theatre, Sheffield.

The three-theatre complex of London's National Theatre is an architectural achievement that clearly acknowledges the need for staging-auditorium requirements that lend themselves more readily to the demands of the classical and modern repertoire than would a single adaptable theatre. It would be fair to say, in passing, that in designing a flexible theatre a degree of compromise has to be made that means that at least one of the forms (proscenium arch, open end, thrust, in-the-round or traverse) is not wholly satisfactory. The Olivier Theatre is the largest of the three theatres in the complex, seating 1,160 in two tiers and the furthest seat is only 70 feet from the stage. The audience is arranged in a 90 degree arc, rather like a fan, and has a very close relationship with the stage, embracing it and having its attention concentrated on the acting area. This concentration is increased by the rather steep rake of the seating. The open stage and raked fan-shaped seating give a sense of being in contact with the action. There is a large fly tower, the front of the stage can be varied in shape, motorized wagons move scenery swiftly into place from backstage assembly areas and a unique drum revolve of 11.5 metres diameter, split into two semi-circular sections, and also trapped, facilitates speedy scene changes and the working of the repertoire.

The Lyttleton Theatre, a proscenium arch theatre seating 895, has, like the Olivier, the audience arranged in two tiers. The height and width of the proscenium arch are adjustable and the stage itself can be fully raked. There is a fly tower over the stage equipped with a power-operated flying system and motorized scenery wagons can effect quick scene changes from the rear and side stages.

The Cottesloe Theatre is the third theatre in the National Theatre complex. It is a studio theatre and holds up to 400 people, depending on the form of staging used. The studio measures 66 feet by 56 feet and has galleries on three sides. The floor area may be arranged for seating and staging with a considerable degree of flexibility.

Supporting the three theatres are unrivalled facilities for design and construction, costume and wig making, lighting, sound and all technical requirements. The theatres mentioned have, of course, been designed following research, consultation and an awareness of the serious shortcomings of many existing theatres. However,

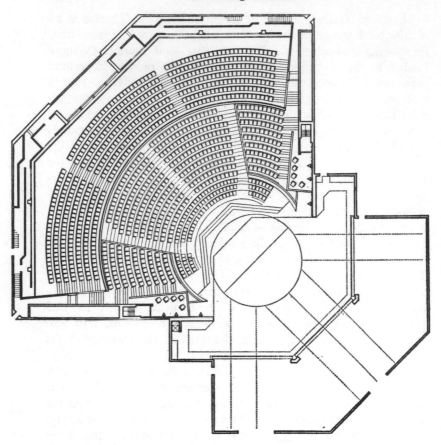

The National Theatre, London. Above: the Olivier Theatre. Facing, top: the Lyttleton Theatre; bottom: the Cottesloe Theatre, adapted for in-the-round (*r*) and end stage (*l*) productions.

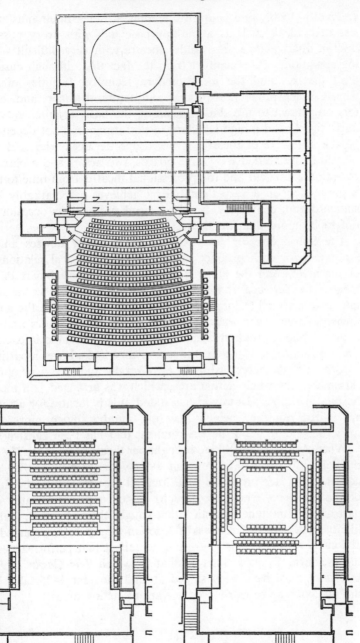

you will probably find yourself directing, at times, in circumstances less than ideal, such as a multipurpose hall with every possible built-in disadvantage or an older theatre with very difficult working conditions. Take comfort from the fact that although custom-built theatres and the most modern technical facilities oil the wheels of the production process and actors, designers and directors are drawn to use these amenities, the basic requirements are fairly simple and a high standard of performance is not dependent on the hardware of theatre. It was Lope de Vega who said that all you really needed was 'three boards, two actors and a passion'. In both the amateur and the professional theatre, from time to time a production on a very tight budget achieves a remarkably high standard and, conversely, lavishly staged productions occasionally fail to be more than mediocre.

The Polish director Jerzy Grotowski normally devises an environment for each production in which the physical relationship of the actors and the audience becomes an essential part of the theatrical experience. In his production of *Doctor Faustus* the spectators were seated at long table-like platforms that were the acting areas, so that there was an intermingling of the actors and the audience and a proximity that intensified the dramatic impact. In *The Constant Prince* the encircling audience looked over a partition and down at the actors, while in *Kordian* the audience were spread throughout the whole acting area, which was arranged as a mental hospital ward. As Grotowski has stated, this is theatre for a rather specialized audience, which may not number much more than forty, depending upon the environment that has been constructed.

When Ariane Mnouchkine brought her theatre company, Théâtre du Soleil, to the Roundhouse in 1971 with their play *1789*, the action took place on raised platforms all around and in the midst of the audience, who were free to sit, or move and watch any part of the simultaneous action that caught their attention. Rather like the audience in Grotowski's *Kordian* they were surrounded by action on all sides. It is interesting to reflect that performances in the medieval Rounds, such as that in which *The Castle of Perseverance* must have been staged around the year 1425, also had the audience spread around the various acting areas.

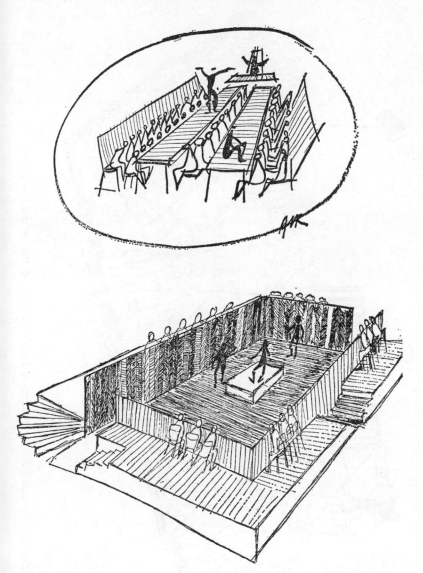

Jerzy Grotowski's staging at the Theatre Laboratory, Wroclaw. Top: Marlowe's *Doctor Faustus*. Bottom: *The Constant Prince* by Calderon-Slowacki.

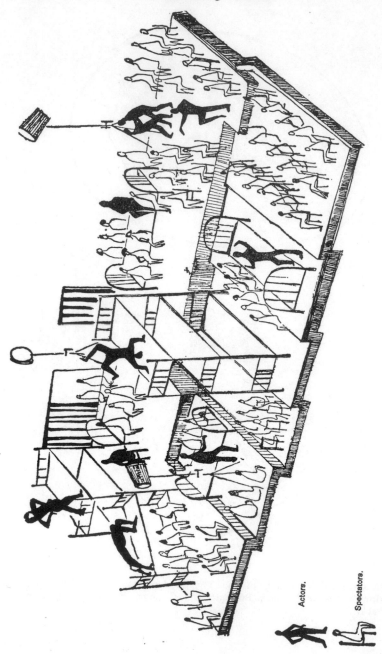

Grotowski's staging for Slowacki's *Kordian:* a mental hospital ward with the audience as patients.

Actors.

Spectators.

6 *The Actor on the Stage*

The acting areas of the proscenium arch stage are as shown below. For speed and convenience in marking scripts the names of the areas are abbreviated thus: DC = down centre, UR = up right, DLC = down left centre, UL = up left, and so on.

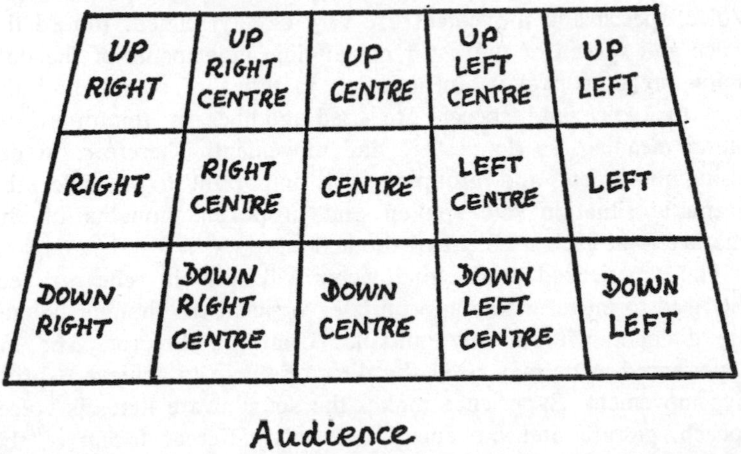

UP RIGHT	UP RIGHT CENTRE	UP CENTRE	UP LEFT CENTRE	UP LEFT
RIGHT	RIGHT CENTRE	CENTRE	LEFT CENTRE	LEFT
DOWN RIGHT	DOWN RIGHT CENTRE	DOWN CENTRE	DOWN LEFT CENTRE	DOWN LEFT

Audience

Figure 1

Note that left and right are from the actor's point of view. 'Up-stage' denotes away from the audience. 'Downstage' denotes nearer the audience. The directions 'upstage' and 'downstage' are dictated by raked stages, which slope up from and down to the audience. The directions 'above' and 'below' indicate that something or somebody is upstage or downstage of a certain point; e.g. 'He is standing above the table,' or, 'The chair is below the fireplace.'

The directions 'on-stage' and 'off-stage' are related to stage centre; e.g. 'Move that bench on-stage another foot,' or, 'Take the lamp off-stage with you when you exit.' 'In' and 'out' usually refer to flying scenery. Scenery is 'flown in' from the flies down on to the stage and 'flown out' up into the flies out of sight of the audience.

MOVEMENT AND THE ACTOR

Planning the movement and grouping of the actors on the stage requires considerable care and deliberation for it should clarify your interpretation of the play, reflect the thinking of the individual characters and give the audience the stimulus of movement and grouping that holds attention and 'points'* the situation.

Movement on the stage can communicate attitudes, relationships and moods as clearly as the actor's speech conveys specific ideas. Voice, speech and movement are very closely related. Indeed the voice and speech of the actor are audible movements of the out-going breath conveying information in terms of sound, and the way the voice and speech are used modifies or reinforces the literal meaning, as do gesture and movement. Therefore, in devising movement and grouping it is important to consider the dramatic situation, the spoken and unspoken thoughts of the characters at each moment of the action.

The experienced professional actor will early in rehearsal feel the need to move, where appropriate, to signal the thought behind the dialogue without any guidance from the director. The inexperienced actor may need the director's help to achieve expressive movement. Experience makes the actor aware that his voice, speech, gesture and movement are only different facets of the total process of communication, so that a gesture, look or slight move can, on occasions, be as eloquent as dialogue.

On the stage all movement attracts the attention of the audience – just as dialogue does. If, for example, there are two characters A and B standing still on opposite sides of a proscenium arch stage engaged in dialogue, you will see the eyes of the audience rove back and forth from speaker to speaker like spectators at a tennis match. If, however, A makes a noticeable move during B's speech A will take attention away from B. If it is the intention of the

* See p. 74.

author that this should happen, all right, but if not the audience may miss an important piece of information.

All movement and grouping should have a purpose, which may arise either from the situation or the characterization. Occasionally, however, the director has to reposition a character and there is no obvious reason why that character should move. In a case like this an unobtrusive move can be devised, if it is motivated by a thought in the actor's mind in keeping with the characterization. For instance, the actor may slowly move towards a desk to look at a letter, or pour himself a drink, or feel that he wants to sit in a certain chair. It will appear natural and unobtrusive if the right thought prompts the movement. Movement must be arranged to allow the audience to concentrate on the important points which you, as director, wish them to observe, whether these points are made by speech, individual action or grouping. All gesture and movement start from stillness in the same way that the sound of voice emerges from silence – even if that stillness and silence last only for a fraction of a second. Complete stillness and silence in a flux of movement and sound can raise the dramatic interest to great intensity for a few moments, after which it wanes and it is very rarely that a dramatic pause can be held for more than five to ten seconds without weakening the audience's concentration. Non-stop movement can be as tedious as complete stillness. Movement is governed by the changing stage situation. Movement for the sake of movement can be very distracting and weakens concentration on the salient dramatic points.

Usually at each moment of dramatic interest one particular character should have the attention of the audience, because of something he says or does. Your job as director is to make it easy for the audience to be aware of what is going on. You must contrive movement and grouping so that the audience is looking where you want it to look at the vital moment. You deliberately focus and refocus the attention of the audience from character to character as the situation changes. An experienced cast who have worked together regularly will instinctively strive to do this. You may either block out basic moves with entrances, exits and other main movements and then refine or change these in rehearsal, or, as some directors prefer, allow the movement and grouping to develop by experiment and discussion with the cast. The success of this second method depends very much on the type of play, the experience of cast, the time available for rehearsal and the working methods of the director concerned.

If, as many directors do, you tentatively block out major movement, you have the responsibility of making sure that all moves arise from the dramatic situations and characterizations and that the actors who have to carry them out understand the reason for the moves and can make the movement a manifestation of their own thinking. If an actor is unhappy about a given move get him to try out his own alternative and see if it works.

There follow some general principles to which there will be, of course, exceptions. Even with the scripts still in hands, moves and groupings that you may have painstakingly devised are sometimes surpassed by the group inventiveness of the actors. Try to utilize this if you can. Even if you are not going to pre-block moves for the cast it is wise to have a possible range of moves or groupings in mind as a possible point from which to work in rehearsal.

The audience usually directs its attention to the character on whom the rest of the cast are concentrating. This gaining of attention can be aided by the positioning of the cast within the three-dimensional space of the acting area. Consider Figure 1a, which represents two actors on a conventional proscenium arch stage.

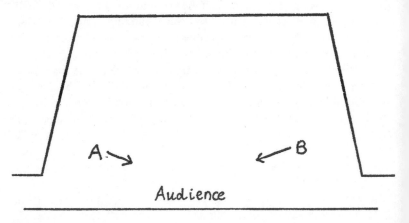

Figure 1a

Actor A is down right and is level with Actor B who is down left. They are presenting the audience with roughly the same proportion of facial and postural communication – so if they are not made-up or costumed to make one more dominating than the other, dramatic interest should be equally divided between them. If, however, Actor B moves to centre stage and looks down right to Actor A, who turns to look at him, the position will be as in Figure 1b.

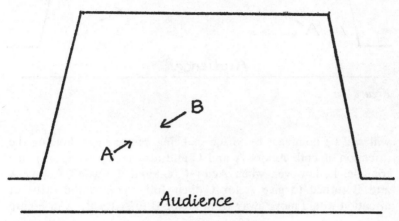

Figure 1b

In this situation Actor A will have weakened his contact with the audience, as he is now facing Actor B and many of the audience will not be able to receive facial or eye reactions from him. Actor B, however, can be seen easily by all the audience. Further, as he has moved to centre stage he should attract more attention, as it is usually an area of dominance.

What has happened in Figure 1b is known as *upstaging*. Actor A is upstaged (has his dramatic position weakened) by being forced to turn away from the audience to act with Actor B, who is upstage of him and is visually more dominant. Grouping and movement patterns must always point the changing centres of interest. Subconsciously the eyes of the audience tend to seek the apex of triangles in the stage image. In Figure 2a Actors A and B have been joined by Actor C. If Actors A and C are respectively down right and down left and both are looking at Actor B, Actor B

Directing Drama

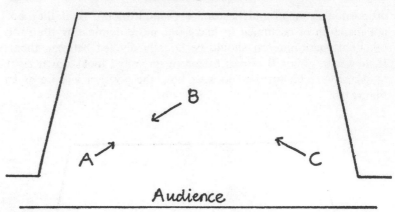

Figure 2a

will still be dominant by virtue of being centre stage, holding the
attention of both Actors A and C and also being the apex of the
triangle. If, however, when Actor C entered down left Actors A
and B turned to give Actor C their full attention the focus of
attention would move away from Actor B to Actor C, as in Figure
2b.

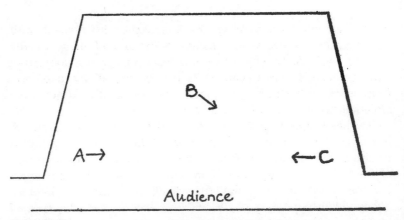

Figure 2b

With Actor D entering up right, as is shown in Figure 3a,

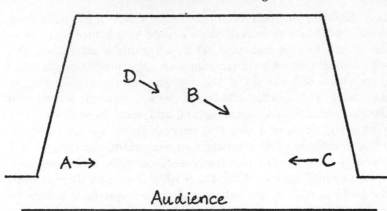

Figure 3a

the focus of attention can still be maintained on Actor C if the entrance is not too obtrusive and Actor D also concentrates on what Actor C is saying and doing. If, however, Actor D makes an entry that commands attention and Actors A, B and C all turn to look at him to hear what he says the new focal point will be Actor D up right, as in Figure 3b.

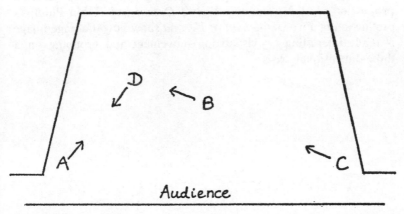

Figure 3b

Here, as in Figure 2a, the dominant actor is upstage and the apex of the triangle. The experienced actor will usually automatically facilitate the shift of attention to a new focal point with some appropriate movement, even if only by a glance that guides the attention of the audience. When rehearsing a naturalistic play with a small cast on a proscenium arch stage the movement often shapes itself with the aid of the dialogue and the arrangement of the setting. The director can accept those moves that accord with the interpretation and appear natural and reject those that do not. With a large cast, or a play that depends for its success on stylization, exactitude or co-ordination of movement, the director will probably have to plan movement very carefully and expect this to be modified during rehearsals. With a large cast there is often the problem of 'masking' where a character upstage is hidden by a character downstage. In rehearsals you have to keep a very vigilant eye on this and check by trying out various seating positions in the auditorium. If masking occurs during a performance sometimes an upstage character can clear it by an unobtrusive movement.

The variety of movement within the acting area necessary to maintain interest and point situations is aided by contrasts in elevation. Characters can stand, sit, kneel, lie on the ground, or use the various levels of the setting, such as rostra, steps, ramps or balconies. In planning movement it is necessary to visualize everything three-dimensionally. The photographs of Peter Brook's production of *A Midsummer Night's Dream* and Robin Phillips's production of *Two Gentlemen of Verona* show how the stage image is made interesting by visualizing movement and grouping on a three-dimensional basis.

7 *Notes on the Actor's Technique*

Although this book is concerned with the work of the director, it is essential for him to have a knowledge of the actor's technique. Many directors have been actors and acknowledge the value of the experience, as it gave them an insight into the actor's mental and physical processes in creating a character and also a common working language.

The actor is his own instrument – he uses himself: his mental faculties, especially his powers of memory and creative imagination, and his entire physique. These factors are controlled by a disciplined approach to his work, so that a process of creative thinking allows a responsive physique, voice and speech to embody a dramatic character.

For the highly gifted few, acting is an instinctual process in which a vivid imagination triggers a flexible body and a naturally good voice to create a fully fledged dramatic character and an analysis of the technical means by which they achieve this could be daunting and perhaps inhibit the natural free flow of imagination. Normally, an actor acquires his technique through training and the experience of performance, but it should be made clear that there is no single 'correct' approach to the creation of a character, any more than there is any one way of directing a play. The working methods of actors, like those of directors, are necessarily individual and will also vary from play to play, but the thinking behind the approach may be influenced to a greater or lesser extent by the work of Stanislavski or other theorists and by productions and performances that have left memorable images. Stanislavski is still the strongest influence on actor training methods. However, in the translations of his books, *An Actor Prepares, Building a Character* and *Creating a Role*, there is sometimes an expansiveness and circumlocution that could make some aspects of his system lack clarity for the beginner. Therefore, perhaps, it might be wiser for the student actor, under the guidance of a drama tutor, to familiarize himself with Stanislavski's theories through the more concise studies listed in the bibliography and later apply himself to Stanislavski's own works at leisure, remembering that Stanislavski himself said in *Building a Character*:

> This system is a companion along the way to creative achievement, but is not a goal in itself. You cannot act the 'system': you can work on it at home, but when you step out on to the stage cast it aside, there only nature is your guide. The 'system' is a reference book, not a philosophy. Where philosophy begins the system ends.
>
> Reckless use of the 'system', work that is done according to it, but without sustained concentration, will only drive you away from the goal you seek to reach. This is bad and can be overdone, unfortunately this is often the case.
>
> A too emphatic, exaggerated care in the handling of our psycho-technique can be alarming, inhibiting, can lead to an over critical attitude, or result in a technique used for its own sake.

The actor is one of the elements the director uses in shaping his production. With his technique the actor attempts to give an interpretation consistent with the director's overall view. We therefore have the director's interpretation of the play subjected to yet a further interpretation by the actor, who because he is working through the inevitable limitations of his own technique, cannot embody exactly the director's original vision of the staged play. A degree of compromise is built into every production situation.

RELAXATION

Relaxation is, perhaps, the fundamental requirement for the actor. By relaxation is meant the absence of mental and physical tensions that prevent the free flow of the imagination, expressive use of the body and full use of voice and speech. The stresses of normal everyday life build mental and physical tensions of which the

1 and 2 The Mercury Theatre, Colchester. Above: open staging with partial thrust; below: end stage with wings and curtain.

3   The Playhouse, Nottingham. The proscenium arch stage with lighting bridge is in the lowered position on the left. The 26-foot revolve can be seen in the centre and the cyclorama lighting bank top right. The partially raised black shutter shows paint frame room beyond. The fly gallery, with lines, is to be seen on the far side. The house tabs, separating the stage from the auditorium, hang behind the lighting bridge on the left.

4   The Festival Theatre, Chichester. Thrust stage.

average person is unaware. The actor should be so trained that as soon as he becomes aware of tensions he can relax himself by means of simple exercises. Even though the acting situation contains its own special pressures, it is nevertheless of vital importance for the actor that he can be relaxed on the stage, even when he is acting a character under stress. Lack of relaxation shows itself in poor posture, awkward movement, hard or inflexible vocal tones and, of course, self-consciousness. Some directors, if time allows it, start rehearsals with relaxation, limbering, voice exercises and games to loosen up the cast and encourage the feeling of being an ensemble. Being relaxed and at ease gives the actor his essential confidence and also the quality of repose, which enables him to be an essential part of the stage image when not dramatically active, by listening and thinking in character. The director can also, by the right approach, instil confidence in his cast as surely as he can dispel it with the wrong one.

VOICE AND SPEECH

The actor's voice and speech are one of the most important aspects of his technique, for no matter how strongly the actor may have conceived his characterization the ideas the character expresses must be projected to all parts of the auditorium. The projection of voice and speech does not simply mean creation of volume of sound, but using what we call 'forward diction' or 'thinking out' to share the ideas with the audience. On the stage an actor may speak fairly quietly and yet be heard distinctly in the auditorium, if he is relaxed, breathing correctly, has clear articulation and uses 'forward diction'. An audience can be irritated if it misses chunks of dialogue because of sloppy use of voice and speech. On the other hand, an over-conscious use of voice, or over-articulation, is also irritating, if it is not a foible of the character.

The voice has to be balanced with the articulation. A very rich over-resonant voice can drown the articulation, so that we can be very aware of the boom of an actor's voice, but not the words that convey the ideas. Variety in the use of voice is essential if the actor is to keep the audience alert and concentrating. Monotony of volume, pace and pitch of voice are not to be tolerated, as

c

they quickly lead to boredom. One sometimes hears a cast echoing one another's tones, this indicates a loss of concentration on characterization and should be checked at once. It is on the amateur stage that deficiencies of voice and speech are more frequently observed, but it occurs in the professional actor, often as a manifestation of tiredness to which the voice reacts by lack of variety and projection.

PHYSICAL FITNESS

It is essential for the actor to keep himself physically fit, as his ability to characterize and to be flexible in movement and voice depends very much on his state of health. Most actors have a private limbering and voice routine on which they work regularly. Apart from fight scenes or fencing routines that have to be rehearsed meticulously, the style of production today often requires the actor to use himself in an athletic or even acrobatic manner. A fit and well-exercised body is also conducive to physical expressiveness, so that movement, gesture and facial reactions may effortlessly reflect the thought of a character. As mentioned in the section on Relaxation, five or ten minutes spent on exercises help to impart a feeling of zest and to keep a cast on the *qui vive*.

IMAGINATION

The quality and strength of the actor's imagination is possibly his chief asset. Without imagination he cannot begin to characterize. Each actor normally has his own method of arousing his imagination and applying it to the stage situation. It is the director's job to create the working atmosphere in which the actor's imagination can flower. By a process of encouragement, suggestion, 'feeding' of ideas and images, the director can help the actor to body forth the character or guide the development where this diverges from the agreed interpretation of the play. The director will learn by experience how to handle the different members of his cast. Most actors value the guidance of the director, but some function best if left alone to work things out for themselves, or until such time as they may wish to approach the director for advice. Knowing when to offer constructive comment on an actor's work and when to defer comment until the actor seems ready to take it is an instinct that the director usually develops over a period of years.

EMPATHY

This is the power of the actor to project his character and emotions to the audience and, of course, to give his fellow actors something to react to. It is an outflow of feeling from a character that is sensed and does not necessarily rely on movement or voice. It would appear to be dependent on relaxation, quality of imagination, concentration and confidence. Although almost impossible to describe, one is aware of its presence or absence. Its effect is not unlike a form of radiation that seems to illuminate some actors. It is a quality very evident in actors of the stature of, for example, Olivier, Gielgud, Peggy Ashcroft, Ralph Richardson, Donald Pleasence, Helen Mirren and Glenda Jackson.

TIMING

Timing is the variation of pace, the speed with which cues are picked up, the use of pauses, the silences and stillness in performance that help to feed the content of the play to the audience. Timing also assists clarity, builds and sustains moods and keeps the play moving at the correct tempo to hold the interest of the audience. It is a skill that is polished over years of performance. In rehearsal the director can be of great help to the actor as he times and shapes the performance. One of the qualities of a good production is the exactitude with which dialogue and movement have been timed to shape each moment of the play to give the audience the opportunity to savour every point of dramatic interest. In a poor production the dialogue and action may drag or sometimes rattle on, perhaps at quite a lively pace, but without the variations, changing emphasis, pauses and momentary silences that transform a stream of dialogue into a stimulating flux of ideas and images. The members of the audience need time to absorb the information a play gives them, whether it's conveyed by dialogue or movement, and one way of doing this is by means of a pause. The inexperienced actor often feels that he is keeping up the tempo by maintaining a swift flow of dialogue without the slightest pause, but the pause is the means by which ideas are clarified. It gives time for the audience to digest information. This is one method of what we call 'pointing'. A word can be 'pointed' by pausing before or after it. The brief pause will make the audience perk up and the following word will have an intensified impact. If the actor pauses both before and after the word the 'pointing' will be even stronger. When you are working on a script preparing it for production it is useful to mark the significant pauses. A convenient way of doing this is to make one vertical line for a very short pause, two lines for a longer pause and so on, as follows:

$$/, //, ///$$

The pause is also necessary to allow the audience to observe the reactions of the other members of the cast to the dialogue spoken. The pause may be very brief indeed, but the momentary break in the flow of dialogue will enable the audience to observe subtle reactions that are often more eloquent than words.

In the following passage from *Hedda Gabler* Ejlert Lövborg has returned to Tesman's house after a drunken night during which he has lost the only copy of the manuscript containing his finest work. Unknown to Lövborg, Hedda's husband Tesman has found the manuscript and Hedda has hidden it. In this scene Lövborg is alone with Hedda. Following is one way in which the timing could be indicated:

HEDDA: And what are you going to do, then?
LÖVBORG: Nothing./Only make an end of the whole business. The sooner the better.
HEDDA // [*a step nearer*]: Ejlert Lövborg,/listen to me. Could you not see to it – that it is done/beautifully?
LÖVBORG: /Beautifully? [*Smiling.*] With vineleaves in the hair, as you used to imagine once upon a time –
HEDDA: Ah, not vineleaves. I don't believe in that any more. But/beautifully, nevertheless. For once./Goodbye./You must go now, and not come here again.
LÖVBORG: /Goodbye, Madam. Remember me to Jörgen

Tesman. [*About to go.*]

HEDDA:/Wait a minute. You shall have a souvenir/to take with you. [*She goes to the writing-table and opens the drawer and the pistol-case. She comes back to Lövborg again with one of the pistols.*]

LÖVBORG [*looking at her*]: // Is *that* the souvenir?

HEDDA [*nodding slowly*]: / Do you recognize it? It was aimed at you once.

LÖVBORG: You should have used it then.

HEDDA: There it is. Use it yourself now.

LÖVBORG//[*putting the pistol in his breast pocket*]: Thanks.

HEDDA: And beautifully, Ejlert Lövborg. Promise me that.

LÖVBORG: /Goodbye, Hedda Gabler. [*He goes out by the hall door.*]

[*Hedda listens a moment at the door. Then she goes across to the writing-table and takes out the manuscript in its package. She glances inside the wrapper, pulls some of the sheets half out and looks at them. Then she goes across and sits down in the easy-chair by the stove with the packet in her lap. After a moment, she opens the stove-door and then the packet.*]

HEDDA [*throwing some of the leaves into the fire and whispering to herself*]: Now I am burning your child,/Thea. You with your curly hair. [*Throwing a few more leaves into the stove.*] Your child/and Ejlert Lövborg's./[*Throwing in the rest.*] I'm burning it –//burning your child.

End of Act III

Apart from the pauses shown, variations of pace within a phrase or line will help to feed the information to the audience and keep the dramatic intensity at the desired level. The movement within this scene, where nothing is said, has to be as carefully timed as the dialogue. For instance, when Hedda goes to the writing-table, the manner and pace at which she moves must be timed to build the tension, which is heightened when we see she is going to give him a pistol. Lövborg's pause before he says, 'Is that the souvenir?' compounds it. After Hedda says, 'Use it yourself now,' if Lövborg does not savour, in a pause, his being ordered to commit suicide before putting the pistol in his breast pocket and before he replies,

'Thanks', the moment will lose force. Similarly Lövborg's exit must be timed exactly to allow the image to register. If he is too fast or too slow the mood will not hold. Again when Lövborg has gone and Hedda is alone on the stage, her movement as she goes to the bookcase and returns to the stove with the manuscript must be timed to reveal her mental state.

From Lövborg's exit to the end of the act there are only four lines of dialogue, but Hedda's business of getting the manuscript must be timed so that the enormity of her action is fully relished and the fact that she has only four lines to verbalize what she is doing must not be allowed to make this scene too abrupt for its dramatic importance. The timing of business must reflect in the rhythm of the movement the thought behind the action.

TIMING LAUGHS

Laugh lines in comedy and farce have to be put across with exactly the right timing and pointing to galvanize the audience into laughter. The basic technique is:

a. To get the full attention of the audience with the first part of the line.

b. Pause very briefly before the key word or phrase, to build up anticipation.

c. Put it across crisply and clearly to trigger the laugh.

d. Freeze while the audience laughs.

e. Kill the laughter before it weakens, by continuing the action.

In comedy and farce teamwork must be very slick and all the actors must be aware of potential laugh lines so that they don't kill them by speaking or moving when the audience has just started to laugh. All the cast must 'wait for laughs' and try to anticipate at which places they must freeze on other actor's laugh lines. Often it is the reaction of a character to a line that triggers the laugh and without the reaction to the line being seen it loses its force.

In the following extract from *She Stoops to Conquer,* by Oliver Goldsmith, the illiterate Tony Lumpkin hands his mother a letter to read for him, which unfortunately reveals the very secret that must be kept from her.

TONY: But I tell you, miss, it's of all the consequence in the world. I would not lose the rest of it for a guinea. Here, mother, do you make it out. Of no consequence! [*Giving Mrs Hardcastle the letter.*]

MRS HARDCASTLE: How's this? [*Reads.*] 'Dear 'Squire, I'm now waiting for Miss Neville, with a post-chaise and pair, at the bottom of the garden, but I find my horses yet unable to perform the journey. I expect you'll assist us with a pair of fresh horses, as you promised. Dispatch is necessary, as the *hag*, (ay, the hag) your mother, will otherwise suspect us! Yours, Hastings.' Grant me patience. I shall run distracted! My rage chokes me.

Amusement will probably build up in the audience to the moment when she pauses before the word 'hag'. If she pauses again after 'hag', in that pause the amusement should burst into open laughter and should be boosted if her facial reaction points 'hag'.

In this extract from Act I of Joe Orton's black farce *Loot*, Fay, a homicidal nurse, is talking to McLeavy whose wife she has discreetly murdered, after getting her to make a will in her favour. The comedy arises from the sense of propriety with which outrageous statements are made. In this extract there are at least ten possible laughs, which are indicated with asterisks.

FAY: Your wife changed her will shortly before she died. She left all her money to me.
MCLEAVY: What! [*Almost fainting.*] Is it legal?
FAY: Perfectly.
MCLEAVY: She must have been drunk. What about me and the boy?
FAY: I'm surprised at you taking this attitude. Have you no sense of decency?*
MCLEAVY: Oh, it's God's judgement on me for marrying a Protestant.* How much has she left you?
FAY: Nineteen thousand pounds including her bonds and jewels.
MCLEAVY: Her jewels as well?
FAY: Except her diamond ring. It's too large and unfashionable for a woman to wear. She's left that to Harold.
MCLEAVY: Employing you has cost me a fortune. You must be the most expensive nurse in history.

FAY: You don't imagine I want the money for myself, do you?

MCLEAVY: Yes.*

FAY: That's unworthy of you. I'm most embarrassed by Mrs McLeavy's generosity.

MCLEAVY: You'll destroy the will?

FAY: I wish I could.

MCLEAVY: Why can't you?

FAY: It's a legal document.* I could be sued.

MCLEAVY: By whom?

FAY: The beneficiary.

MCLEAVY: That's you.* You'd never sue yourself.

FAY: I might. If I was pushed too far. We must find some way of conveying the money into your bank account.

MCLEAVY: Couldn't you just give it to me?

FAY: Think of the scandal.

MCLEAVY: What do you suggest then?

FAY: We must have a joint bank account.

MCLEAVY: Wouldn't that cause an even bigger scandal?

FAY: Not if we were married.

MCLEAVY: Married? But then you would have my money as well as Mrs McLeavy's.*

FAY: That's one way of looking at it.

MCLEAVY: No, I'm too old. My health wouldn't stand up to a young wife.*

FAY: I'm a qualified nurse.*

MCLEAVY: You'd have to give up your career.

FAY: I'd do it for you.

MCLEAVY: I can give you nothing in return.

FAY: I ask for nothing. I'm a woman. Only half the human race can say that without fear of contradiction.* [*She kisses him.*] Go ahead. Ask me to marry you. I've no intention of refusing.* On your knees. I'm a great believer in traditional positions.*

MCLEAVY: The pains in my legs.

FAY: Exercise is good for them.*

[MCLEAVY *kneels.*]

Use any form of proposal you like. Try to avoid abstract nouns.*

If you attempt to squeeze the maximum laughter from each possible laugh you may slow the performance and 'milk' it too much, therefore you have to decide which you will treat as moments of silent amusement and which you will treat as major laughs. This is called 'storing laughs'.

Towards the end of the extract the laughs tend to bunch up. This is where you should be selective. This can be contrived simply by not pausing before and after the ones you wish to play down, but give the full treatment to those you select.

In the following extract from Act III of Molière's *The Imaginary Invalid*, the quack Purgon is terrifying the gullible hypochondriac Argan with a list of the dreadful things that will happen to him for refusing to take his expensive remedies.

As Purgon swiftly piles disaster on disaster and Argan quails with each imaginary affliction the comic effect will build until Purgon's last speech.

PURGON: I declare that I abandon you to your evil constitution, to the disorder of your bowels, the corruption of your blood, the bitterness of your own gall and the feculence of your humours.

ARGAN: Oh Lord!

PURGON: I foretell that in four days you'll be in an incurable condition.

ARGAN: Oh mercy!

PURGON: You'll fall into a state of bradypepsia.

ARGAN: Mr Purgon!

PURGON: From bradypepsia into dyspepsia.

ARGAN: Mr Purgon!

PURGON: From dyspepsia into apepsia.

ARGAN: Mr Purgon!

PURGON: From apepsia into diarrhoea and lientery.

ARGAN: Mr Purgon!

PURGON: From lientery into dysentery.

ARGAN: Mr Purgon!

PURGON: From dysentery into dropsy.

ARGAN: Mr Purgon!

PURGON: And from dropsy to autopsy* that your own folly will have brought you to.

[*Purgon exits.*]

If 'autopsy' is pointed as the ultimate of all the grisly horrors, with a pause before it as a 'get ready to laugh' warning and a pause after it for the audience to relish Argan's reaction of terror it will trigger the 'stored' laughter into one big laugh. Purgon can then kill the laughter before it wanes when he continues, '. . . that your own folly will have brought you to,' and make a splendid exit in high dudgeon.

POINTING

Pointing is the technique the actor uses to clarify or emphasize an idea, word or action for the audience. There are various ways in which it can be achieved. As we have seen when considering timing, pausing before or after, or before and after the salient word, phrase, sentence or action makes it stand out.

The actor can also point by making a word, phrase or sentence stand out from its context by changing the volume with which it is spoken, making it louder or softer; by using a different vocal tone; or even by using a different pace, pitch or inflection. Pointing demands a subtle and flexible use of voice and speech.

An action can be pointed by ensuring that the attention of the audience is momentarily directed at that action. This is achieved by having momentary stillness everywhere else on the stage, so that the slightest movement catches the eye of the audience; the image is made to impinge by virtue of its isolation.

An example of pointing an action would be in Act II of *Hedda Gabler*, where Lövborg (who has forsworn drink) takes one of the glasses of punch and says, 'Your health Thea!' to Mrs Elvsted. If Lövborg were to speak as he reached for the glass the gesture would not convey the full significance of his reaction to his belief of Mrs Elvsted's lack of faith in him. However, if all on stage, including Judge Brack and Tesman in the small room up stage, are still and silent for those seconds, Lövborg's action of taking the glass in his hand before he speaks can be a very powerful moment.

CHARACTERIZATION

Every actor has a different approach to the job of creating a character. Some actors like to find their own way into the character and need to have the liberty to experiment without feeling that the director is doing too much of the thinking for them. Others are much more open to suggestion and some ask for positive direction. You must be sensitive to the way in which it is necessary to handle the individual members of your cast. Too firm a style of direction with an actor brimming with ideas may inhibit his creative spark. The comparative freedom you may give to a well-cast and polished actor may leave the actor, who needs the constant guidance of the director, floundering. As director you have to monitor the development of every character; in some cases you will need to do it with subtlety, in others you may be very explicit.

From early rehearsals, by discussion and information the director gives, the cast should be aware of the following:

1. What the play is about. (Theme, message, ruling idea or super-objective.)
2. The plot of the play, with its sequence of events, climaxes and individual involvement in the action.
3. The style or convention of the play. (Comedy, tragedy, farce, fantasy, romance, thriller, play of ideas or a mixture of various styles.)
4. The proposed treatment of the dialogue.
5. The stage settings, furnishings and essential properties.
6. The leading character, what makes him tick and his relationships with the other characters.
7. The other characters in the play and their motivations and inter-relationships.
8. Their own character's physical appearance, attitudes and relationships and, of course, the background of their character so it can be developed in depth.
9. The mood or atmosphere of the play and what creates this.
10. Any relevant details that will help them to visualize their characters, such as: period in history, architecture, costume, music, or social, political or literary background.

In rehearsal the actor may try out various ways of creating his character, such as Stanislavski's advice to think and react 'as if' he were this character in this situation, allowing the dialogue and the physical situations to trigger his reactions and using recollected emotions to fuel the character's emotions, or he may use the stimulus of impressions gathered from any literary or art form, or indeed simply rely on the power of his own imagination and common sense to create a credible character.

The furniture, setting, properties and costumes can, in themselves, be a powerful stimulus to the actor. These external tangible items can, on occasion, fire the imagination and foster that essential quality of truth in the dramatic situation. For instance, a certain chair, walking stick, hat or picture may prove to be the talisman that leads the actor to the full realization of his character. The development of his character will inevitably be influenced by the reactions of the other members of the cast and the guidance of the director. In the early stages of rehearsal he will probably be ultra-sensitive to criticism, although he may not show it, and therefore need very considerate handling by the director. He will also be influenced by the setting within which he is working, the properties he uses, costume, make-up, lighting, music and effects.

Rehearsals are a time for experiment for the actor in which he will gradually, from rehearsal to rehearsal, as the production gains momentum, transform from an actor holding a script to a fully-fledged character. The director will need to assist him with patience and an understanding of the actor's psychology. During rehearsals a rapport often develops between actor and director, so that without words being used the director can guide and encourage the actor by the quality of his attention and sense of appreciation.

8 *Preparing the Production*

THE DIRECTOR AND HIS DESIGNER

The director and his designer usually have a series of discussions at a very early stage of the production to decide how the play will be presented. Sometimes a director is his own designer. Normally, however, the planning of the setting with its décor is a matter of collaboration in which all aspects of the play are discussed prior to the designer making drawings and models of the setting for approval or modifications.

The director needs to have a ground plan of the setting agreed as soon as possible, so he can be certain it will allow the cast to express the play in movement and grouping. It is imperative to be strictly practical and understand what will work in terms of theatre and what will inhibit movement or distract from the content of the play by drawing attention to itself as a piece of scenery. On occasions there is applause for a beautiful set as the curtain rises. This will no doubt gratify the designer, but it may detract from the main fare of the occasion which is the action of the play. Settings should not be too obtrusive, unless, of course, one is aiming for spectacle, but should be a stimulating working environment for the actor. Sometimes an originally splendid idea can 'grow' and obstruct the acting area, cramping movement; like a recent production of *The Cherry Orchard* in which the orchard itself was so thoroughly represented that the settings in which the actors performed were unnaturally cramped and this affected the movement of the entire cast.

There seems to be a feeling these days in favour of simplicity of design, although, naturally, some plays demand elaborate settings for their interpretation. Settings should normally reflect the period, mood and convention of the play, although in recent

77

years there have been many brilliant productions which have made older plays more significant to contemporary audiences by a completely fresh approach to the décor and costuming. Notable examples are the Royal Shakespeare Company's productions of *The Man of Mode* directed by Terry Hands and designed by Timothy O'Brien, and *A Midsummer Night's Dream* directed by Peter Brook and designed by Sally Jacobs.

In the early meetings with the designer there may also be preliminary discussions on lighting, costume, projected scenery, effects and pyrotechnics – such as the use of smoke boxes, flash boxes and maroons for explosions. Pyrotechnics require stringent safety precautions and space within the stage area for their deployment.

From the start the cost of the production must be kept in mind in case the design plans become too expensive. The production manager is normally the person who supervises the costing of set construction and he must be consulted to advise on the practicability of what is proposed and whether it is within the budget for the production.

When the design of the setting has been approved the designer gives working drawings to the master carpenter or construction crew so work may start as quickly as possible. The designer, if not actually designing the costumes, will want to be consulted about those that are hired or taken from the wardrobe. Similarly the designer will be interested in the lighting of the play, because both the setting and costumes will be influenced by the type of lighting used.

WORKING ON THE SCRIPT

The early stages of preparation involve a study of the script to clarify your approach to the whole production. You must satisfy yourself that you have a thorough understanding of the following: the theme, the style (convention), the plot with the dramatic climaxes, the characters, the language, the subtext, the period, the sound, music and effects required and, of course, the essential requirements of the setting, which you are discussing with the designer. It is also wise to familiarize yourself with the dramatist's background, his preoccupations, and his other plays.

As you read the play visualize it in action. The series of mental images you receive should give you ideas as to how you can stage it. Try to see the play from the point of view of each character. Put yourself in the shoes of each of them, in the situations in which they find themselves. Remember each character is the centre of his own world, with aspirations, virtues and failings.

In this phase of work you will probably be making notes on all the above-mentioned aspects of the production as well as diagrams and sketches of possible movement and grouping. Don't allow your director's text of the play to become too cluttered with a multiplicity of notes. You can if you wish keep notes on themes, characters, situations, subtext, etc., in a separate notebook, cross-referenced with your director's copy, and keep the latter free for diagrams, sketches, sound, light, effects, curtains and scene change notes, which are the physical happenings in a production. Careful preparation of your director's text will help to make your rehearsals efficient and progressive. It is the working blueprint for your production.

Some directors note every minute detail of what they want to happen on stage; others do not block any moves or groupings before rehearsals and allow the movement of the play to sort itself out in rehearsal as a result of discussion and experiment with the actors. Coming to rehearsal with no blocking in mind demands plenty of rehearsal time and absolute confidence that you can sort out the movement flow with the actors in discussion and experiment fairly smoothly. It also demands a very experienced director and highly professional cast.

What many directors do is to arrange a tentative blocking of the scenes they are rehearsing, but are prepared to alter or abandon it if it doesn't work and devise something better on the spot. If you do block out basic moves it helps to visualize what you feel are the most effective groupings at the climaxes of the play and plan moves that make it easy for the characters to find themselves in that position at the desired moment. If you start planning moves without knowing where all the characters should be at a certain point you may have to scrap those moves if you find you have put actors in the wrong position, and go back to a point where you can manoeuvre them into the correct strategic placing for the important moment.

When blocking in your copy of the text you must visualize what your moves will look like from all parts of the theatre and check that characters do not mask one another and that all members of the audience will be able to see into the stage picture. It is advisable to use pencil when making sketches or indicating moves, as there are bound to be many alterations made in rehearsals. Blocking for arena and thrust staging calls for particular care and the director has to arrange movement to give the audience a fair share of the viewing, especially of the leading characters.

If you do pre-block moves it is vital to arrange every move in accordance with the thinking of the character. You have, as it were, to get inside the skulls of the characters and to plan moves accordingly. In a particular situation a particular character would probably want to sit, stand, cross the stage or rise to express in movement what he is thinking. In blocking you mentally become each character and act out the scene in your head. Some directors like to use a model of the stage with small figures to represent the actors so that they can get a three-dimensional impression. If your thinking really probes the mind of the character the moves you devise may be excellent, but remember that you, the director, are not the actor you have cast. He is the person who has to make the moves, therefore suggest to your cast that the moves are something to try out, to be modified by them or completely changed if unacceptable. With this approach most actors manage to make given moves their own. However, if an actor says firmly that a move feels very awkward and it is throwing him, invite him to devise his own move and see if it fits into the shape of the scene.

Some play texts include the moves of the original production. These are the work of another director and cast and were also devised within a different setting; they may be quite unsuitable. It is far better to plan fresh moves and business based upon your interpretation of the play. In preparing the production, however, one has to guard against indulging in what the critics will tell you are extravagant gimmicks. Innovations must spring from valid interpretations of the text, as was the case with Peter Brook's highly praised production of *A Midsummer Night's Dream* with its circus stilts, trapezes and juggling.

The period of preparation will be one of fairly intensive work and may occupy several weeks (or months in some cases). This is the time when you will, on your own, apart from conferences with the designer, steep yourself in the text until you feel that you have a firm grasp of the play, an understanding of its inner life, and know how you will arrive at your interpretation.

Many directors prepare their copy of the text by interleaving each printed page of text with a blank sheet of paper on which diagrams and notes may be made. These are usually cross-referenced by numbers, starting at number one for each page. A handy way of arranging this is to get an A4-sized ring file and remove the sheets of the text from the binding, leaving enough unprinted paper to allow holes to be punched for inserting the sheets into the ring file. The blank sheets of A4 paper are inserted between each sheet of text and may be divided into two columns with a vertical line: a narrow column on the outside of the page for notes for the stage management on curtains, lighting, music and effects, and a broad column on the inside of the sheet for diagrams of movement or groupings and notes describing each move (this is shown in the blocking examples). Some directors include their detailed notes on the interpretation of the play on this sheet. If you do this it may clarify things if you make a third column so that stage management instructions, movement information and notes on interpretation are all kept separate. You must find the best arrangement for your own methods of work. Quite a few directors, it is fair to state, do not pre-block in any way and let the movement and grouping evolve in rehearsal, although naturally they have made notes and have a fund of ideas.

The examples of blocking, for a proscenium arch stage production of *Hedda Gabler,* an in-the-round production of *The Rules of the Game* and an open-air thrust stage production of *The Jew of Malta,* show one way of preparing the director's working copy of the play. Also included is a list of symbols commonly used to denote stage furniture and abbreviations of stage positions.

CASTING

The success of a production is heavily dependent upon the quality of the cast. It pays to take time and care to assemble a cast that have not only the necessary temperamental and physical attributes – quality of voice, speech, movement, stage presence and dramatic imagination – for their individual roles, but can balance and work agreeably with the rest of the cast.

For most actors auditions are a nerve-racking business and

Common Symbols for Settings

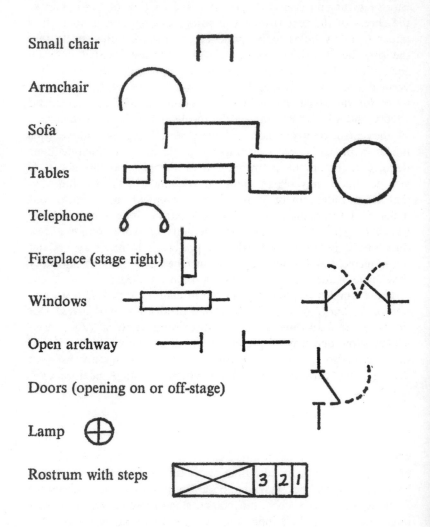

Small chair

Armchair

Sofa

Tables

Telephone

Fireplace (stage right)

Windows

Open archway

Doors (opening on or off-stage)

Lamp

Rostrum with steps

Abbreviations used in Blocking

Cross	X
Cross left	XL
Up right	UR
Right	R
Down right	DR
Up centre	UC
Centre	C
Down centre	DC
Up left	UL
Left	L
Down left	DL
Up right centre	URC
Right centre	RC
Down right centre	DRC
Up left centre	ULC
Left centre	LC
Down left centre	DLC

The directions are from the actor's point of view as he stands on the stage. Left is the actor's left.

EXAMPLE OF BLOCKING FOR THE PROSCENIUM ARCH STAGE

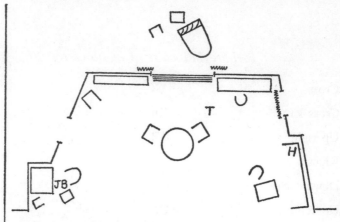

① H sitting sofa DL. JB has back to stove DR. T is UL of table centre.
② T to H a few steps.
③ T move away again.
④ B enter R above armchair.
⑤ B exit.
⑥ L enters to UR of table

⑦ T X R to L.
⑧ L x below table C to UR of H.

⑨ H stays sitting.
⑩ T x L below table to R of Lövborg.

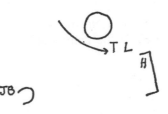

BRACK: ① What do you mean by 'the worst'?

HEDDA: If he won't go with you and my husband.

TESMAN [*looking at her dubiously*]: ② But, Hedda dear, do you think that would quite do, for him to stay here with you? Eh? Remember Aunt Julle can't come.

HEDDA: No, but Mrs Elvsted's coming. So the three of us will have tea together.

TESMAN: ③ Oh, that will be all right, then.

BRACK [*smiling*]: And perhaps that might be the wisest plan for him too.

HEDDA: Why?

BRACK: Good gracious, my dear lady, you've often enough said hard things about my little bachelor parties. They weren't suitable for any but men of the strongest principles.

HEDDA: But surely Mr Lövborg is a man of strong enough principles now? A converted sinner –

④ [*Berte appears at the hall door.*]

BERTE: There's a gentleman, ma'am, who'd like to see you.

HEDDA: Yes, show him in. ⑤

TESMAN [*quietly*]: I'm sure it's he. Just fancy!

⑥ [*Ejlert Lövborg comes in from the hall. . . . He remains standing by the door and bows abruptly. He seems a little embarrassed.*]

⑦ TESMAN [*crossing to him and shaking his hand*]: Well, my dear Ejlert, so at last we meet once more!

LÖVBORG [*speaking with lowered voice*]: Thank you for your letter, Jorgen ⑧ [*Approaching Hedda.*] May I shake hands with you too, Mrs Tesman?

⑨ HEDDA [*taking his hand*]: I'm glad to see you, Mr Lövborg. [*With a gesture.*] I don't know whether you two –

LÖVBORG [*with a slight bow*]: Mr Brack, I think.

BRACK [*returning it*]: Of course we do. Some years ago –

⑩ TESMAN [*to Lövborg, with his hands on his shoulders*]: And now you're to make yourself absolutely at home, Ejlert. Mustn't he, Hedda? For you're going to settle down in town again, I hear. Eh?

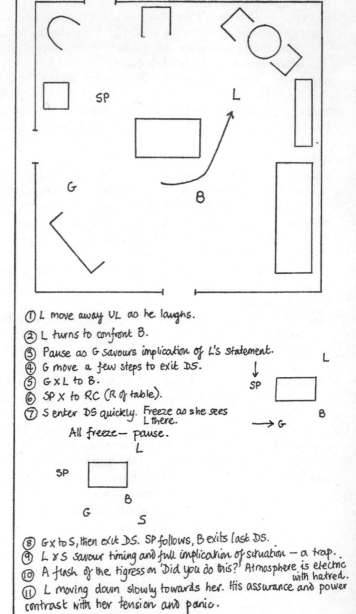

① L move away UL as he laughs.
② L turns to confront B.
③ Pause as G savours implication of L's statement.
④ G move a few steps to exit DS.
⑤ G X L to B.
⑥ SP X to RC (R of table).
⑦ S enter DS quickly. Freeze as she sees
              L there.

     All freeze — pause.

⑧ G X to S, then exit DS. SP follows, B exits last DS.
⑨ L & S savour timing and full implication of situation — a trap.
⑩ A flash of the tigress on 'Did you do this?' Atmosphere is electric
                                     with hatred.
⑪ L moving down slowly towards her. His assurance and power
contrast with her tension and panic.

LEONE: – No, no, my dear Venanzi! Not mine: your own!

GUIDO: Very well then: mine! But *you* will be dishonoured!

BARELLI: Disgraced! We shall be forced to expose your dishonour!

①[LEONE *laughs loudly.*]

BARELLI: How can you laugh? You'll be dishonoured, dishonoured!

LEONE:② I understand, my friends, and I can still laugh. Don't you see how and where I live? Why should I worry my head about honour?③//

GUIDO:④ Don't let's waste any more time. Let's go.

BARELLI: But are you really going to fight this duel?

GUIDO: Yes, I am. Don't you understand?

BARELLI: No, I don't!

LEONE: Yes, it really is his business, you know, Barelli!

BARELLI: You're being cynical!

LEONE: No, Barelli, I'm being rational! When one has emptied oneself of every passion and . . .

GUIDO⑤[*interrupting and gripping* BARELLI *by the arm*]:   Come, Barelli. It's no use arguing now. Come down with me, too, Doctor.

SPIGA:⑥ I'm coming! I'm coming!

⑦[*At this moment* SILIA *enters. There is a short silence during which she stands still, perplexed and amazed.*]

⑧GUIDO [*coming forward, very pale, and grasping her hand*]:   Goodbye, Silia. [*He turns to* LEONE.] Goodbye.

[GUIDO *rushes out, followed by* BARELLI *and* SPIGA.]

SILIA: Why did he say goodbye like that?

LEONE: I told you, dear, that it was quite useless for you to come here. But you were determined to.

SILIA: But . . . but what are you doing here?

LEONE: Don't you know? I live here!

SILIA: And what is Guido doing? Isn't . . . isn't the duel going to take place?

LEONE:⑨ Oh, it will take place I suppose. It may be taking place now!

SILIA: But . . . how can it be? If you're still here?

LEONE: Oh, yes, I am here. But he has gone. Didn't you see him?

SILIA: But then . . . that means . . . Oh God! Why has he gone? Has he gone to fight for you?

LEONE: Not for me, dear – for you!

SILIA: For me? Oh, God! Did you do this⑩

⑪LEONE [*coming up to her with the commanding, disdainful air of a cruel judge*]:   Did I do this? You have the impertinence to suggest that I am responsible for it!

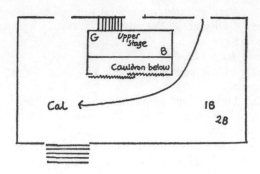

① G offer gold.

② G to UR of upper stage.

③ Cal and 1 Basso and 2 Basso enter UL. Cal to RC.

④ B to C of upper stage — above cauldron.

⑤ G hold up knife. (On trumpet cut cable.)

⑥ On trumpet 1 Of and 2 Of fast entry (UL & UR) to open curtains.

⑥ Quick sequence
a - trumpet
b - cable cut
c - B into cauldron
d - explosions
e - light cauldron
f - Officers open curtains
g - cauldron thrust forward

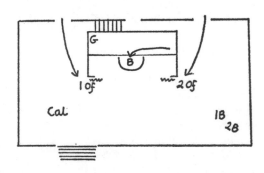

GOVERNOR: Oh excellent! ① Here, hold thee, Barabas!
I trust thy word, take what I promised thee.

BARABAS: No, Governor, I'll satisfy thee first:
Thou shalt ② not live in doubt of anything.
Stand close, for here they come. Why is not this — *to audience*
A kingly kind of trade to purchase towns
By treachery, and sell 'em by deceit?
Now tell me, worldlings, underneath the sun
If greater falsehood ever has been done. ③

[*Enter* CALYMATH *and* BASSOES.]

CALYMATH: Come, my companion bassoes, see I pray
How busy Barabas is there above
To entertain us in his gallery;
Let us salute him. Save thee, Barabas!

BARABAS: ④ Welcome, great Calymath.
Will't please thee, mighty Selim-Calymath,
To ascend our homely stairs?

CALYMATH: Ay, Barabas;
Come, bassoes, attend.

GOVERNOR: Stay, Calymath;
For I will show thee greater courtesy
Than Barabas would have afforded thee. ⑤

KNIGHT [*within*]: Sound a charge there! ⑥

[*A charge, the cable cut, a cauldron discovered into which*
BARABAS *falls.*]

although an actor's technique may enable him to appear relaxed in most circumstances it is possible that under audition conditions the actor may do himself less than justice. It is therefore up to you as director to ensure, as far as you can, that actors are put at ease and do not feel that they are caught up in a rushed, impersonal process where they have only a brief time to display their talents. The mass auditions held by some managements are typical of this and are an off-putting experience for a sensitive player. Amateur companies usually have a more considerate approach.

If possible, let the people auditioning have a copy of the script in time for them to read the play and decide on an initial approach to the part for which they are auditioning. Ideally they should be aware of the style, the nature of the language, the period and their own role in the context of the play as a whole. On occasions a fluent and lively reader at an audition cannot develop a fully rounded and projected character in rehearsal, because movement and physical attributes don't match up with the impression given by the use of voice and speech. If possible, therefore, include one or two improvisations and also several audition pieces that the actor feels represents his best work.

Type-casting – that is using actors who are very similar in temperament and physique to their stage roles – is still fairly common in both the professional and to some degree the amateur theatre. This is something that many actors resist – unless they feel that steady work in the same type of part is better than long periods of unemployment. It is also sometimes the penalty of excelling in particular 'type' roles. The late Sonia Dresdel often found herself playing dominant and ruthless women because she was brilliant at it and it was rarely that she was offered parts where her true warm nature could be revealed.

It occasionally happens that you make a mistake in casting; the actor belies the impression made at audition and during rehearsals it becomes clear that a change must be made. This is a painful decision to have to make and there are bound to be strong feelings generated, but your duty is to the success of the production. You must also consider the rest of the cast, because one character who is not correct can upset the balance of the whole production. It is essential to make any cast change as soon as possible.

Casting in small established companies is often limited to members of that company, but it has the advantage that the talents and potential of everyone will be known and there is an opportunity to give actors the chance of broadening their range. Also in the small established company it is possible to create very good working relationships, which are not so easily achieved in an *ad hoc* situation.

Don't attempt to direct and act at the same time, unless you have the calibre of a Gielgud, because the points of view are, as it were, 180 degrees out of phase. The director is out in the auditorium tuning the performances of all the cast and gauging the possible reactions of an audience from all parts of the auditorium, while the actor's main concern is the development of his character within the stage situation and projecting this to the audience. It is unusual for one person to fulfil both functions satisfactorily.

THE PRODUCTION CONFERENCE

When the production has been planned and the setting and the physical arrangements for the production have been decided, it is necessary to have a meeting of the production team, where everyone will have an initial briefing about the production and be given details of setting, décor, rehearsals, lighting, costumes, furniture, properties, sound effects, music and a look at the set model. This meeting puts everyone in the picture and subsequently the production manager will see people individually and co-ordinate the work of the team and check that all items will be ready on the dates required.

A Progress Check is a useful way of ensuring that everything goes smoothly, that nothing is overlooked and that deadlines are observed. This check can be enlarged or cut according to the scale of the production. You will see that most of the items concern the work of the production team and business management, but as director of the whole operation you may want to ensure that everything is on schedule and all is going smoothly. Efficiency helps to give the cast a feeling of confidence, while last-minute delays and panics are demoralizing.

Progress Check

1. Costing ....by :
2. Scripts available ....by :
3. Set design completed ....by :
4. Production Conference ....by :
5. Casting completed ....by :
6. Rehearsal Call Sheets ....by :
7. Furniture/Props ordered ....by :
8. Posters ordered ....by :
9. Programmes ordered ....by :
10. Tickets ordered ....by :
11. Handbills ordered ....by :
12. Preliminary publicity ....by :
13. Costumes ordered ....by :
14. Wigs ordered ....by :
15. Licences : play/taping ....by :
16. Advertising in ....by :
17. Furniture/Props ready ....by :
18. Posters/Handbills ready ....by :
19. Tickets ready ....by :
20. Set completed ....by :
21. Costumes/Wigs received ....by :
22. Sound ready ....by :
23. Lighting ready ....by :
24. Photo call ....by :
25. Programmes received ....by :

THE REHEARSAL CALL SHEET

In consultation with your production manager and stage manager you will need to prepare a Rehearsal Call Sheet that gives full information about the place, day, date, time, scenes to be rehearsed, costume parades, photo calls, dress rehearsals and opening performance. This gives everyone, cast and production team, a clear view of the work in hand and the time available. Of course, between the commencement of rehearsals and the opening performance there will be the inevitable alterations that the stage manager passes on to all concerned.

SCENE AND CAST ANALYSIS

With a large cast, especially if there is to be a lot of doubling of parts, it is often useful to make a scene and cast analysis. This also shows the rehearsal units into which the play has been divided. Many classical plays and some modern ones (for example, those of Brecht) are often written in fairly short scenes which are often units of convenient rehearsal length. For a full-length play not written in short scenes you will find that each act can be broken down into rehearsal situations. Most plays can be divided into approximately twelve to thirty situations for concentrated work in rehearsal. An example of a scene and cast analysis is shown for a production of Marlowe's *The Jew of Malta*. An analysis like this allows you to call only those members of the cast needed for the scenes you are rehearsing. It can be very frustrating for actors to hang about, sometimes for hours, waiting to rehearse.

The number of hours available for rehearsal will govern the quality of the production. There is no hard and fast rule about rehearsal time. It depends very much upon the play, the cast and the working methods of the director. In the professional theatre from two weeks in a regional repertory company to twelve weeks in a major theatre company, working a five- or six-hour rehearsal day, seems to represent the range. In the amateur theatre rehearsals at evenings and weekends can be spread over a longer period of time than the average professional production, but in most amateur companies an intensity of rehearsal is called for to acquire and polish techniques that the professional has as a tool of his trade. When working with amateur casts you have to gauge how much rehearsal they can beneficially take. The director of an amateur company will often find himself in the role of drama tutor as well as director, which will absorb some of the available time.

CAST ANALYSIS FOR THE JEW OF MALTA BY CHRISTOPHER MARLOWE

Page	Scene	Rehearsal Unit	Situation	Machiavel	Barabas	1st Merchant	2nd Merchant	1st Jew	2nd Jew	3rd Jew	Governor	2 Knights	2 Officers	Caymath	2 Bassoes	Abigail	Friar Jacomo	Friar Bernardine	Abbess	Nun	Mathias	Lodowick	Del Bosco	Ithamore	3 slaves	Katherine	Bellamira	Pilia-Borza	4 citizens
9	Prologue	1	Prologue. Profit by guile and force.	✓																										
11	I.i		B reveals wealth. Turks arrive.		✓																								
18	I.ii A		Turks demand tribute. Jews money.		✓			✓	✓	✓	✓																		
26	I.ii B	2	A becomes nun to find B's cache.		✓											✓													
33	II.i		A finds cache.		✓											✓													
36	II.ii		D-B brings slaves. Counters Turks.		✓						✓												✓						
38	II.iii A		Slaves. B plays bankrupt. M & L to A. False challenge.		✓							✓	✓								✓	✓		✓					
45	II.iii B	3	B sends false challenge.									✓	✓								✓	✓							
54	III.i		P-B gives Bell. silver. I desires Bell.																					✓				✓	
55	III.ii		M & L kill each other.																		✓	✓		✓		✓			
57	III.iii		I tells A of murder. I enters convent.								✓					✓								✓					
61	III.iv	4	B and I poison porridge.		✓											✓	✓							✓					
65	III.v		G refuses to pay Turks.								✓	✓		✓	✓														
67	III.vi		Nuns dead. A tells Friars.													✓	✓	✓											
69	IV.i		Friars try to blackmail B. Are killed.		✓												✓	✓						✓					
78	IV.ii		P-B and Bell. con I to rob B.		✓																			✓			✓	✓	
84	IV.iii	5	P-B extracts more money.		✓																			✓			✓	✓	
86	IV.iv		B disguised. Poisons flower.		✓																			✓			✓	✓	
90	V.i		B betrayed. B helps Cal.		✓						✓	✓	✓	✓	✓									✓		✓	✓	✓	as Turks
95	V.ii		G prisoner. B now Governor.		✓						✓	✓		✓	✓											✓	✓	✓	as Turks
99	V.iii	6	Mess. invites Cal. to feast.		✓																								as mess
100	V.iv		G prepares to defeat Turks.								✓	✓											✓						as Turks
101	V.v		G traps B in cauldron. Cal. is prisoner		✓						✓	✓		✓	✓								✓						as ctz

9 Rehearsals

'The director is a one-man audience through whom
I prepare for a real audience. He is the focal point
at which, during rehearsal, I aim my performance.'
PAUL SCOFIELD

Before rehearsals commence your planning should be completed. During rehearsals the various members of the production team, apart from those assisting at rehearsals, should be occupied ensuring that the set, furniture, properties, costumes, lighting, sound effects and music are ready on or before the date required.

Rehearsals may be on the stage where the production will be presented, or in a hall or rehearsal studio. Substitute furniture and properties – usually anything suitable the stage management can lay their hands on, will be used for some weeks and the acting area, entrances, stairs, windows or other features, will be marked on the stage with chalk or adhesive tape to give the actors the feel of the proportions and disposition of the setting. This work should be completed before the cast arrives so that no time is wasted. Punctuality is of prime importance. The first rehearsal is important because you can set the tone of the working atmosphere, make introductions, start welding the disparate members of the cast into an ensemble, subtly instil enthusiasm and make the company aware of your confidence in the play and casting.

Most directors commence proceedings by talking about the play and the way in which it is proposed to stage it. At this first rehearsal the designer is usually present with ground plans and a model of the set. Everyone gets a chance to inspect these and see how they have been represented for rehearsal purposes by odd tables, chairs and markings on the floor. There may be some preliminary discussion about costumes, properties, furniture, lighting, effects, music and other things that will receive more attention in later rehearsals.

The next step is usually a reading of the script to mark cuts and alterations, to begin to sort out the ideas and relationships and to settle queries. In this first reading the actors are getting used to the voices and personalities of the rest of the cast, the language of the play and its dramatic situations. It is usually a good idea for everyone to read quietly to pick out the sense of the dialogue and not to attempt to characterize at this stage. A few directors do not give their actors a script at first, but use the cast as a group to explore the situations in the play by means of improvisation. When the dramatic situations are clarified in this way, they then turn to the script. Of the vast majority who start from the script, most have only one or possibly two readings and then start moving the play, but there are those like Roger Planchon of the Théâtre National Populaire at Villeurbanne who like to do extended work on the text itself. In his rehearsals for *Gilles de Rais*, Planchon had the cast reading the play round a table for three weeks, during which time the set was built; only then did the cast start to move the play inside the actual set. This is an extreme example and most actors would get restive if not under the spell of a director of the calibre of a Planchon. You may have to spend more time on readings if the text is a complex one or if the language and style of dialogue demand detailed attention and you feel it is better to tackle this in readings than when you have the play moving. Sometimes a director reverts to a few readings to work on certain aspects when the play has been fully blocked.

When you are ready to start moving the play, if you have already blocked out major moves in your director's copy of the text, it is a good idea to phrase your directions to the actors in such a way that the cast understand you regard your blocking as tentative and if after trying your given moves several times the actors are still uncomfortable, then you want them to say so and you and the actor concerned will devise something better. So you might, when giving your pre-planned moves, phrase your instructions, 'I thought you could come downstage on that line,' or, 'Try crossing right after she sits down.' This sounds more open than a directive. If you are autocratic about pre-planned blocking the actors may feel constrained and perhaps have some difficulty in approaching their roles with free-ranging imagination.

5   The Phoenix Theatre, Leicester. Open stage.

6   The Crucible Theatre, Sheffield. Thrust stage.

7 The Royal Exchange Theatre, Manchester. Theatre in-the-round.

8 The Victoria Theatre, Stoke-on-Trent. An in-the-round production of *Circus Adventure*, a play for children by John Ambrose Brown.

You are more likely to obtain performances of depth from your cast if you work as a team and devise an environment in which discussion, experiment and encouragement lead the actor to characterize from a body of inner truth and understanding that has surfaced in rehearsals, than if you adopt a dictatorial attitude. The usual practice is to block the basic movement of each situation or unit and then for the cast to walk it through to see if it feels right, while the director checks if there is masking, or if any move or grouping looks unsatisfactory on the stage.

If you firmly establish the style of the production during the time when you are rehearsing the first units it will set the tone for the rest of the play and you should find that the concentrated work on early rehearsals makes subsequent rehearsals go smoothly. If you are working on a play in which the women wear long skirts, arrange for rehearsal skirts to be worn. It will help movement and sense of character.

During rehearsals the stage manager, or assistant stage manager, who is acting as prompter, will be noting moves in the prompt book. This is the working copy of the text which will contain every practical detail of the production including cues for lighting, sound, music, effects, and fly gallery. It will be used by the stage manager to run the show from the prompt corner. There are a few points worth mentioning here. Some companies do not use a prompter if the stage manager runs the play from a control room at the rear of the auditorium. This makes the actors responsible for getting themselves out of a 'dry'. With productions on a thrust stage, or in-the-round, the prompter frequently sits in the front row. In very small or amateur companies the director's copy can serve as a prompt copy if it contains all necessary information.

If you are working on a three-act play, for example, it is necessary, as rehearsals proceed and you start rehearsing scenes in, say, Act II, to go back and spend a rehearsal on Act I to keep it fresh. In the same way, when working on Act III you will periodically have to run Acts I and II to keep them going and to build continuity. When you and the cast are happy with the basic movement of a rehearsal unit you can then start concentrating on the finer points of production. It is advisable to have a clear aim for each rehearsal. Each situation in the play will have its own theme or objective, relevant to the main theme or super-objective of the play. Bear this in mind as you work in detail on scenes

D

dealing with the characters and character relationships, dramatic climaxes, timing (pace, pauses, silences, stillness), variety (pace again, volume, pitch, voice), pointing, audibility, teamwork and development of business.

During early rehearsals, if you are rehearsing in a theatre, you may be on the stage with the actors or in the front seats, so that you are in close contact with the cast, to discuss aspects of the production as they arise and devise the basic blocking. When the blocking is completed and the whole play is moving, it is advisable to reposition yourself further away from the stage so that you can check that what is happening on the stage is registering at a distance. You will have to monitor audibility (some theatres have 'dead' spots) and also view the pattern of movement and grouping. It is wise to vary your position and try out the extreme left and right stall seats and also to sit as far back as you can get and as high as you can at the back of the circle or balcony. If you have been working in a rehearsal room you will have to check these points as soon as you can after you get on to the stage, because the intimacy of the rehearsal room has probably toned down the scale of the playing, which may need to be adjusted for the theatre.

During rehearsals the lighting designer should watch the play through, be given a ground plan with the main areas of action indicated, be briefed about the setting, hear the director's views on lighting requirements, special effects, the time, season and the atmosphere of the locale and of course the colour of costumes and settings. He should have discussions with the designer and the more thoroughly he is briefed the more efficiently he will be able to light the play.

BUSINESS

'Business' is the small movement personal to a character that is developed during rehearsal. It is unwise to attempt to impose business on an actor as it arises from his characterization and situation. You may have visualized a comic routine that an actor can carry out with some property, which seems to you quite brilliant, but the actor has to make it work. Therefore, feed the general idea to the actor and if he thinks it's a good one let him work on it himself so that the carrying out of the idea is his own creation. In rehearsal, of course, you can comment on and polish his business.

Some play texts have the business of the original production printed as well as the basic movement. Consider very carefully before you use any of this and make sure it agrees with your production and the characterization. The best thing is to let the actor invent his own business, but you will have to view it with your directorial eye to ensure that it is in key with the production and that he has not elaborated it out of proportion. Business can give an added dimension to a production and imprint memorable images. For instance, in Lindsay Kemp's production of Oscar Wilde's *Salome*, Salome's ecstasy when she had been given the head of John the Baptist was portrayed in a brilliant bit of business when the severed head emerged from a slit in the side of the skirt of Salome's shimmering costume. This was contrived by an actor being inside the voluminous skirt. The image was unforgettable and in a moment conveyed more information than any words could have done.

IMPROVISATION

Improvisation is an invaluable tool in training the actor. It can also be used in rehearsal to aid the development of character and to give a fuller appreciation of situations that in their scripted forms have not fully stimulated the imaginations of the cast, so that they can return to the script with fresh insights and an understanding of the implications behind the dialogue.

If, for example, the actor and actress playing Lövborg and Hedda in Ibsen's *Hedda Gabler* were having difficulty with the scene quoted earlier, where Hedda is persuading Lövborg to commit suicide, setting up a similar situation, where one person is prevailing upon another to similar purpose, but inventing fresh characters and improvising dialogue, could supply the appropriate mental images to help the actor and actress to characterize Ibsen's characters with greater depth.

However, improvisation is a tool to be used with discretion in rehearsals. On occasions a session spent on an improvisation, especially with amateurs, generates valuable insights into situation and character, but it will take time out of your rehearsal schedule and not all actors will find it the best way of using their rehearsal time. Working with the author's script supplies the exact thoughts, language, reactions and situations for that particular play and the subtle director can feed ideas, images and suggestions that will fire the imagination of the actor as surely as improvising a comparable situation. Indeed, working and reworking a scene giving difficulty in an exploratory manner is in itself a form of improvisation.

The director must always strive for spontaneity of thought and action. Although dialogue is printed and movement is planned they must be invested with absolute freshness at every rehearsal and performance. There is always an apparent set-back when scripts are first put aside and fluent rehearsals with scripts in hand are temporarily replaced by an emphasis on remembering the words. This is where the director needs patience to allow the cast to slowly think their way through the scene and take as many prompts as are needed. When fluency is gained your prime task will be to see that the thoughts behind the words are revealed and that the actors don't simply deliver a fluent stream of dialogue. It may take a few rehearsals from the word-perfect stage to reach the point where the ideas behind the dialogue are absolutely clear.

Some directors want words to be learned as soon as possible, but most directors want the characters and the situations developed first, so that the thoughts of characters in the dramatic situation can give the dialogue greater subtlety and depth and the words are acquired from a sense of full dramatic involvement.

The words 'open' and 'closed' are sometimes a useful way of describing the success of an actor in projecting the thoughts of his character in the dramatic situation. The 'open' actor allows us to, as it were, see into his mind, to share his thoughts and feelings. There is no barrier between him and the audience; all is clearly revealed. The 'closed' actor, on the other hand, while possibly very audible and outwardly polished, does not allow the audience to share his thoughts and feelings so easily. The audience have to probe in an attempt to find out what is going on inside him. The director needs to check that an outer gloss does not hide lack of content in performance.

Occasionally, when time is short, there is a temptation to show an actor how to achieve a certain effect. Usually it is better to give him the impression of what is needed by feeding ideas, imagery, similes and metaphors, and allow him to find his own way of expressing it. In this way the final performance will have the authority of the actor behind it. On the other hand there are actors who ask to be shown what you mean and there are also highly successful directors such as Ingmar Bergman and Samuel Beckett (when directing his own plays) who do demonstrate, when an exact piece of timing, intonation or movement is required.

When you have got to the word-perfect stage you can try running scenes as 'stoppers', in which you tell the cast that you are concentrating on certain aspects of production, such as cues, timing, pointing, variety or climaxes and not to be put out by being halted for a quick note, before continuing with no loss of momentum. After a 'stopper' have a 'non-stopper', in which you keep quiet, to restore the flow, and give notes only at the end of the scene.

If for some reason a rehearsal is becoming lifeless you can try what I call a 'shake-up' run, in which the scene is played very fast, very loudly with large gestures and exaggerated movements with the cast doing just what they like. It is relaxing, often great fun and certainly shakes the actors out of a rut. As you can imagine, there are plays with which you would be loath to try such tactics, but as in love and war – so with directing – all is fair if it achieves success.

The director receives the transmission of the actor from the stage, savours what is given and sends back his impressions in much the same way as an audience, for whom he is the substitute in rehearsal. Sensitive actors can feel the quality of your attention and respond to it, although you may say little or nothing. It is, as Reinhardt called it, a psychic evocation of performance from the actor. Be attentive, courteous, decisive and encouraging. Use your sense of humour, the leaven of labour, and try to keep interruptions to the minimum when a scene is going well – give notes at the end.

If one or two members of the cast are experiencing a problem it is better to give them a special half-hour rehearsal on their own, rather than hold up the rest of the cast while you deal with it. Also some comments are better made in private than in front of the whole cast.

Occasionally an actor becomes spiky or argumentative. If this happens let him free-wheel for a short time – say nothing and don't comment on his work. Eventually, slightly anxious, he may approach you for your opinion. Actors don't like to be ignored.

As rehearsals proceed and the production begins to take shape it is wise to check with the production manager that all the jobs under his control are on schedule and all will be ready for technical and dress rehearsals.

As soon as the set is up, view it from all parts of the auditorium, particularly from the extreme left and right seats of the front stalls and the back of the highest circle or balcony to check lines of sight, the set itself and setting of furniture. It will pay to check from all angles even if you are working in-the-round or on a thrust stage. Also invite the cast to try out the set, opening and closing doors, using practical windows, sitting in armchairs and on sofas and generally familiarizing themselves with the working environment. If possible have a dress parade well before the dress rehearsal to give time for any costume alterations. At the technical rehearsal the cast will adjust to the stage management working through a routine, operating music, sound, effects, curtains, lighting and scene changes to see that all function smoothly. Both cast and director will need infinite patience, as hitches inevitably occur, and lighting and sound levels have to be adjusted, scene changes rehearsed and timed, curtain and lighting cues timed, and a multitude of other details attended to.

Some directors like to have a word rehearsal before the play opens. A convenient time is usually when the setting-up is taking place and it is not possible to rehearse on the stage.

In the late rehearsals the actors take over. You feel, to use a metaphor, that the garment you have designed has been woven by the cast with so many personal contributions that it is theirs to display.

DRESS REHEARSALS

The dress rehearsals are another time when patience, tact and humour are needed by all. They are the occasion when every element of the production is conjoined in sequence of performance: music, curtains, sound effects, pyrotechnics, costumes, wigs, scene changes, lighting, make-up and special effects.

As the stage manager will be in charge of the running of the show you will be free to sit well back in the auditorium and take notes. Try sitting in a different place for each act to check visibility and audibility.

If all is on schedule everyone will be saved the irritation of people still sawing, hammering and touching up the décor. It is quite maddening trying to conduct a dress rehearsal with work that should have been completed still audibly in progress. This is why deadlines must be observed. When all is ready an air of efficiency prevails and this gives everyone a feeling of confidence. Last-minute panics are very unsettling to a cast, apart from being a waste of time. If all is well-organized and your first dress rehearsal runs smoothly subsequent dress rehearsals will allow time for the cast to consolidate their performances.

There will, of course, be various stops during your first dress rehearsal. Although you will have given curtain, lighting, sound, music and other timings in the technical rehearsal, there will be adjustments.

Your concentration will be mainly on the technical matters, while the cast will be incorporating all the new factors into their performances. As in the first rehearsals without scripts, there may be a set-back, but do not be dismayed, the new circumstances have only momentarily impaired concentration.

When you stop the action of the dress rehearsal for a necessary re-timing of an entrance, cross, lighting cue or sound effect make your remarks briefly, clearly and cheerfully. Don't allow a minor point to develop into a time-wasting debate. Also check that people have had time to note down what changes you have requested. For a 'dry', ensure that the member of the cast is re-cued so that they get the link-up and not just the prompt. Often for the first dress rehearsal there is no make-up, but the wardrobe people will be in attendance to make any further changes to costumes. In this and other dress rehearsals there are so many items that have to be noted that it is helpful to have a production secretary with you, so you can quietly dictate notes on items for which you are not going to stop the action. If you yourself try to write and watch and listen some fault may pass unobserved. A cassette tape-recorder is a useful substitute.

Three dress rehearsals are recommended. An invited audience for the last dress rehearsal helps the cast to get to grips with audience reaction, especially for the timing of laughs.

The curtain call is an essential part of the performance and should be rehearsed. Audiences need to release their feelings of appreciation in applause and a well-rehearsed curtain call is the professional way of returning the compliment.

10 *Directors at Work*

In this section seven contemporary directors talk about their methods of work. Six are professional directors and one is from the amateur theatre.

I asked each director approximately twenty questions concerning their personal approach to the staging of a play. Not all the questions were phrased in the same way and frequently the answers were extended to include valuable comments on theatre generally.

What emerges clearly is that each director has his own individual attitude and method, and that his approach is different for each production. Also it is clear that the experienced director achieves his best results by creating working conditions in which the actor is given a creative freedom within the bounds of the agreed interpretation for the particular production.

I should like to express my gratitude for the enthusiasm and openness with which all these directors have discussed their working methods – often in the middle or at the end of a busy rehearsal day.

DAVID BUXTON

David Buxton is the Artistic Director of the Mercury Theatre, Colchester, which opened in 1972. He has worked in the theatre for many years and was an actor and stage manager before he became a director.

How long do you like to work on a text before starting rehearsals?

It's difficult to say; usually I've been ruminating on a text for months. This *Reluctant Heroes* thing we decided to do as the opener for a new season as long ago as last November. It's true that when we made the decision it was left a little bit loose, so we could have changed it. When I read it last November I already saw its possibilities as an opener. I tend these days to do quite a bit of intensive work on a play for about a fortnight and then leave it at that and go into rehearsal.

Does a lot of the thinking crystallize in rehearsal with the practicalities in front of you?

To a degree, yes. One has, regrettably, to make certain decisions before the company starts rehearsals, because of practical difficulties with the construction of sets and costumes. Ideally, what I would like is for the company to do a fortnight's work on the play, then for me to talk to the designer, and for the company to talk to the designer as well, and hammer out how we are going to do it and then start a further three-week rehearsal period. This is not economically possible, so I have to make decisions about how something or other is done at least three weeks or so before we go into rehearsal. I find that I get fairly confident about the sort of decisions I make and I very rarely have to change something, but I like things flexible as far as the actors are concerned.

Do you follow any routine in this pre-rehearsal work on the text or does it vary from play to play?

It's very hard to say. In some ways it's easier to do intensive planned work on plays that I don't like very much. Plays I'm very fond of I tend to read. I start at the beginning and think, 'Would this work well if we had two entrances up there, or do we need a third?' And even at the sixth time of reading the play, after about four pages I find that I am caught up with the excitement of reading it. And it's very difficult to sort out how the excitement is in fact working – what is in fact making it exciting. In plays I am ambivalent about, I can do rather more disciplined and scholarly work.

You've got to dig out the way to make it work?

Exactly. One, as it were, makes a list of the problems implicit in the play.

At what stage do you bring in the designer?

We have two designers. And before we went on holiday we discussed in vague shape the three major productions that I am doing this season. I am doing the productions of *Reluctant Heroes, The Importance of Being Earnest* and *Hamlet*. I went on holiday on 14th June and came back on the 26th or so, and *Reluctant Heroes* had hardened off very nicely. The designer showed me the designs when I came back. However, we had both gone off the original idea for *The Importance* and we had a brand new plan. She came back with this new scheme a fortnight ago and I was rather wild about it. She then did some sketches and a few days ago she gave me the ground plan and I've taken that away and looked at it. *The Importance* goes into rehearsal just two and a half weeks from now.

Do you collaborate – giving the designer an equal say?

The designer has a pretty equal say. We get our best results if I make detailed notes. About *Hamlet,* one knows the play so well it is surprising to realize how long it is since one has actually read it. During the last three months I have started to read it through on various occasions, but have been distracted by urgent things that have cropped up. So I had to start from the beginning each time.

Do you ever find yourself saying to a designer, 'I want three doors and I want them there, there and there. I want steps, rostra and various levels, this is definitely what I want?' Do you ever dictate what you require?

I tend not to. Naturally with *The Importance* one works out how many entrances there are and the designer sketches very freely in the first instance and I understand the direction it's going to take and I felt that there must be a central entrance for Lady Bracknell in Act I and Act III and the bookcase must go over there, for example. I do insist on some things, such as not wanting this play done in a realistic set. We must find some way of stylizing it. One of the best bits of design we did was for *The Cherry Orchard*. This took a lot of experiment before we found exactly what we wanted.

So you always have a ground plan before rehearsals start?

Yes, and there is a model that we can all look at, otherwise the tradesmen – carpenters, electronics and the wardrobe – are going to be desperately behind.

Working to a schedule you have got to have everything exactly on time.

Very much so, but one always has to allow for some things to be altered, even at a late stage. It's a mug's game trying to keep carpenters waiting.

Do you have your major movements blocked before rehearsals start, or do you like to leave everything open, if you have the time to spare?

There is no spare time to spend, but I find more and more I am leaving things open, because the final result is better. I used to block things rigid. What I do now is to block things roughly and I do this before the ground plan is finally approved, so that I know that if the worst comes to the worst I can refer to notes. What I thought originally was that on this line you walk down there and he moves over there and then you go over there, then we've got people where we want them. Now I find it much better, even in plays I know have to be highly stylized, to try to make the actors find the moves 'right' for them. It's not that one leaves them entirely without suggestion. I am constantly making suggestions, but I encourage the actors to move about themselves.

For general grouping no doubt you would have to use your director's eye and not leave it entirely to the actors?

Oh, yes! One is trying during the blocking, even at a blocking rehearsal, to make some sort of sculptural shape, but if it is clearly not going to seem right to the actor, it's just not going to work, so that one has to compromise.

So large basic moves you might have blocked, whereas minor moves will be left to the actor?

It's difficult to be hard and fast about this. In the set for *Macbeth* we had quite a tall staircase with a gallery and it would be damned silly if, because of what the actor said, we played the dagger scene on the floor and did not use the gallery. One has to make a decision and carry it through. The possibilities of the set must be used.

Apart from your director's copy of the text, in which you have presumably made some drawings and notes, do you have your stage manager or prompter record moves and business?

Yes. I find this very useful. Because neither the actors nor I have infallible memories and if the prompter can say, 'Last time he was down there,' it is a great help. We find that it is invaluable to have a meticulous record of what we had decided at the last rehearsal. Moves that are changed very late may not be in the book. We don't make a fetish of it.

How many hours would you say you manage to put into a production, including the technical and dress rehearsals?

We try to rehearse all the hours there are, within the three weeks. We don't rehearse in performance time. I don't go a bundle on evening rehearsals when the theatre is closed. People get very tired in extra evening rehearsals and you don't get good work out of them and the chances are that you won't get good work out of them on the next day either. We start work in the morning at a quarter past ten and rehearse until one o'clock and then rehearse from two fifteen until five o'clock, except when there is a matinée.

Do you normally give a preliminary talk to the cast at the begin-

*ning of rehearsals about the author, the play, the period, the cos-
tumes, etc.?*

I get self-conscious doing it, but I believe very firmly that it is
a good thing to do. I should say why, because I have thought
about this quite a lot. At the beginning of the rehearsal it is the
director's responsibility to point everybody in the right direction.
Then I like to block it – some people don't like blocking, but I
like to block the play from beginning to end. This takes a couple
of days and as you get the cast piecemeal during blocking, so a
preliminary talk is the only opportunity you have of trying to get
something across to them as to how you want it to be done. When
they are rehearsing with a book in their hands they want to know
where I want them to stand, or where we decide, as I like to put
it these days, and they're not going to be thinking about the play
in general – they're going to be thinking about trees rather than
woods. Then, it seems to me, the director's job is to start something and be somehow the chairman, as it were, of a committee,
and he has to blow the whistle and get it together at the end. The
beginning and the end are terribly important. So I always say a
word or two, sometimes not very much. I feel it is important, on
the sergeant-major principle, when you're doing an army play
for instance, that you can show the troops that you have a very
firm idea how the play can be done.

So you may give an example of the style.

Exactly.

*Would it be fair to say that you have a variety of approaches –
some things you block, while some things are free, you like to
experiment and the approach is pretty democratic?*

I should hope so. I have little opportunity these days of seeing
other directors at work. I trained myself as a director by first
being a stage manager, and I saw an awful lot of directors working. Only someone observing me at work could comment on how
I do it, but I am conscious of approaching different plays in
different ways.

You just said you trained yourself to be a director by working a great deal in stage management. Do you feel this is the best way to learn the fundamentals of directing?

It's one way. I came into the theatre with ambitions to be a director. I was an actor, perhaps I wasn't a very good actor, and as I wanted to be a director I went into stage management. It was work I liked doing. I liked being on the book. I was a good prompter and sensitive to the actors and found it fascinating. I worked with many directors, so I was able to pick their brains, as it were. When I first started I used to say, 'Don't you think it would be a good idea if . . .?', but I soon learned to shut up. I learned a tremendous amount by just watching what people were doing.

Many directors I have worked with have tended to be autocratic, but things seem much more democratic in the theatre now.

Yes, that's the way that suits me really. I'm not much good at being an autocrat. I'm a confidence man. A confidence trickster. I persuade the actor that he can do it. I suppose it's a process of encouragement. It's not in me to be really rude to a man. I can on occasions be pretty firm, but I find the new open method of directing suits me rather better. I've no doubt that the actors in the pub might characterize me as being rather easy-going in rehearsals, but I don't really mind, it's the results on the stage that matter.

How many readings do you like to have before you start moving the play?

We usually only manage one, because of the time factor, of course. Sometimes it's useful to read a play more than once; usually not. It depends on the play. With *The Importance* one could well read the play several times during rehearsal. I don't think it would be much use reading it twice, straight off the reel.

But you might stop moving the play and go back to a few readings?

Yes. I find this useful with authors who write highly stylized plays. If a play doesn't seem to be coming out in the right style, I might go back to a complete reading of the text to get at the style and the rhythms.

Do you usually keep moves as they have been blocked out, or do you change things – even up to a late moment of rehearsal?

If necessary, up to the last moment, but certainly not for the sake of it. With moves, sometimes you have to backtrack to a point where you can arrange the grouping more satisfactorily. You might say, 'When you move, don't go down there, go up there and then you can move across here.' I find that one of the things about devising moves is that I often get better results if I work backwards, as it were. I might be rehearsing and then visualize this fabulous grouping, where there is a central character, and there is a 'pull' from this character here and a 'pull' from that character there. Then you have to backtrack to see how you can arrive at this particular grouping that exactly reflects the tensions between the characters. Perhaps, for example, you may want a character to be in the middle and able to look right and left and able to exert the maximum 'pull' – that is a triangular situation. You then work backwards to see how you can get the characters into those positions. I've been doing this instinctively for years, but it's the first time I've actually expounded the idea. With younger directors, I do notice that they are not so conscious as people of my generation where the strong points on the stage are. If you want to get somebody to do something good and strong you've got to not only get them on to a good position on the stage, but you've got to group the other characters to maximum advantage for the situation.

Do you mean they don't have such a strong pictorial sense?

No, not just pictorial, but in the sense of appreciating the forces that are made by sculptural shapes in groupings. I am more interested in forces than in the picture. One can make the picture look pretty quite late by arranging minor details. For me the pentagram of forces on the stage is important, so that you've got strength in the dramatic situation.

At what stage in rehearsals do you expect your actors to be word perfect?

I never ask people to come in next morning word perfect. I like them to learn at their own rate. I employ actors who are not lazy, but if somebody doesn't know it then everybody else suffers. I find that actors vary as to when it's good for them to drop the book. It is important that they can 'give' to the other actors as soon as possible, so that they have something to react to; of course, it's difficult for them to do this when they're still holding the book. If someone still has his nose in the book and time is getting on, I might say, 'You should, by now, be giving something back to your fellow actors, either by eye, face, gesture or body movement.' I believe it's a big mistake to allow actors to go away to study their parts and think, 'Here I have these lines; how can I make them live?' What you've got to do is to get the actor to learn his lines so that he gets a reaction from the other people in the play. It's not what lines mean that is so important, but the reaction they will cause, which is progressive. What lines mean is subjective. It is surprising how quite experienced actors ask how a line should be spoken, when the reaction that is implicit in the reply to that line clearly indicates how the line should be said to get that certain reaction.

How many dress rehearsals do you like to have?

We now open on a Wednesday. We cut Sunday work to the minimum, Monday is a normal working day, no costumes, and normally we have the possibility of two run-throughs in a rehearsal room away from the stage with all the props while the set is being built. On the Tuesday morning, somehow or other, by working overnight and in the morning, by twelve o'clock noon, we should have finished lighting. We then immediately start a technical rehearsal with the cast and all costumes and we do a stopping dress rehearsal. I don't usually cut to cues or entrances, because if you do that you may find you have cut out the moment when you take your coat off and you haven't got a peg to hang it on. Then not later than eight or half-past we start the full dress rehearsal. On the Wednesday, one has on occasions done a word rehearsal, or bits of the play, but usually we have a dress rehearsal at a quarter past two on Wednesday afternoon which finishes at five or half-past, leaving just time for everybody to have a bite to eat before we open.

Helen Mirren, in a letter to the press, stated that she felt that the technical side of theatre – computerized lighting, scene shifting, music and effects, and elaborate costuming – militated against the all-important relationship of the actor with his audience. Do you feel that there is any truth in this?

Yes, it's a trap one can easily fall into if only because the more elaborate the staging is the more time the technical effects take – the technical rehearsals and the dress rehearsals. So in the time when the actor should be warming up and getting ready to face the audience, he is, instead of concentrating on the basic thing of his performance, worried about all the technicalities. It's as simple as that. Obviously it depends on the show, but it's a very easy trap to fall into.

If you can't have three theatres in a complex like the National, although here you do have a main theatre that adapts from prosce-nium arch to open and a studio theatre, is there any theatre form you particularly favour?

This theatre was built as an open theatre with possibilities of closing it in to a proscenium arch style, if there is a play for which proscenium arch staging is particularly suitable. I much prefer it as an open stage. But it poses problems in certain plays which are easier to do in a proscenium arch theatre. But they are all challenges which are worth overcoming. It works marvellously for two sorts of play. It works marvellously for the epic play like Shakespeare, where you have a group of people who react one to the other and then one of them breaks off and directs the audience to another aspect of the action, or for Brecht, or where music is introduced. It works marvellously where the actors relate strongly to one another, like *The Caretaker* for example, where you have three characters who bring on their own preoccupations and react one to the other. The challenge is when you are doing Wilde, Coward or highly stylized comedies where the actor appears to be playing with the other actors, but in fact has an ear cocked for audience reaction and is consciously aware of the audience all the time. This is true of most high comedy and is true of a farce like *Reluctant Heroes*. This is where the open stage presents a challenge, because it is much easier to do it on a proscenium arch stage, where it is very easy for me, say, as the actor to feed you, and you just turn your head slightly downstage and make some flip remark and all the audience can see you raise your eyebrows. I find it most invigorating to change over from proscenium arch to the open stage, for most of our productions.

RICHARD COTTRELL

Richard Cottrell is the Artistic Director of the Bristol Old Vic Company, which is comprised of three theatres, the Theatre Royal, the Studio and the Little Theatre.

How long, in an organization such as this, do you manage to work on a text before starting rehearsals?

I like to know as long ahead in advance as I possibly can what I am going to do when I am producing a play, because although one may not be consciously thinking about it, and it may sound a little high-flown of course, but you do carry it around with you. For instance, I've known for about nine months that I'm going to be doing *Hamlet* in September. I suppose that for actual reading and work on the text one doesn't get more than four weeks before one starts rehearsing. I generally try to lock myself up for two weeks before I start rehearsals to do some really concentrated work.

Is there any routine you tend to follow in this pre-rehearsal work?

It varies a bit depending on the play, but certainly I tend, with scenes that have more than three or four people, to pre-block them before I start rehearsals. That is a sort of security for me really. It gives me a feeling of security and it gives the actors something to react to and generally saves a great deal of time. If I had a six- or seven-week period of rehearsal I probably wouldn't bother with pre-blocking at all. But in a three- or four-week rehearsal period you've got to get a move on. I generally start, certainly with classical work, with a certain amount of academic reading, which again very frequently isn't awfully helpful, but it gives one something to react to. I try and cut the text as late as possible, if it has to be cut, and I'm a great rewriter and changer of words.

I am interested to hear you say you do some pre-blocking because so many people today say they don't pre-block, but with a tight time schedule one has to do a certain amount.

You have to have plenty of time to be in a position to come to rehearsals without some pre-blocking in mind.

At what stage do you bring in the designer?

As early as I can. Once I have a vague idea – it may only be a single image in my head. Then that's the time to throw it to the designer and get his imagination working.

When you get the designer in, do you, as director, say to him, 'This is what I want and this is my ground plan and I'd like you to execute something on these lines,' or do you say, 'This is an idea and use this as a starting point for your own ideas'?

Mostly the latter. If it's a naturalistic play then I may not. I may stipulate that the table, say, is in the middle, but if it's not a naturalistic play then I leave the designer as free as I can. The designer goes away and gets his imagination working and comes back with his ideas and we talk about those. He'll then go away again and then, depending on the designer, start producing sketches or models and then we'll go through three, four, five or six of those perhaps until we've got it right. So that when we start rehearsals we know precisely what we're up to. The set will be agreed, especially because of the building and painting time schedule. The set has to be agreed and it's got to be costed apart from anything else, at least three weeks before rehearsals start. When the basic set has been arranged, if it's a naturalistic set then one can start putting the furniture into the room.

So you always have a fixed ground plan at the start of rehearsals?

Yes. That's partly of course because of the time element, particularly in an organization like this which once the season has started – we go from the end of August to the end of June – we're producing three plays every four weeks, so it's a bit like a factory. All the departments work to a careful schedule. It has to be very carefully organized and if we have a very big show coming up they'll sometimes start making that particular wardrobe and wigs the production before.

Apart from your director's copy of the text, do you have the stage management record your blocking?

Yes. They record this in the prompt book, yes, because the pre-blocking is something that one alters, throws away, modifies the whole time. It's just my flask of brandy, but the record of what happened at the rehearsal has to be in the stage manager's book.

How many hours of rehearsal do you manage to get in on an ordinary production?

Well, the average play rehearses here for three weeks and is rehearsed for about thirty-three hours a week, not including technical and dress rehearsals. So we get over a hundred hours on the average production. We rehearse from ten in the morning until one and then from two until five on Mondays to Fridays and on Saturday mornings.

When you are starting rehearsals do you give a preliminary talk to the cast about the period, costumes, settings, style, etc.?

Yes, always.

What sort of working atmosphere do you as a director set up for your cast in rehearsal? Do you give them a certain amount of freedom to move as they will and experiment with their characters and relationships, or is time so short that you have to define things rather closely?

No. I give them as much freedom as I can. With somebody who's playing a leading part I would generally discuss the broad lines of the character before rehearsals had started, particularly if you are dealing with somebody who is, say, playing the title role in *Hamlet*. You don't have time to discuss the 'why' in rehearsals – you have to devote rehearsals to 'how'. The 'why' having been decided before.

Do you feel you have a distinctive or very individual approach to directing?

The one thing I do feel, very strongly, is that the well-directed play appears not to have been directed. The best compliment I was ever paid was when somebody once asked one of the critics why – because this person was kind enough to think that I wasn't too hopeless at it – why I didn't have the kind of image that a lot of other directors have. And this critic said that he thought that it was because with my work you never saw the director's hand on the work. You were simply shown the work. That I took as a compliment.

How many readings do you like to have before moving the play?

Generally, only one. We read the play then we get on with it. Sometimes we'll read a scene and we'll discuss it before we start putting it on the floor. Sometimes we won't start with the text at all. Sometimes we'll start by improvising. Improvisation is just a means to an end; it's not an end in itself. It's only useful if you use it to get somewhere.

Do you continually change your basic moves up to a late stage of rehearsals?

One's continually changing.

Right up to the last moment?

Yes.

Gielgud does this doesn't he?

Yes, but I don't drive the actors mad, like Sir John! He drives them into a frenzy by altering things the whole time. One's always modifying the whole time, because one has to try to keep, as Hobbes said, 'working in a steady direction towards an approved end.' At the same time you have to try to look on every rehearsal as a fresh experience. When you come back to rehearsing a scene, you say to yourself, 'Now what am I being shown?' So obviously that will allow for continual modification, because you may not like what you see.

At what stage of rehearsals do you like people to be word perfect?

In the sort of period that we work in, by the last week. It varies slightly, depending on who the actor is. I don't have a lot of hard and fast rules, because every actor is different and has different problems. Every actor has to be treated in a different way.

About improvising – do you use this a great deal to try and reach inner meanings and resolve relationships in a production, or is it only a thing you use occasionally?

It's not something I use invariably. Occasionally, really. I use it if we have a problem. I use it to solve problems.

Do you find that older actors take to this easily or are slightly diffident?

Not really. I find that older actors are sometimes quite brilliant at improvisation.

How many dress rehearsals do you feel are necessary?

Our schedule here, for plays in the Royal Theatre, which is the main house, is that they open on Wednesdays, so we do a technical dress rehearsal, which takes all of the Monday. Then we do three dress rehearsals after that. In the other theatres it's a technical and two dress rehearsals.

What sort of breathing space do you manage to give your casts between the last dress rehearsal and the opening?

I am required by Equity to give them a breathing space of two and a half hours.

If you remember, Helen Mirren wrote to the press some time ago about actors being burdened by the techniques of dramatic presentation?

Yes, I remember that extremely clearly.

She felt that a great deal of over-elaboration, with computerized lighting, scenic techniques, music, sound effects, elaborate costuming, etc. militated against the actor-audience relationship. What do you feel about this?

I think the actor can get swamped by production effects and certainly the relationship between the actor and his audience is the most important thing. I don't like scenery. With the classics I try to keep the stage as empty as I can, but I feel costumes are important.

As a director are there any changes you'd like to see in working conditions in theatre?

Longer rehearsals. Not like the Moscow Art Theatre necessarily, but there is an optimum rehearsal period for a play and that is different for each play. I remember reading in Tyrone Guthrie's autobiography once – he was talking about *Hamlet*. He said, 'If you and your Hamlet really know what you really want to do, the optimum rehearsal period for the tragedy of *Hamlet* is three weeks.' I'm not sure I quite agree with him, but I do see what he means. I think there is a tendency in the theatre for people to talk, rather than do and I'm a great believer in saying to actors, 'Don't tell me, show me.'

If you couldn't have three theatres in a theatre complex, which you have here in Bristol and the National Theatre has, can you suggest a form or even name a theatre that does accommodate itself to most forms of drama?

I personally don't think that the eighteenth-century theatre design has ever been improved on, because it seems to me to give a very good actor-audience relationship.

Is there any particular ideal in the theatre to which you aspire?

I believe very strongly in the permanent company – the ensemble. It's very much a matter of the actors trusting and respecting each other. If they trust and respect each other they will be more pre-pared to take risks and the theatre, it seems to me, is all about taking risks. You have to try to create a working atmosphere in which the actor is prepared to make an absolute fool of himself and not feel that he has failed, because in rehearsal what you often do is fail – often.

I think it was Peter Hall who remarked, 'One has the right to fail.' Do you agree with that?

I think the right to fail is very important, because it is the same kind of thing as the right to take risks. The pressure of having to have a success every time can be intolerable.

Is there any advice you could give a young director wanting to enter the profession?

See a lot of plays. Get to know a lot of actors. The more you know the better. Get a job doing anything, absolutely anything, in the theatre. I think the director is not a sort of *deus ex machina* figure. He is one of the workers in the theatre and therefore the more he knows about every aspect of how the theatre works the better he's likely to be. The other thing, I think I would say, is don't bother what *you* think the play is about, try and discover what the author was intending the play to be about. Our job is to interpret the author.

ALFRED EMMET

Alfred Emmet, O.B.E., is the founder and former Artistic Director of The Questors Theatre, Ealing, London, which is one of the most successful amateur theatre companies in the United Kingdom.

How long do you like to work on a text before starting rehearsals?

This does vary, of course, because it is very much a practical matter. But I would normally hope to work on a text for the minimum of three months.

Do you have any regular routine that you follow on that work on the text – a series of points that you want to resolve?

It varies from play to play. The most important thing I like to do is as much research as I possibly can. My last production was *Three Sisters* and I spent a great deal of time re-researching – because I had done the play before – into the background and various productions of Chekhov's plays and so on. I think research is the most important aspect – the rest depends so much upon the play. Obviously one is trying to probe into it in the greatest possible depth that one can.

Do you work with the designer from the very first opportunity?

Yes.

Do you give the designer a firm outline of your basic require-ments, or is it a collaboration on a fifty-fifty basis, or do you perhaps give your designer a completely free hand?

I think in practice it's a matter of discussion. With some plays one may have a very firm idea of how one wants to direct it, because that may be the reason why one is directing that particular play – but in giving directions to the designer I'm always very careful to give them in very general terms, because the last thing I would want to do would be to block out the possibility of a creative contribution by the designer. So I think the design of the staging evolves as a result of quite a lot of prolonged discussion with the designer.

At your first rehearsal do you normally like to have a firm ground plan and a model, or do you like to keep things flexible for a short time?

Both. I have a ground plan and a model. That is absolutely essential, but everything is kept, to a certain degree, flexible, right up to the last dress rehearsal.

To what extent have you blocked the basic moves before the first rehearsal?

I always block the basic moves before I start rehearsals of any particular scene or act that I'm going to block in rehearsal. I would never come to a first rehearsal in which I'm going to block the moves without having planned it out in detail beforehand, but that doesn't mean to say that that's rigid in any way – one may normally change that quite a lot.

How many hours of rehearsal do you manage to put into the average play, including technical and dress rehearsals?

I suppose one hundred and twenty to one hundred and thirty rehearsal hours. That's what I would say for an average play. In my last production, *Three Sisters,* I was able to get and use about one hundred and seventy rehearsal hours, excluding technical and dress rehearsals, and I found that invaluable. Certainly when I started directing, years ago, I couldn't have made full use of that length of rehearsal time. But I find as I go on I can use more rehearsal hours, that is, make something out of them. On this last production, for instance, I felt that there was not a lot more I could have done even if more time was available, and that was after one hundred and seventy rehearsal hours.

Over what period of time are the one hundred and seventy hours spread?

April 4th to June 19th – about eleven weeks, with a short break for the Easter holiday, but that was exceptional.

Do you usually give a preliminary talk to the cast on the author, the play, period, costumes, mode of staging or do you leave these things to arise in rehearsals?

I think a preliminary talk is important, with discussion as one goes along. I believe it is important for everybody to have at least a general idea about some common aim or direction from the beginning. I find if one talks at great length and in great detail and thinks to oneself, I've covered all that, one deceives oneself very much, because at that stage of rehearsal a great deal of all that information will probably go in one ear and out of the other, because they have not been working on the play enough to assimilate it and take it in, so one has to keep on coming back to quite a number of, even major, points. But I wouldn't like to go into rehearsal without some talk, discussion and preliminary guidance. I certainly think it's important at the first rehearsal to be clear about the mode of staging, the costumes and basic information.

How many readings do you manage to have?

Three Sisters was a special case and in another way too – with enormous success. I tried something I've never tried before and that is I got the cast to read the play very very slowly without any attempt to express it, quite monotonously. This is an idea I've had in my mind for a long time, because I've always been begging actors in early rehearsals, 'For God's sake don't act – I don't want a performance. I want you to discover things.' Then I was very much encouraged when I read in an article that Roger Planchon adopted precisely this method of very, very slow reading over a period of three weeks, before he allowed the actors up on their feet at all. I found this approach immensely valuable. Of course, the cast thought I was quite crazy and it was a mad idea, but after we had done it a bit they found it tremendously valuable. The point being, I think, one has to explore as one reads, and as one listens to other people reading in that way one is really listening to the words with time to understand them, to consider and think about what is behind the words, to get the basic background. I found this very valuable. For many years my basic method of rehearsal has always been to take a section of the play, for example the first act, and to rehearse that intensively for quite a long time before I start any work on the second act. In this instance, first of all I did very slow readings of the whole play then slow readings of the first act and so on. Occasionally, even after we had moved it, we sometimes went back to very slow readings again, which the cast welcomed and found very valuable and then we repeated that process with Act II. So Act I was already learned and working and then we started with the very slow readings of Act II. I found this worked out very very well indeed.

So you set the style that fed into subsequent acts?

Yes. There's a lot you can learn about a play only by a great deal of detailed work and if you establish that at the earlier part of the play it carries through the whole play. Also it means that actors are having to cope with a small section of a play at a time. It's my job as director to see that it is all working into a whole. Of course one has to give it time to get running again, to cohere again, after you have finished with detailed work and start the last fortnight or so of rehearsals. This slow work means that the actors are able to concentrate on studying one single section of the play at a time, and you never have this appalling business of suddenly having to do Act I without books on Monday and Act II without books on Tuesday and Act III without books on Wednesday, which inevitably means an enormous amount of prompting. Working in this way actors are able to arrive at a word-perfect stage without any problems or difficulties at all. This is an enormous help with regard to the progress of rehearsals.

What sort of working atmosphere do you like to create – do you favour a rather disciplined or a free and easy approach?

I think these are two objectionable extremes. I think they must be disciplined. I would think it appalling if any actor were ever late for rehearsal. That sort of discipline is of prime importance. During the rehearsals for *Three Sisters* there was only one occasion when an actor was late and that was when there was a real snarl-up in London traffic. I find that actors accept this sort of discipline without any sort of problem whatever. What I do dislike is discipline in the sense of telling the actors all the time what to do – you do this, you do that, you move here, you move there – in an authoritarian sort of way, because I don't think for a moment that gets the best out of the actors. So, if by 'free and easy' you mean an atmosphere in which the actors are encouraged and helped to be creative and come out with their own ideas and thoughts then free and easy is the way.

Do you find that you tend to change movements or groupings at quite a late stage in rehearsals, or do you regard basic blocking as fixed after a couple of weeks?

I am always prepared to change moves in rehearsals – right up to the last moment, if necessary. I find that if I have really prepared the blocking well, with a subjective feeling from the actors' point of view of what they are being asked to do, I don't often have to change a great deal. But one does come up against scenes which are being difficult and don't work, then very often one will find that a small change in a move or group provides the key that helps the thing to work. This can happen right up to a very late stage. I think it's very important to keep an open mind about that. I would never ask an actor to carry out a move, if I had not, in my own imagination, identified myself with the actor in the character. I imagine myself carrying it out and feeling right.

At what stage of rehearsals do you like the cast to be word per-fect? You have, of course, partly answered that one.

Stage by stage. For instance I would probably, for intensive re-hearsal purposes, break an act up into three sections. For *Three Sisters* the first act, which I see from the timing took a little under three-quarters of an hour on its first run-through – this I broke into three sections, so that for each section I would spend six to nine hours of rehearsal on a scene that might be expected to play for, say, fifteen minutes and then expect no books for the next rehearsal. This means that by the time you come to rehearsals without books the actors are very familiar indeed with the scene, as it has been worked over in such detail.

How many dress rehearsals do you usually like to have?

We normally have three. The first one is about six days before the opening night.

What sort of breathing space do you give your casts between the last dress rehearsal and the opening?

I like to have the last dress rehearsal the night before. When the actors are still in top gear.

Do you feel that there is a particular type of play that gives you scope to use your individual qualities as a director?

One likes to think of oneself as a director for all kinds of play. I think it is the fact that I have been more successful with the plays of Chekhov and plays of that kind, not that any play is necessarily the same kind as Chekhov. I have of course directed a very wide range of plays, some reasonably successful, some less successful, but I don't know how far the less successful productions are due to my own inadequacies in that particular field or due to other circumstances.

If you didn't have a flexible theatre, such as you have, The Questors Theatre being capable of use as proscenium arch, open, or thrust stage, is there any one form of theatre that you feel lends itself satisfactorily to the majority of productions?

As you know I'm very keen on the flexible theatre and worked to create one here at Ealing. If I were told, 'You can only have one form, so which form is the one that is most generally used for all kinds of plays?' – then I think I would say a thrust stage. If I were setting out to create another theatre for myself I am very inclined to think I would have a very simple theatre in-the-round. I find the challenge of that very exciting and when I've seen it work it seems to work extraordinarily well. But there are some plays that are a little difficult to achieve in-the-round.

Quite a good case in point was when I did *Uncle Vanya*. I did that in-the-round and I thought that worked very well. There was only one purely technical practical problem and that was the map of Africa in the last act. I substituted for the map of Africa a globe of the world. Not as satisfactory as a map of Africa, but it worked reasonably and it was a small price to pay for all the other advantages of being able to do it in-the-round. When I tackled *Three Sisters* I realized it really was not practicable to do that in-the-round, because in the first act you must have the counterpoint between what's really basically the drawing room in the front and the dining room at the back with the counterpoint of characters in one with the other. This couldn't work in-the-round, because for part of the audience one stage would be in the foreground and the other one in the background, but for the other part of the audience that would be reversed and they would get a totally different picture of the play in consequence; so I don't think for that reason that *Three Sisters* would work in-the-round. So there are plays which don't really work as well in-the-round. Theatres in-the-round, of course, have been working for years and years and years and don't really seem to have any insuperable problems.

Do you, like Helen Mirren in her letter to the press some time ago, feel that the technical side of theatre – computerized lighting, scene shifting, music, effects, cues and elaborate costuming – militate against the relationship of the actor and his audience?

Personally, I am inclined to think so, but I think it depends upon what kind of theatre you want. If you want theatre of spectacle all these things are quite important and that's what you go to see and you need gorgeous costumes and transformation scenes and super lighting and fantastic sound effects and so on. And if that's going to be achieved then technical improvements to make it better are a good thing. It just happens that's not the theatre that appeals most to me personally. I like a theatre that is for hearing and sharing with the actors what they are bringing to life on the stage and for that kind of theatre too much spectacle rather gets in the way. And of course the more elaborate, the more complicated, the more finished all the technical possibilities are the more people want to use them and there is a tendency in that direction. I have often felt this in shows that I've seen in some of the more prestigious theatres, such as the National, in which one would have liked a much simpler presentation, where one could really share with the actors to a greater degree. I think it depends upon what one, personally, wants from the theatre. One can enjoy a spectacle from time to time too, of course.

What sort of experience do you feel would be most useful to a potential director?

I think this is a very difficult question to answer in a clear way. Obviously anyone who is going to direct needs experience of all aspects of the theatre. He may sometimes have to have theatre in his blood. I think that experience as an actor is really quite important to a director, because, it seems to me, that what a director is doing is working with the actor in the actor's own imagination, as it were. If he hasn't experienced acting he doesn't understand how the actor works – even understanding the kinds of personal blocks an actor can have that make some things difficult for him. So I would have thought that experience of acting is perhaps one of the most important things, but any kind of theatre experience is valuable. One has to widen one's whole experience of theatre by visiting theatres of all kinds. Also widen one's experience of life, by being aware of people – what makes people tick and so on, which is what an actor has to do. If you are suggesting that there is some specific kind of key or course or training, which is essential and would do the trick, I don't think that is so, but that does not mean that a director can't learn a great deal about his actual job. I think there are far too many directors about in the professional, as well as the amateur theatre, who simply don't know their job.

DAVID KELSEY

David Kelsey is the Artistic Director of the Royal Theatre, Northampton. He has lectured and directed all over the world and is the author of several plays. He is currently Artistic Director for the Ludlow Shakespeare Season.

What sort of theatre experience did you have before you commenced directing?

9 The Théâtre du Soleil's Paris production of *1789*. The action took place on five rostra, around which the audience sat, stood or wandered at will.

10 A production of *Chinchilla* by Robert David MacDonald at the Glasgow Citizens, 1977. An example of very sparse staging lending an elegance and power to the actor on the stage. The deployment of the cast in depth, breadth and elevation creates a three-dimensional image reflecting tensions between characters. The design is by Phillip Prowse.

11 Peter Brook's 1970 Stratford production of *A Midsummer Night's Dream*. In the plain white setting, by Sally Jacobs, movement gained a special significance. The acting area was fully used as a three-dimensional space, with Titania flown in on a crimson bower of ostrich feathers, actors flown in on trapezes, and a catwalk around the top of the set walls to accommodate actors and musicians.

I commenced in the theatre as an acting ASM, and because I was ambitious and determined, managed to slip off the cloak of stage management and then became an actor. And then about twenty years ago I fell into the job of directing, because a director was having problems dealing with a cast, who were not responding to him. In a general discussion he asked me, 'Well, can you do it any bloody better?' So I said, 'It won't be better, it will just be different.' So I fell into directing, then I started writing. In my opinion it's useful to have a knowledge of all departments, because when you come into conflict with an author about a situation and he says, 'Well that's the line I've written', it's useful to have the actor's mental tuning fork to be able to say, 'Well I'm sorry, it may be an accurate and grammatical phrase, but it's not speakable, the rhythm of the line is wrong.'

So the basis of your work comes from having been an actor and stage manager, which gave you a thorough grounding in the theatre? And of course you write plays yourself.

Yes. Having a basic knowledge of the technical design and geography of the stage is essential, as it is the crucible for your creative work and if you know something about lighting it becomes a collaborative process. It is useful to be able to say to your lighting designer, 'Could we try this, that or the other?', naming lanterns and colours and directions – revealing that you know something about shadow and light. You make his job much more productive, because he feels that you are on his wavelength and it isn't a matter of your simply liking or disliking something.

How long do you usually manage to work on a text before going into rehearsal?

In my present working capacity it's either a three- or four-weekly cycle. Every three or four weeks we have a change of programme. In some theatres it's possible to have a six-weekly turnover. It may be possible for a director to do one play in every three-month period. At the moment at the Royal Theatre, Northampton, I'm doing one in three productions, the other two may be done by a guest director or my assistant director. I have heard to my surprise that in some theatres the director, poor sod, still has to do

E

almost every production. I just don't know how they do it.

There was a time when I first came into the theatre, you may remember this, when the resident director peddled out play after play after play in what was then called 'repertory'. Mercifully that has come to an end. The audience these days is discerning and comes to the theatre expecting to see a high standard of work. A different attitude is being taken from the home into the theatre largely on the strength of good TV drama, and I think there has been a general improvement in drama work in education, so much so that I hope there will be a deep and lasting appreciation of drama. Ten years ago that was not the case.

It needs at least three weeks to actually chew through a script and find its merits and its faults – how you are going to carve it up and how to assemble it. In other words, we have to take the jigsaw to pieces. Without that dissection in that preparatory period the director is lost when he comes into rehearsal. For that period of investigation I would like more time. I can imagine for example if we were to dig up some rare Jacobean play, or having to work on a Greek play, or a new translation, that would, for me, demand two months' work. Of course, our bosses don't recognize this. They think everything comes quickly off the shelf and you just blow the dust off a script, get some actors sitting around and the whole thing springs to life in a short time. The director has to be informed; he doesn't necessarily need to have all the answers, but it's very important that the actors should have a sense of security with him, knowing the director has a head full of ideas and the actor, too, needs a head full of ideas – then it's a question of what is suitable to be selected for use during the course of rehearsal.

Is there any routine you follow in the pre-rehearsal work on the text? Do you have in mind a series of points you want to resolve?

Yes. One looks for objectives in collaboration with the author, either present or on paper. One is looking for the author's intention. There are 'moments', skeletal shapes and points the author wishes to make. The rest is a steam-up to reach that climactic point and after that it may be simple exposition, or a slide down to the final curtain. But there may be several climactic moments in a well-wrought piece of work and that's where the director may say to his cast on that first day something like, 'I've come up with this shape, I've got a red light here and a point there, a sharp precipice here, at this point I think there is a crucial explosion, here is a positive blister and there an assault course.' The actors get those images in their minds, however they may be translated. That is a very rough outline of what I might say to the actors.

Do you give your designer a firm outline of your basic require-ments, or is it a collaboration on a fifty-fifty basis, or perhaps you give your designer a completely free hand?

At the moment I've got a designer, who, fortunately, seems to reflect my own ideas. I haven't always worked with someone who was so collaborative. I would insist, in every case, that before we go any further on how the play is to be presented we should de-cide on one thing, and that is not colour. People can talk wild and woolly about, say, the drawing room in a play like *The Doll's House*. I had a fierce argument on that particular play some years ago when I did it – and it was silly because we had forgotten for the moment what the fundamental idea of the play was. We should really have been thinking about something like a cage, something claustrophobic. We should have discussed much more relevant things, instead of which we got into a fierce argument as to whether we should use Scandinavian blue or some other colour, and then we burst out laughing because we realized we had sidetracked ourselves and had started at the wrong end of the stick.

In arriving at a design it's often useful if the director and designer sit together and look at a blank sheet of paper and write down ideas that come to mind. This is what I do with my present designer. We ask ourselves, What are the main points? Is there a fight? Do people have to come through doors carrying large parcels? One has to think of practical things like that. Light sources are very important. One has to visualize the geography of the house, that is if we are thinking about a naturalistic interior. How far away is this house from a main road? This is important because of the window space and the sound and whether people come into a room with their overcoats on. Is there an ante-room? One must study the play very thoroughly – the designer too will, of course, have examined the script. Then the designer and director come together with their blank sheet of paper in front of them and write down what they remember – what images come to mind about this particular play. My present designer might say that the table in the middle of Act II has to be big enough for six people to sit around and have a four-course dinner, so a set of chairs of a certain period has to be found and so on. Those are just mere practical things, but it is important to get the practicalities right, because it is maddening in rehearsals to find that, say, a couple of big armchairs are in fact an obstruction and interfere with the actors' movement around the stage.

After considering the strictly practical issues I would expect any designer to go away and produce a sketch, so that I can see the dimensions, projections, recesses and the acting areas, so I can study these very quickly. Then, of course, the next thing is that he must make a model. When the model is made you may look at it and see that the ceiling piece is going to make it very difficult to light, because you can't get a bar over it, you can't get the lanterns in. So the designer may have to do two or more models before one finally decides. Some plays, unfortunately, are not as flexible as that. I want an air of flexibility when I'm working with a designer, because if you have to do the occasional West End release, which suddenly finds itself in a Samuel French paperback, it seems that the stage manager and the designer want to do all our work for us. I can understand that in the case of an amateur company who have limited facilities and don't have the opportunity of putting A, B and C together as well as they would like to. But in the professional theatre, because we have a director, because we have a designer on the payroll and, of course, design assistants, if it's a theatre of any repute at all, they would want the opportunity of looking at that play with fresh eyes. Just because Pinter's production of *No Man's Land* with Gielgud and Richardson had that certain setting, it is not the *only* way it could be designed. I was with a designer when I saw it. It was a fascinating text and the designer said to me, 'I wonder if Pinter's been as accurate about how he wants that set as he is about the balance and timing and punctuation?' I suspect he isn't. I don't think he's as punctilious about his sets. I hope not, because when I do the play I want, with my designer, to work out my own setting.

The ground plan is very important. In the ideal theatre, where I want to work, and try to make possible where I am at the moment, I think the presenting of a play should be a collaborative movement. If an ASM suddenly says in the middle of a rehearsal,

'Excuse me, but shouldn't that line be so and so,' I want the actor on the stage, and the stage manager and the director – whoever it might be – to acknowledge him or her as being a useful member of that company. I know you've got to have a hierarchy. Eventually you've got to have a referee, someone to say, 'Just a moment please, I must take a final decision on this, because the curtain goes up in three days' time.' It's very important that one doesn't over-indulge, but I do like the idea of a designer coming to the reading, because the area in which this is going to be performed is very much dependent on him. So, why shouldn't he, or anyone working within the framework of the rehearsal, come out with a very good idea?

To what extent have you actually blocked basic moves before you start rehearsals?

Well, my actual script is as virgin as the day I get it. Of course I go on reading it and reading it, until, say, a recipe begins to formulate in my mind. Now actors, of course, are invited to write down things in their scripts – textural alterations, moves, shapes and ideas in the margin and also notes, as they may be given by the director or wardrobe department, but I don't write anything down when I read a play. I recently directed *Habeas Corpus* and the designer and I got together and worked on a basic design for it. Although it's a very fussy play – I use that term deliberately – I found I didn't need to write anything down. The reason for that is that I have worked as an actor and an actor, whichever side of the mirror of the stage he happens to be on, whether he is looking at it from the stage or the auditorium – I suppose it's kinesthetic – kinesthetically you carry in your mind a sort of choreography. Now if it's written down in the script before rehearsal, and I had some experience of this from other directors I worked with when I was an actor, they are rather loath to change something. They might say, 'Well I've worked all this out and you do come on there and stand here' – for example. It's more likely to be printed on the memory as a stubborn shape. If it's left open in the director's mind he may find that his actors can generally collaborate and create something extra special, rather than be a definitive, final conclusion.

How many rehearsal hours do you manage to put into the average play, including technical and dress?

Let's take an average day. If it's a three-week schedule the day starts at 10 o'clock in the morning with one hour for lunch. Then we continue rehearsals from 2 o'clock until 5 o'clock. That's six hours a day for three weeks. It may be that the actors are working in a play in the evening. If they are not working in the evening that gives one another three hours and, as you know, we have to abide by the Equity rule that no one session will go on longer than three hours, so at the most we can get in nine hours' rehearsal out of the day. If you are in repertoire or presenting a play in tandem with a rehearsal schedule, then you're cut down to six hours of rehearsal a day. Besides, one cannot start earlier than 10 o'clock in the morning, the average is 10 o'clock, because you can only call the actors twelve hours after the fall of the curtain the previous night. It's lovely at the beginning of the season, because it means you can play around with those time schedules and get more mileage. So that's, in the normal way, thirty-six hours a week. Then we have the production weekend, because we don't open until the middle of the week, so there's all the Monday, Tuesday and Wednesday. So we have thirty-six hours for three weeks and the production weekend.

Do you usually give a preliminary talk to the cast at the first rehearsal?

I think it's better to lay your cards on the table and declare yourself to a cast – not, of course, to make any kind of lecture out of it, because actors should be intelligent people and sift out what they require. Without that initial introduction it's rather like throwing people into water and they don't know which way to swim.

How many readings do you usually have before you start moving the play?

I would say a minimum of four readings. That would take about two days – including time for discussion, especially on a difficult play: that is a play that has more substance and requires deeper analysis than a lighter piece of writing. Of course, all plays deserve as much attention as possible.

What sort of working atmosphere do you like to create? Do you favour a disciplined or a very free and easy approach?

A very disciplined approach. That may seem to negate what I said before about everyone being in a collaborative framework. I think you can have both. I think you can have a concentration on the actual product itself, so that all eyes and ears are giving the maximum attention to the main idea. But discipline is all. If you call an actor to rehearse at a certain place and time he must be there. Anarchy has no place in art as far as I am concerned. The actor's craft seems to me to be the most disciplined of all – save for dance and music. It always astonishes me that so many people want to get involved with it, considering the society we are living in at the moment. There seems to be a queue to get into drama schools and dance schools and this is an answer to some of the more pompous voices in our society at the moment saying that there is a turning away from discipline. I find that, generally, actors and dancers are the most disciplined people I know. They have to be, because they know what time the curtain goes up and they have a certain sense of shame about not fulfilling a professional task.

In rehearsing do you use improvisation as a way of investigating something?

Yes. I find it useful to unknot or shake up what may be a dull rehearsal. If two people are wrestling with a difficult patch of text and other actors are feeling a little bit limp on the side, I think it's a good idea to say to people, 'All right I know you're only playing Tom and Jerry, but you two do it.' Now if there's time – I wouldn't say it's the most essential part of rehearsal – I welcome the opportunity to use improvisation whenever it occurs.

Do you find that you tend to change moves and grouping at a late stage of rehearsal, or do you regard things as set after a certain time?

I want to be as flexible as possible. There must always be room for improvement or a change of heart – not major, but I do want to keep things flexible. You can change some things at the very last minute, but only minor things. If you happen to be doing *Waiting for Godot* you can't ask the SM to give you a different tree just before the 'half' on the first night. If you make changes it must be as early as possible – otherwise it's not fair and anything that savours of a panic measure gives the wrong sort of vibration and can be unsettling.

Do you have any personal method of getting your cast to achieve your intentions without too much 'direction'? Do you have any subtle things you say, or infer, to feed ideas?

A very good question. I'm glad to answer this one because it is something that has been levelled at me by way of, I think, praise. The immediate answer is yes. To digress a moment, because this is a very interesting question, I was on a theatre Brains Trust panel recently in the Midlands and this question came up. Because we are all trained differently, because there is a vast difference between the techniques of the RADA, the Central School, the Webber-Douglas, the Rose Bruford, Drama Centre, that is the major schools. They all have a different approach. Shall we say there's Tom, Dick and Harry in one company. Tom went to RADA and he's had a year's experience in the theatre, so he's probably worked with a couple of directors, but in the back of his mind he still carries that approach, that method he had at RADA. Now he and his colleagues – all three of them incidentally trained in a different way – are now, shall we say, side by side in *The Cherry Orchard* and they are having to cultivate a scene with extraordinary subtleties of character. One can't use an umbrella approach to those three actors. There are certain areas where they will find common ground, but I may find that I have to use an entirely different approach to get some ideas across. At the moment I have a man who is advanced in years, over the age of retirement. He is an extremely useful character actor. Now this particular actor, as far as I know, did not receive any initial formal training. Now the thing about him is that he does understand certain fundamentals, but there are certain areas that I would not dare tamper with, because I know I would be wasting my time. But I can get him, metaphorically, by the hand and sometimes guide . . . shame him into an attitude, or humorously direct him towards a line, a figure, a sentence, a move, a prop, so that that becomes an anchor for what I want and the compromise is a useful substitute.

Could you say at what stage of rehearsals you like your cast to be word perfect?

Well, again, some actors can act marvellously with a script in their hands and it doesn't get in the way. The actual business of digesting lines is a miserable process for some actors. I like the actor – this is where trust comes in – to hold on to the book for as long as he needs it. Of course you've got to watch the chap who is using the book and the prompter as an excuse for a bad memory, but if I'm reasonably sure that that actor is going to digest it and is going to give me some of that fire that is necessary at a dress rehearsal, I don't mind him carrying the book until, say, the technical rehearsal. I don't *want* a book at a technical rehearsal, because a book will get in the way, especially if you've got a lot of props to handle and doors to navigate and elaborate costumes. But if I can trust the actor I don't mind how long he carries the book.

I worked with an actor very recently, an actor I would thoroughly trust, but he doesn't like putting his book down until he's absolutely sure he's found the key. After that he might put the book down and improvise his way through it. I don't mind him doing that, because I know that he will eventually be using the original text. Now that's a very rare animal. It may annoy other actors and I say to them, 'Well at least he does know what this scene is about.' 'Ah', they say, 'but is he going to talk all that improvised stuff in performance?' 'No', I assure them, 'he won't do that.' Gradually he finds his way to the original text. I like that.

I worked for a long time with a director called Harold Lang, who didn't like people using texts at rehearsal. You had to use your own words, but never to forget what the author's words were. In a strange sort of way, we discovered, in the early stages of our company, an overseas touring company, that one got to know the original text so much better, because one was being forced to paraphrase. If an actor can paraphrase sufficiently, if he can have authority and carry the objective through each scene, by going through those points we were mentioning earlier; if he can give me the red light, and the blister, and the precipice and the car accident and the fugue – if he can give me all these things with a paraphrase, then I know jolly well I'm going to get a performance out of him, which is certainly going to be a damned sight better than from someone who can perhaps learn lines overnight and never get any further than that. The actor who has a mind full of paraphrase, which he may not necessarily use, but has flexibility – there is the actor with a range of interest.

I am rapidly coming to the conclusion that you can often see it in the face. There are some actors who seem to think they need to do some radio rep acting in the first reading and they mumble through lines as though to say it's all rather boring – we'll read it through for the director, just to let him know we can sight read and punctuate – now that actor is a bore, because he's not really helping himself. He seems to be saying to himself, in some mild rather pompous way, 'I'll do them all a favour, but I've been acting for over twenty-five years and I don't like these readings. I want to get on with the bloody job.' Those sort of actors are a bit of a yawn, because they are doing damage to themselves. If only they would open their mouths at a read-through and use their faces, however crude it may be – just bark a few lines in the face of his partner, even with a book in his hand and sitting in a rehearsal room. Then you think at least there's someone who's going to have a go. There's somebody who's got a bit of fire in his belly.

How many technical rehearsals do you have?

Well first, of course, the stage management have their production rig, that is the setting of props, furniture and all the other accoutrements that are necessary for the play, and then we have one full technical rehearsal with the cast, who for the sake of the play have to go through the slow motion process of a lighting rehearsal, because you can't light satisfactorily without seeing the cast on stage – otherwise you're just lighting blind.

How many dress rehearsals do you usually manage to fit in?

Two, but I'd like three. I get two full dress rehearsals where absolutely everything has to be ready, including sound and wardrobe, and all production facilities have to be there to be viewed, corrected and rehearsed for the first performance.

Are there any changes or improvements you would like to see in working conditions?

All directors are going to say that they need longer time to prepare. They want a much more processed schedule for all the various departments, between wardrobe, design, lighting and the rest of the production side. From an actor's point of view I think we must look at backstage facilities in all theatres – even new theatres that have only recently been constructed.

If you can't have a flexible theatre, is there any form of staging that you feel lends itself to most types of drama?

I've worked in most of the dimensions – proscenium arch, Greek open theatre, in-the-round – and I am coming to the conclusion that you cannot live in the theatre generally without being able to construct a proscenium arch. At the Northcote, Exeter, which is the widest stage in Britain, it is wonderful to have that great space and the hydraulic lift at the front and a huge flying area, but I found that, for the productions that I did there, ultimately what I wanted was, for the purpose of set design and to focus the eye of the audience, not a constricting framework, but some form of proscenium arch stage. Naturally one wants an all-purpose theatre really, where for Aeschylus or Brecht the actors can feel a certain freedom and be in touch with the audience where necessary. I would like a proscenium arch stage that is not constricting and has some flexibility.

A few years ago Helen Mirren wrote a letter to The Guardian *about computerized lighting, scene shifting, elaborate costuming and technical effects coming between the actor and the audience. Do you feel that this is sometimes so?*

Yes. We are spending far too much time trying to streamline our activities and in doing so we are forgetting the fundamentals. I sometimes find myself doing this. I know it can be done on a much grander scale in our large playhouses. I would like a theatre with a little more improvisation in all departments and with less emphasis on the streamlining of events. I think I have a pretty good sound desk where I am working at the moment and I've worked with three very, very good sound engineers in the last two years – at the Northcote, Haymarket and the Liverpool Playhouse. All those theatres, including my own, are very fortunate in having high-powered stereo sound desks and they still have problems. We're still discovering – I'm not a technician – that the balance, this, that and the other thing are not quite what we need, so sound reproduction is getting in the way; it's taking up far too much time honing the damned thing down to exactly what you need. I certainly don't want to go back to the old idea of the Bishop's cueboard, where you dropped a needle on a chalk mark on a revolving disc – we don't want to go back to that, but maybe when we start putting a play together we should think, 'What can we do without? Do we need this huge battery of lighting or sound desks?' Somebody told me the other day at Covent Garden – of course it's a very big stage there and I realize that they are doing operas in repertoire – that with innumerable cues and lamps the lighting designer is becoming not so much part of the whole, but is dictating disproportionate aspects of the enterprise. People do not leave a theatre – I know this will offend lighting designers – talking about the lighting. They leave the theatre, or should do, talking about the play. I don't particularly like them leaving the theatre talking about the stars, or how good X, Y and Z were. Ideally one wants the audience to leave the theatre with a satisfied feeling, feeling enriched or ennobled by the experience, but pleased they don't go out of a musical whistling the scenery. I certainly don't want the audience to leave any production of mine saying they thought the lighting saved the day, because that would mean we have our priorities wrong.

What sort of experience do you think would be most useful to a potential director to give insights and skills?

Obviously to go as often as possible to see theatre of all kinds, from amateur to the productions of the large national companies. To engage himself in as much dramatic activity as possible. To read about the theatre is vital, especially the history of the theatre, because without that the young director comes up with what he fondly believes to be new ideas and we older folk have to say,

'Actually I'm sorry to disillusion you but that was thought of by Gordon Craig in 1911,' or 'Grotowski has been peddling that one around for a year or two.' I think he should eat and drink theatre before he starts putting actors together and an important thing that young directors need apart from practical experience as an actor is a basic understanding of human psychology. I think a director should have the capacity of someone who hosts a genial party with a cross-section of people. Let him, for example, imagine how he would entertain, say, a seafaring captain who's just come back from a long voyage, with a woman in the room he's trying to avoid and a woman who is about to have a nervous breakdown because her husband's left her, with a backward child who needs attention. Let him put a group of people like that together in his imagination and see if he can generate less than a boring afternoon. He becomes a father confessor, a psychologist, judge, advocate, guide, counsellor, detective all rolled into one. Actually detective novels are quite good reading for directors, because one's mind is always alert looking for the clue.

JONATHAN MILLER

Jonathan Miller, who first made his name in Beyond the Fringe, *started directing at the Royal Court Theatre in 1962. Since that time he has been heavily engaged directing for the stage and television and in recent years has been directing opera.*

How long do you like to work on a text before getting down to rehearsals?

I don't do an enormous amount of textual work before I start. Usually I become interested in a play without necessarily having a view to producing it. The main issues of the text have made themselves fairly clear to me by the time I have decided to do it. I do the main part of my textual work during the rehearsal period. It's empirical really. I go at it on the floor and resolve points in the process of discussion with the actors and thinking it out in the evening after I've finished rehearsals – sometimes reading things which have been suggested in the course of rehearsal. It's very unplanned in many ways, although I've usually read fairly fully around various aspects of the play by the time I come to rehearsal. I don't do specific homework on a play. The reason why I think a play worth doing is that I happen to have reached a point in my reading which, somehow, crystallizes the play as a topic for production.

In your lectures at the University of Kent, you said you worked from a very strong sense of visual imagery. How important is the visual image to you in your productions?

For me it is certainly one of the important factors. It often provides a defining framework about how it's going to be staged. It's either a visual image simply about the physical space in which the production is going to occur – whether it's going to be a shallow stage, or a deep one, or whether it's tilted. Then there are some very specific iconographic images which come from, say, a study of the art and historical issues of the period and images taken from pictures, which seem to me to be relevant, or certain themes, or certain ways in which the thing is structured and dressed. This will have a very strong effect upon the way the whole thing is produced.

When you meet your designer do you give him a firm outline of your requirements, or is it a collective effort, or perhaps you give him a free hand?

I have a very firm outline before I start. I know the sort of painters that I'm thinking of. I know the certain colours, tones and even the way in which I want it lit, so that we will discuss and pore over certain works of certain painters, look at them and get the feeling of the style and the stance and the particular grouping and the décor from those pictures, then we will look at certain works of architecture together and out of it we'll produce a double idea which will be fused into one work.

But as director you have the final word on the design?

Yes – one is bound to in the end.

When you start your rehearsals do you always have a firm ground plan or do you like to keep things flexible for a little while?

I have a firm ground plan and I always have a model of some sort. The furniture is often fairly movable. Sometimes I will start with a very fixed piece of furniture around which the whole production revolves. I did a production of *Eugène Onegin* very recently, in which I quite deliberately made provocative problems for myself by placing the dining table right downstage, across the front of the stage, in order to create the sense of being excluded from a room. This created a tension from which some exciting things arose in the course of rehearsals and I didn't anticipate them all.

To what extent have you blocked basic movement before you start rehearsals?

Not at all. There are, perhaps, one or two moves which I think of as crucial; certain ways in which people will come into a room, which I already have in mind before I come to rehearsal and sometimes a whole scene will crystallize around those tiny images, but usually I let the whole thing happen as we go along. But I write nothing down at all.

What length of rehearsal time do you feel is necessary for a play to develop and reveal its full texture?

About a month. I get bored after a while and I think that the actors work well under pressure. I don't like scamping things, but I find that if you let things happen spontaneously, rather than imposing things, since the experience comes from inside it happens much faster. You only have to take a long time, I think, if you impose the idea entirely from the outside and they have to incorporate it. Whereas, if it starts to grow from within them it develops very rapidly. Sometimes a whole scene can be almost fully blocked and the whole idea fully worked out in about half an hour.

Presumably this is with a fairly small cast?

Yes. Once you have large casts, or choruses, or mass movements, then, of course, you do add to rehearsal time considerably and the moving of it is a much more complicated procedure. But I don't like to block in advance. For example, there are some very big party scenes in *Eugène Onegin* and I just let the cast improvise a party and then supervised and watched it and then edited it.

Improvisation, then, is one of your tools?

Yes, but not self-consciously, but I certainly let things happen by using the creative energies and ideas of the actors. I provide them with an outline, an idea, a notion, a tone. Then having given them the tone they are almost forced to respond in the tone that you provide. It's like saying what the key note is in music.

At the beginning of rehearsals do you talk to the cast on the author, play, period, costumes and staging, or do you allow some of these points to arise during rehearsals?

I used to give long talks and I used to find that they were falling asleep. Now, I may give a little talk about the set – what it's going to look like, their costumes especially, because I think they like to know what they are going to wear. But I've become much less didactic and hectoring as I've gone on and I find I do talk a great deal through the rehearsals, but in the course of conversations we're having together, rather than simply talking at them. I find that that becomes less and less profitable. I favour action rather than talk.

How many readings do you like to have before you start moving the play?

Often I like to read it over and over again – a large number of times, so that they become un-selfconscious about the words and just simply to hear the meaning. Sometimes I don't know what the play means until I have heard it read through. The full meaning emerges from the reactions between characters. When I did *Three Sisters,* we read and read, perhaps between ten to twenty times before we got up on our feet and did it. Sometimes I have no readings at all. It depends what the spirit of the meeting is.

What sort of working atmosphere do you like to create – disciplined, or fairly free and easy?

Oh, I like a very free and easy, convivial rehearsal, broken frequently by coffee breaks and talk, and I like living together with the actors a great deal while I'm doing it. I like going out to meals with them, so that we are living in each other's pockets, so that the rehearsal period is, as it were, almost indistinguishable from the ordinary life that is going on.

So you're creating something like an ensemble during that time?

Yes, almost a family atmosphere really.

So you can create the style of an ensemble in the period of one production?

Yes, if you choose your actors carefully and you cast convivial people, as well as talented people, then they enjoy reacting off each other and meeting each other and it's out of that that it comes really. I like discipline in the sense that I don't like chaos and I don't like inattentiveness. I like everyone to be watching what everyone else is doing. I'm not authoritarian. I won't sit behind a table and I don't like to read the text while I'm rehearsing – I listen to what they are doing.

Do you tend to change moves and groupings at quite a late stage in rehearsal?

Sometimes I do, but they are usually minor adjustments. I rarely have major upheavals. The production is growing organically all the time and therefore as one part is beginning to grow you sometimes have to lop off something somewhere else. It's a continuous process of growth. Any changes are almost by implicit consent. People begin to feel, I can't move there, so don't you think we can change it to something like this? It arises out of the collaboration.

Do you have any personal technique for getting an actor to arrive at your interpretation without too much obvious 'direction'?

No. It's usually done by amusing them. I have a humorous approach to anything I do on the stage. Simply by creating an atmosphere of amusement and laughter people start to relax and to be truly creative. You create such an amusing atmosphere, where everyone is amused by everyone else, and out of that experience of creating a myth, which is private to that group, then a sort of coherence and loyalty comes from which work arises.

Do you like your casts to be word perfect as soon as possible?

Yes, I do really. It's mainly because I think that books are terribly inconvenient. Once you are up on your feet I do think that books get in the way. I am perhaps spoiled by having worked in opera for four or five years, because singers always come knowing the words and knowing the music. I think it would be very salutary if the actors knew their words before rehearsals actually begin. They pretend that they can't, because they find out what the text means by learning it in rehearsal, but I think that a rough, crude learning of it is actually very helpful. After a series of readings, of course they do have the gist of it.

Do you find that there is a genre, a type of play, that presents a particularly enjoyable challenge to you?

I know the ones that *don't* present me with an enjoyable challenge. On the whole I'm not very interested in modern plays. I work best with classical plays, Chekhov and Shakespeare for example. I've not done very many modern plays. I don't rule them out, but the ones that really set my juices moving are classical texts with very rich allusions. With classical drama you don't have to go through the crashingly boring process of reading hundreds of plays before you find something that you feel is worth doing.

If you can't have a flexible theatre, is there any form of staging that you feel lends itself satisfactorily to the majority of productions?

I've worked on practically every sort of stage and they each have their problems and they each have their virtues. I rather like the proscenium arch stage. There are certain things that I could not have conceived doing on a thrust stage. I don't like large theatres in-the-round. I think it's very hard to get a decent view. I like small theatres in-the-round very much indeed.

How sacred do you feel the author's text is?

I don't think anything is sacred in literature at all. It has become sacred by being performed, that's what makes it sacred. I don't think one owes it any more than having shown one's awe of it by doing it again. I think one is honour bound to try and find out what the author meant and not to ride roughshod over his obvious meanings, but interesting and important plays have such richness and ambiguity that it is often a matter of discussion as to what was meant. That is really what one is doing by producing a play for the nth time. One is trying to open another door.

When you know exactly what you want from an actor do you ever demonstrate what you want, as Samuel Beckett and Ingmar Bergman sometimes do, or do you leave it to the actor to find his interpretation?

I will sometimes demonstrate, if I feel it's important. If you demonstrate something convincingly the actor will often see what it is that you are getting at. It isn't that one wants complete imitation. Very often certain gestures will symbolize something, which if they can understand why you are using it, they can then reproduce. If you simply ask them to copy a movement that's no good. They have to understand why the movement is being done and also understand the phrasing of it. I don't believe entirely that an actor has got to feel the emotion which is associated with a movement. He has to feel the meaning of the movement in its connection with the emotion, but it isn't necessary to feel the emotion itself. He has to know what he is trying to convey with the movement.

What sort of experience would be useful to a potential director to give the necessary insights and skills?

He needs an intuitive sense of human conduct. He needs to be sensitive and humorous and alive to human encounters, which really means keeping his eyes open on buses and trains and watching how people behave. He should have almost an ornithologist's interest in human conduct and that interest should be carried on into other people's descriptions of human conduct, therefore I think he should be well-read. I don't think it's very useful to spend all your time in the theatre, it's much more important to read novels and visit art galleries and enrich yourself by as many other ways as you possibly can. If you get all your experience from the theatre, you will simply repeat what you see in the theatre. The business of directing plays is to introduce new themes and new ideas and the only way to do that is to constantly nourish them with the life of which they are meant to be a reproduction.

JAMES ROOSE-EVANS

James Roose-Evans founded the Hampstead Theatre Club in 1959 and Stage Two Experimental Workshop in 1969. Since 1973 he has worked as a freelance director. He has directed in the West End, in regional theatre and in the USA, and has travelled the world directing and conducting drama workshops. He is the author of Experimental Theatre *(Studio Vista, 1970);* Directing a Play *(Studio Vista, 1968);* London Theatre *(Phaidon Press, 1977) and numerous children's books.*

How long do you usually like to work on a text before you commence rehearsals?

As a professional, one can, on rare occasions, be given a script only a few days before and have to bring all one's skills to bear in going straight into rehearsal with it. Ideally, from a creative point of view, I like to know months ahead. I usually read the play many times, then put it away and do other things and then come back to it. I find that organically the whole direction and style of the production grow over a period of time and therefore ideally one likes to work with one's designer over a period of several months. One has initial meetings, one makes sketches and models – then one may, as happened with *Romeo and Juliet*, tear it all up, knock it down and start all over again. I think, creatively, one does need time.

I remember you mentioned a book of sketches that you make for each production. Do you say to your designer, 'This is what I have in mind and you can interpret these sketches as you feel', or do you give a fairly firm indication as to what you require?

I don't have any one method of working. For me working in the theatre is a pragmatic experience. It's like a surgeon doing an operation – you've got various skills, it depends upon the individual which of these skills you employ. I have a very strong visual sense and usually, when I am reading a script, I do sketches of groupings, or ideas for the set. Equally, there are times when I have no visual ideas for the set at all and I am totally dependent on the designer to bring me sketches or a model. The sketches or model may be it, or they may spark off something else in me and bring out alternative solutions. One can digest the concepts, the characters and the motivation from the text, but the actual work of beginning to prepare the production I cannot do until I have an actual model in front of me. When I've thrashed out those problems of design – then I can start to see it. Once I have the final model I play with it – like a child with a doll's house. Every day when I get home from rehearsal I play with the model, moving characters about on it, as well as reading the text each night for the next day's rehearsal. Professionally, one wouldn't go into the rehearsal situation without knowing the setting beforehand, unless it was a production where you were given two or three months in which to rehearse, which would allow time for the set to evolve. That has happened a few times. That is the way Joan Littlewood used to work. At the start of rehearsals no one would know what the set was going to be.

To what extent do you block basic moves before you start rehearsals?

Again there's no one answer. I tend to do a great deal of homework and try to anticipate every move, every permutation of movement, but I don't burden the actors with those. I think through all the problems. In any one scene there might be six or seven ways of doing it, of moving the actors about the stage.

The director must have done his homework, because then he is open to all sorts of possibilities the actors may bring. I think it's awful if a director 'ums and ahs' in rehearsal and keeps actors waiting because he hasn't thought it through. When I was a young director I used to block very tightly and impose that on actors, but that was only because I was insecure. I think that with maturity one learns to be quite open and not possessive about one's ideas.

You do block some things, major images in your mind?

Oh yes! There may be certain scenes, which are key scenes, and I may have a very strong concept and they will probably stay like that. Such as the way I conceived the ballroom scene in *Romeo and Juliet,* which was a very complex and exciting way of doing it. I was very strict about achieving this so that the whole thing looked like a Velasquez painting.

How many hours do you hope to rehearse to reach a satisfactory standard with the average straight play?

That's a question that I find difficult to answer. As you know Equity lay down a standard of hours, after which you enter into overtime and actors tend to be very strict. I would like to rehearse as long as is necessary. I believe like Guthrie that if you rehearse for ten hours one day you might have the next day off or only work for four hours. I think it's a fallacy that you've got to work so many hours each day, for the number of hours rehearsed bears no relation to the intensity of the work.

When you're starting rehearsals do you usually give a preliminary talk or lecture to the cast on the author, play, period, costumes and general background, or do you allow these points to arise during rehearsal?

I have given long talks on occasions. I remember with *An Ideal Husband,* in the West End, I gave quite a lecture before we began. I did a lot of research into the period. But I think now that I wouldn't do that again, because I think if you are skilful you weave your own research into rehearsals or encourage the actors to do their own research. You can make books and pictures available to them, or weave all this in during the process of rehearsal, otherwise there's a danger of treating actors like students and giving them a seminar or lecture, and I think that's rather insulting to them and they resent it rather.

How many readings do you like to have before you start moving a play on the stage?

I vary from play to play. The readings I don't like, and I don't think that actors like either, are those old-fashioned ones with everybody sitting round the table and giving a reading of the play. I think on the whole that that can be damaging. If I talk of readings, it is having three or four actors sitting quietly examining the text, *sotto voce,* and on those occasions we will ask questions, discuss and analyse. That might go on for a day or two or three days, before we start to move it on the floor. Then there are other plays where one begins with quite different techniques. There might be exercises, games, improvisations, or we might just start blocking it. Much depends upon the play, the actors, the theatre – the actual situation in which you are working.

What sort of working atmosphere do you like to create? Do you favour a disciplined or a free and easy atmosphere?

I think there always has to be discipline in theatre. Theatre is a complex and difficult art involving so many people, so there has to be respect for each person contributing. If it's too free and easy a lot of time can be wasted. I think you have to learn to carry your authority with ease, so that the actors don't feel that you are being paternal or dictator-like. You are there to guide, to draw out from the actors. I think the director's task is to engender a very creative atmosphere in which everybody wants to work, wants to give of their best, wants to make discoveries, to explore, to experiment and therefore everybody is working very hard, because they are working creatively and therefore the discipline is engendered by the actors as much as by the director.

Do you find that as a director you tend to change moves and groupings at quite a late stage in rehearsal?

The director is outside; he is the only one ultimately who can judge the overall orchestration and pattern and design of the production and it may seem to the director that it is absolutely right. Some actors hate things being set and constantly want to change and sometimes with that kind of actor you have to be very tough and firm and say, 'No leave it at that, that is absolutely right.' At other times if you feel you haven't yet found the solution, then, I think, you must go on changing right up to the last minute; except it depends very much on the actors – it's a nerve-racking business and some actors, if you keep on changing up to the last minute, they may get so rattled that you will undermine their confidence. It depends on the situation and the actors with whom you're working. But I think that one should be able to go on changing. Of course, the actors do need to run a production in. That is the point of previews and public dress rehearsals. If you change too much before the first night they are going to be too insecure. It's a matter of fine balance, of the director sensing just how far he can go.

At what stage of rehearsals do you like the actors to be word perfect?

As soon as possible, but again one has to adapt to human nature. I find that while the actor has the book in his hand it's difficult for him to relate to other actors, the furniture, to props, objects and attend to business. One thing that I always insist on, but don't always achieve, is to have all props and costumes as early as possible.

Bruno Santini, with whom I worked, was always marvellous at making the costumes at an early stage of rehearsal, handing them to the actors, even if it were only a hat, or part of a costume, or a prop. He would watch the actor working with it and then perhaps adapt or change it, or give it to another actor. I think it takes the actor time to relate to objects and if the actor still has his script in his hand he is impeded. Some actors are, of course, lazy, but others do have genuine difficulties in learning the actual text until they're sure of the characters. You have to sense the needs of each individual.

Is there any particular type of play that you feel gives full scope for your individual qualities as a director? Are you a man for all plays or are there plays that you are especially drawn to?

No. No. I doubt if any director is a man for all plays. I suppose a genius might be, but on one hand I do enjoy comedy, because I love the simple form of entertainment and the marvellous, but highly complex skill of comedy, which is really of course the actors. The director has less to do in a sense, because given very good comedic actors they know instinctively about timing and the length of a pause and the pointings of a line to get a laugh. It's a wonderful form of theatre with the release that it gives to an audience when there is wave after wave of laughter. But my own talents as a director are most stretched and used to the full in plays that I always think of (it may be the title of the next book I will write), as 'theatre of the imagination', such as Shakespeare, Greek plays, plays that call for an imaginative response, where the director contributes very much to the style of the production. An example was Peter Brook's *Midsummer Night's Dream*, which was very much a director's creation, with all the exercises evolved for the actors and the way it was staged stemmed from the director's concept. But in comedy the director has less to do. He is assisting. It is very exciting working with highly skilled technical actors. That is a great joy and privilege.

Is there a form of staging that you think lends itself satisfactorily to the majority of productions?

I think probably that's the end stage, because think of the Mermaid, or the Hampstead Theatre Club where you achieve the overall composition of a picture that you would get on a proscenium arch stage, but you have the intimacy of theatre in-the-round, so that there is a close physical relationship between the audience and the actor, which you don't get in the proscenium arch stage, whereas theatre in-the-round, which although it is very exciting, has its own limitations, as you have to keep moving the actors about. Also, some plays call for the contribution of the designer and theatre in-the-round is very limited in a pictorial sense. The proscenium arch stage can be rather suggestive of the two-dimensional painting. Therefore, I think that the end stage provides for either a relatively bare stage, like theatre in-the-round, or for the full contribution of the designer.

Do you feel, like Helen Mirren, that the technical side of theatre with computerized lighting, scene shifting, music, effects, cues and elaborate costuming militates against actor-audience relationships?

Yes – I quote it in my book, *London Theatre*. The lines of hers that I quote are 'that all one needs is a space, a few actors, an audience and a leader'. I think that it's a matter of balance. Obviously technical equipment can achieve marvellous effects, but I think that the most potent force in the theatre has always been the actor on the stage communicating with his audience. The actor is the most important element and I think where the actor is subservient to computers and electronic systems and grids this is frustrating and crippling to the actor. I question it. Technical equipment is valuable, but it should be kept in its place.

What sort of experience do you feel would be most useful to a potential director to give him the necessary insights and skills?

I was fortunate in that I began as an actor, with no idea of being a director. One learns so much from working with actors. One should be open to actors and willing to learn from them, because the good director is one who anticipates the needs of his actors and senses the solutions to their problems. Every actor has different problems and needs different handling, so to some extent the director has to be a good psychologist. I think that a director who is just a university man and has a too academic approach might not always get the best out of his actors. Actors are not intellectuals; they are instinctive creatures and I think you have to learn how to talk to actors, which is very different from the way in which you'd talk to students or scholars or anybody else. There is a certain kind of shorthand, a jargon, that one uses with actors. I remember the marvellous story that Guthrie told about someone going along to see Reinhardt direct and watched him at rehearsal one morning. At the end of the scene all he said was, 'Let's run it again, shall we?' He said he realized that it wasn't anything that was said, but it was the vibrations passing between the director and the actors. The director did not need to articulate. Often one uses private words when working with actors. They know telepathically what is going through your mind. I think you have to use this non-verbal communication. If you do say anything – what is the right thing to say? I suffered as an actor sitting through the seemingly endless note-giving of verbose directors who kept the whole company waiting, fumbling, 'er'-ing and 'ah'-ing, because they didn't know their own minds. This deflates and exhausts actors. You have to have the skill of a brilliant diagnostician, a specialist, to go to the heart of the actor's problem.

CLIFFORD WILLIAMS

Clifford Williams has worked for many years in the theatre and at one time ran his own mime company, before concentrating on directing. He has directed a very great range of work in the UK and around the world. He is probably best known for his work with the Royal Shakespeare Company.

How long do you like to work on a text before going into rehearsal?

It varies enormously. If one's doing a complex play often you don't have enough time. I find the main work I do on a text is not so much the reading of a text, but the periods of discussion with the designer on how one is going to design and mount the piece. I find I discover more about the nature of the play – what it is about, what its intentions are – in the talks with the designer than I ever do in the study looking at it and reading it through. I'm not very good at just reading the text. I find it a bit boring at times – just reading through a play time and time again. Nevertheless I suppose one would hope to have, before one goes to the first rehearsal, a period of perhaps five or six weeks. At the beginning of that six-week period one reads the play for the first time and cogitates a bit and meets the author and a few changes are made; a fortnight's gone by and one now meets the designer and talks with him. He designs the set. That usually takes about three or four weeks and that brings you to the first rehearsal. So it's usually spread over about six weeks, sometimes a little longer. If it were not a new play, but an established play – a classic play – probably slightly less time.

Is there any routine you follow in this preliminary work on the text? Do you have in mind a series of points you want to resolve?

I really do most of my thinking with the designer, I really do. One works out whether the play is going to be performed naturalistically, or in some form other than naturalistic. One has to come to that conclusion with the designer, because he's got to know if he has to build four walls, or use a piece of white plastic. To come to that conclusion you've got to resolve a number of points. At the moment I'm working on a production of *Rosmersholm;* I have to come to a conclusion with the designer whether we are going to put that into a naturalistic turn-of-the-century setting or a more abstracted setting. To make that decision we do have to resolve a number of points. If someone asks me to do a production, certainly the first decision I have to make is, who is going to design it? Often I say I would like to do that production providing I can get such and such a designer and we can engage that person, because I need that designer to do that show. In this I'm probably a bit conservative. There are about half a dozen designers I work with and I work only with them. I go to whichever one seems best suited to the text, not necessarily because one goes to the one who's good at box sets, because one has a box-set play. But on the whole the decision whom one's going to have to design is almost more important than who's going to act in it.

When you have your discussions with the designer, do you give him an outline of your requirements or is it very much a matter of collaboration?

It's collaboration. A designer might ask me, 'Have you got anything to say about it?' and I might reply, 'No, I haven't got anything to say about it.' We look at each other and drink a glass of wine, and gradually a conversation starts up. If you know your designers well, they tend to read what they think is in your mind and you tend to react to odd things they say. It's very, very unscripted – not much vocabulary in it but a great deal of gesture perhaps. No, I don't lay down a brief, or very rarely. We might have two or three discussions, before he puts pen to paper or cuts off a piece of balsa wood. Most designers today do work through models. I think he's likely to construct a very primitive model and will use that as a starting point for further discussions. As a result of seeing something in more concrete terms one can say, 'Now I see absolutely, that's wrong,' or 'That's right.' He may defend or agree as the case may be and go on to another model. One might go through a series of models before one comes to the final solution. It depends on the amount of time you've got.

So at your first rehearsal you always have a firm ground plan?

Oh, absolutely. The luxury of going to the first rehearsal and subsequent to that settling one's scenery – that is a luxury that can be done by flexible and lightweight organizations. If you've got no money in the kitty to build scenery then in a way you can go on changing your scenic devices until the bitter end, because all you've got are chairs and minor items. But if you're in a heavier situation – that is, within a conventional theatre situation where you've got to spend money on your scenery and you can't make do with agitprops – when you are in that situation you do have to say, 'Well that's the set and that's what we're sticking with.' You cannot change it, partly because of time. Time plus money. To build a bit of scenery to see if we like it and then build something else – that's out of the question financially. We used to do that. As recently as ten years ago at Stratford we used to try a longer rehearsal period to see if we couldn't keep some options open, vis-à-vis the scenery, until the actors had joined in the discussion. Today that is quite out of the question. Whether you are in an institutional or commercial theatre, everyone needs to know what the set is and how much it is going to cost, before you go into rehearsal.

To what extent have you blocked basic moves before rehearsal?

Not at all. It used to be different at Canterbury, when I was there. It was weekly rep when we began and then we made it fortnightly. Then, of course, one wanted the security of knowing what one was doing; with literally only six hours to block the play, you'd have to work out the moves. I used to religiously do all that, but I don't any longer, partly because I suppose I know my way around a bit more – I don't get scared by not knowing what to do next. I would have been scared then, now I don't care. Today one wants to leave it open and get the actor's contribution. But I suppose it's also because I'm not particularly interested in the geography of the show, only its inner life, and once one's got that right the moves become very easy.

So all this work is done in collaboration with the actors?

Absolutely.

Presumably you have to have your fixed points of entry and exit?

Yes. You've got that settled. I find now that once the designer has created the area, or perhaps the room in which something is going to take place, then, possibly with the designer, one has looked to see where the grand piano will go. Obviously the grand piano can't go in the middle of the stage; it has to go into a corner and you look to see where the grandfather-clock will go – well that can't go in the middle – that must go in a corner. But apart from those obvious things, and I tend to find designers agree with this, we know we may need a sofa, and three or four chairs, or what have you, but one tends to leave even the placing of those until one gets into rehearsal, rather than saying, 'Well that's the room.' On the grounds that, perhaps, if you are working with a good actor and he's playing Solness in *The Master Builder,* one tends to want to say to that actor, 'You're Solness. This is your room. Where have you put the furniture?' So he puts it around and you say that would work if it were real life, but we've got to take away one wall as we're in a theatre, so we shove the things around a bit – I tend to improvise with the positioning of furniture. I wouldn't recommend it to everyone; I don't mean this immodestly, but you actually have to have the confidence I didn't always have. One has to have the security. If one goes into rehearsal and you say to the actors, 'I don't know where the hell the furniture goes,' you can lose their confidence. The actors have got to know that you know what you're doing.

This approach, of course, demands an expert cast and plenty of time.

Of course, but a lot of actors, and good ones at that, just don't want to know where the furniture goes. They want to be told where things are and get on and use it as it's set, but others welcome a certain amount of flexibility. I think it is vital to leave as many bridges open as you can until the last possible moment – until you've made up your mind that you're going to have three chairs and a table; that is the item of expenditure you've already allowed for. You can indeed leave them where you put them until a bit later on. So, frequently, during the first week of rehearsal I will shift around the whole room – not where the windows are, not where the doors are. That's the *sine qua non*, but the actual geography of the furniture I often shift around.

How many rehearsal hours do you normally manage to put into the average play? I say 'hours', perhaps you may think in weeks?

One can work it out in hours. It depends if you are doing a commercial show, where it is likely the actors are completely free, or whether you are doing a show in a repertoire system, where the actors are performing at night. Where they are completely free, theoretically you can work eight hours a day. In fact, any actor after he has rehearsed six hours, if he has worked well, has had enough. On the whole one can say one works five and a half days a week for six hours a day, so that's about thirty-three hours for the week, and you have a varying period between four and five weeks to rehearse so you've got anything between one hundred and thirty and one hundred and sixty hours of rehearsal.

Part of the point of my question was that if under the very best professional circumstances this amount of time is necessary, then it is very important for people in the amateur theatre not to curtail rehearsal time.

Oh, God, yes! I think we have a very small amount of rehearsal time in the British professional theatre. We have considerably less than the average continental theatre. If you do have more time you must be able to use it properly.

How many readings do you usually have?

It is very, very rare that I have more than one reading. Sometimes none. We may go straight in, having shown the model and talked, or not, about the play. It depends on my assessment of the situation. On the whole actors say they don't like first readings, it makes them nervous. Really, I think they do, because it puts off the evil hour. I would see no point in sitting down and solemnly reading through *Hamlet*. I think it would be much better to be doing something.

So in this type of situation, from the first moment you and the cast are improvising and experimenting with moves?

Yes. Absolutely. You can always do a week of that and then reverse the process and sit down and read the play, or take a week talking about it, depending on your timetable.

Could you say what sort of working atmosphere you like to create? Are you in favour of a disciplined type of approach or a very free and easy experimental approach?

A bit of both I suppose. It is work and one can't waste time. One has to be advancing in some way all the time, if one is going to get one's work done properly. There has to be a certain amount of discipline from the company. They've got to be on time. They've really got to try and learn their lines as soon as they can, consistent with the type of material they are doing. They've got to keep quiet while other actors are rehearsing. They've got to be in every sort of way alert and disciplined. At the same time, I hope they would accept and subscribe to that discipline as fellow professionals without bullying or shouting and therefore that discipline would be congenial, because within it we would work freely. I think people looking in on rehearsals I take would, on the whole, say that it looks pretty free and easy, but if they think that, it's probably because we are being very exact with each other and very disciplined. One can relax when one is disciplined.

Do you find you tend to change moves and groupings at quite a

12   An example of simple but effective staging by means of a ramped stage, steps, shadows on screens and lighting in Robin Phillips' 1970 production of *Two Gentlemen of Verona*, designed by Daphne Hare.

13   This photograph of the 1975 National Theatre production of *John Gabriel Borkman*, directed by Peter Hall, shows how Wendy Hiller, down right, is the focal point of the action by virtue of having the attention of the rest of the cast. Observe how the cast is positioned to make it easy for the audience to see right into the stage image and also how the linear effect, sometimes noticed on a proscenium arch stage, is broken up by subtle variations of spacing and grouping to reflect the 'pull' between characters.

14   In this production of *Summerfolk* by Maxim Gorky at the Lyttleton Theatre
in 1977, adapted and directed by Peter Stein, the characters do not freeze their
individual actions momentarily to create focal points for others, but rather, as
the Schaubühne programme states, scenes 'arise and disperse in the midst of an
enduring community'. There was a continuous flux of life on the stage to which
the audience directed its attention as it chose.

late stage in rehearsal, or does a time arrive when you consider these things set?

I think a time arrives when three-quarters of it is set and you're modestly happy with it. But for me there is always 25 per cent I am never happy with and go on fiddling with, if the actors don't get thrown, until the last possible moment. I don't actually know when the last possible moment is; it must be sometime well after a show has opened. There is possibly no such thing as a last possible moment. I go on fiddling until I'm content, or rather the actors and myself together are content. And that can take a long time. It can take till well after the first performance.

Although you did say something about this earlier, at what stage of rehearsals do you like the cast to be word perfect?

The sooner the better, as far as I'm concerned, but one has to accept that actors differ in this respect. Some actors say they like to come to the rehearsal with every word learned, while others say that's anathema, it'll come out like a parrot if you do that. Others like to learn gradually and some I know pretend they don't know the script, although they know it perfectly well, in order to keep their own options open. They go on stumbling. You think, they'll never get there, but actually they know the lines perfectly well. I don't think there is any easy answer to that. It is a completely personal one. I find the period of time when you're waiting for the actors to learn their lines a fairly boring one on the whole. I feel I can't work at full stretch until they've got over that hurdle. So the quicker the actors learn their lines the happier I am.

How many dress rehearsals do you usually manage to have?

It varies, but one would expect to have between two and three dress rehearsals and then normally, whether one's in the West End or not, with an institutional company one has a certain number of previews after that, in which you play to an audience without the actual first night having come upon you.

And these previews have a flavour of dress rehearsal about them?
F

A flavour, yes, but as people pay these days you've got to give them the best you can. We don't have enough dress rehearsals on the whole, but a dress rehearsal in terms of labour charges, staff and dressers, and so on, is a very expensive commodity and when you're dealing with a dress rehearsal, as far as a management is concerned, you're doing something that gets no income, so they tend to want to reduce the number of dress rehearsals. If you can put an audience out front with your dress rehearsal they get an income.

So you are pressurized to some extent?

Very much so.

What breathing space do you normally give your cast between the last dress rehearsal and the opening performance?

Oh, I think the time between the end of the last dress rehearsal and the first public performance, if I can put it that way, is approximately an hour and a half. You find yourself in a situation in which the theatre is dark for four days. The scenery is put up, you do your technical rehearsals, your first dress rehearsal, you change a few things, you complete the lighting, you have your second dress rehearsal, if you're lucky you have your third dress rehearsal on the afternoon of the first public performance.

Do you still light yourself? I remember you used to be rather keen on that.

No. I was enormously keen on lighting and used sometimes to light other people's shows. I remember lighting a couple of shows Bill Gaskill did once at the Arts Theatre for the RSC and one at Stratford. I lit one or two of my own shows at Stratford as well – *The Comedy of Errors*, I remember, was one. But over the years there has grown up this group of lighting designers and therefore we've started in our own time the tradition of employing a lighting designer. There are some very good lighting designers and some very bad ones. Although I would like to go on lighting my shows I don't any more and perhaps one gains a bit of time. For instance, the play I'm working on at the moment by Alan Bennett called

The Old Country, which opens in Oxford next week, is being lit at Oxford at this very moment by Glen Tucker, the lighting designer. He's been lighting it all day and I've been rehearsing all day. Of course you can't be in two places at the same time. So, he'll go on lighting tomorrow, I'll go on rehearsing tomorrow. Tomorrow evening I'll go and see what he's done. If it's been done well I've saved two days of rehearsal. But if it's not been done well, then we'll have to pull it apart again. So there are advantages about having a lighting designer to whom one can talk about what one needs and just let him get on with it. But again one would always want a collaboration with one's lighting designer, and since I have quite strong ideas on lighting, I would insist on it being a collaboration. I know, if there has to be any yelling, who would yell the loudest and it would be me.

Do you feel there is a particular type of play that gives you scope to use your individual qualities as a director, or do you feel you are a director for all plays?

I suspect that there are plays that I am not very good at doing, but apart from those – I'll think what they are in a moment – I suppose I've been lucky enough to do an extremely wide range of plays. I've done political stuff, overt and less overt, and nude revues and classical plays and quite a lot of new plays, like all the mime stuff I used to do, which had no text at all. So I suppose I'm lucky to have done a very wide range of stuff and perhaps there are some things which I am not awfully keen on doing – I've nothing against them as such, but I'm not keen on doing obvious revivals, unusual revivals yes, but I'm not keen on revivals of Somerset Maugham or Terence Rattigan. But on the other hand I do do revivals – Barrie's *What Every Woman Knows*, which is thought of as a sentimental play. I enjoyed reviving that because I thought it wasn't a sentimental play and it would be interesting to do it in a tough manner. Actually it worked rather well. On the whole I do most things. I try to avoid doing bad things.

If one cannot have a flexible theatre, lending itself to proscenium arch, thrust, in-the-round, or other shapes, do you feel there is any one shape of theatre that lends itself satisfactorily to most styles of drama?

I think the proscenium arch theatre does this. I don't know of anything that is actually imperilled by being done in the proscenium arch theatre, although it's fashionable to want to employ other forms of theatre. I've seen every possible type of drama I can think of, from the Greeks through English medieval, up to the present day, ranging into expressionist drama and God knows what, done very satisfactorily on the proscenium stage, so I don't think one can say that the proscenium stage can only do certain things. On the other hand I can think of a number of open stages on which I wouldn't want to do certain plays, so it seems to me, strange to say, that the proscenium arch stage is possibly the form that is most adaptable.

Do you feel there is an element of truth in Helen Mirren's letter to the press about the technicalities of theatre creating a barrier between the actors and the audience?

They can when they go wrong. I remember I was doing a production of *The Flying Dutchman* at Covent Garden and Sean Kenny designed a most marvellous stage which actually lifted away from the main stage of the house – lifted very high, thirty feet into the air, like a great ship rising out of the sea, and rocked and turned as well – it was a fearsome sight and on top of it was the entire Opera House male chorus singing the sailor's chorus from *The Flying Dutchman.* Thank God this was a dress rehearsal – the thing rose up and broke down with them suspended thirty feet above the stage with no way of getting them off it. That, I suppose, is the technical thing going wrong, but then I mean the most simple things can go wrong and it didn't go wrong in performance – we got it right. But I suppose because we've been moving through a period of considerable economic crisis it is natural that one can be very critical of what one thinks to be wastage. I think that is one thing. It is possible to go a step further and to say what is required is just the text and the space and the actor and that's all you need, you don't need the rest of the blarney, the lights and what have you. It is possible to say that. But I don't know how much that is the sort of theatre the audience will always want, because it seems to me that it is just one of the forms of theatre – a bare austere form of staging – but, equally, the popular theatre has always demanded its fairy lights and its tinsel and its make-up and its glamour and lots of people on the stage, rather than a few people, and lots of smashing scenery rather than no scenery. It's a question of varying the diet, I would have thought. If you've had a very rich meal there's nothing more acceptable than a bit of bread and cheese, but if you live for a couple of weeks on bread and cheese a bit of steak is very acceptable. I think everyone ex- aggerates the attitudes they take – it's very understandable.

What sort of experience do you feel would be most useful to a potential director to give the necessary insights and skills?

A very difficult one to answer. I think that our theatre, on the whole, is a theatre deeply rooted in the psychological realism that Stanislavski talked about. Of course, the greater part of the British theatre heritage is not naturalistic. There's not much naturalistic about any play written earlier than 1900, and a great deal that is not naturalistic about quite a few plays written after that date. Take the whole of renaissance dramaturgy in this country, it's not a naturalistic dramaturgy in the sense of the form. However, not- withstanding that, I would say in the time we've been living through during the last thirty years of the theatre it has been primarily realistically motivated, so it seems to me that what you're going to be talking to actors about a great deal is character and beha- viour and therefore you really have to be a dab hand at divining what it is that makes people function and behave the way they do. You may not be able to do it with yourself, or your family, but you've got to be able to do it with other things. You have to be able to say, 'I know what makes that character tick!' and you have to be accurate about that because the actor at the same time is trying to find out what makes that character tick. The remarks you make to him will only be helpful if they really illuminate the character and he thinks that yours is an interesting analysis that he wants to follow further. Then you are animating the actor and putting him on the right psychological lines. So first you've got to be interested in what makes people tick and also you've got to have the capacity to be awed and amused by human behaviour. I think you have to have the capacity to find human behaviour and actions extraordinary and sometimes horrifying and sometimes incredibly funny. You've got to be able to take an objective view of the way people behave, not necessarily individuals, but also groups of people – because plays are normally about groups of people and you've got to have some sort of clearly held attitude from the outside towards the behaviour of society as well as the way individuals are prompted.

I suppose the other important thing is that you've got to be able to communicate with the actor. It seems to me that you can have all the things I talked about, such as psychological alertness and the ability to analyse a situation and still not be able to direct because you lack the manner, the aptitude, God knows what it is, to win the sympathy and the ear of the actor. It seems often that we have a director who's saying all the right things and the actors just close their ears, because something is not clicking between the director and the actor and when that happens, all too frequently, that sort of chap never gets across to any sort of actor. It happens with a good director, an established director, occasionally he runs into a blockage with an individual actor, but on the whole a good director, almost by definition, has to be someone who gets across with most of the actors he works with.

Understanding what life is about on the one hand and knowing how to talk about that with the actors are the two important things.

Bibliography

DIRECTING

Braun, Edward (ed.), *The Director and the Stage,* The Open University, Milton Keynes, 1977.

Clurman, Harold, *On Directing,* Collier Macmillan, London, 1974.

Cole, Toby and Chinoy, Helen Krich, *Directors on Directing,* Peter Owen, London, 1964.

Cook, Judith, *Director's Theatre,* Harrap, London, 1974.

Fernald, John, *Sense of Direction,* Secker & Warburg, London, 1968.

Gorchakov, Nikolai, *Stanislavski Directs,* Grosset & Dunlap, New York, 1962.

Roose-Evans, James, *Directing a Play,* Studio Vista, London, 1968.

ACTING

Barker, Clive, *Theatre Games,* Eyre Methuen, London, 1977.

Benedetti, Robert, *The Actor at Work,* Prentice-Hall, Englewood Cliffs, N.J., 1976.

Hayman, Ronald, *Techniques of Acting,* Eyre Methuen, London, 1969.

Hodgson, John and Richards, Ernest, *Improvisation,* Eyre Methuen, London, 1966.

Moore, Sonia, *The Stanislavski System,* Penguin Books, New York, 1976.

Seyler, Athene and Haggard, Stephen, *The Craft of Comedy,* Garnet Miller, London, 1958.

Stanislavski, Konstantin, *An Actor's Handbook,* Theatre Arts Books, 1963.

167

168   *Bibliography*

—, *An Actor Prepares*, Geoffrey Bles, London, 1937.
——, *Building a Character*, Eyre Methuen, London, 1979.
——, *Creating a Role*, Theatre Arts Books, New York, 1961.

VOICE

Berry, Cecily, *The Voice and the Actor*, Harrap, London, 1973.
Turner, J. Clifford, *Voice and Speech in the Theatre*, revised by Malcolm Morrison, Pitman, London, 1977.

LIGHTING

Bentham, Frederick, *The Art of Stage Lighting*, Pitman, London, 1976.
Pilbrow, Richard, *Stage Lighting*, Studio Vista, London, 1979.
Reid, Francis, *The Stage Lighting Handbook*, Pitman, London, 1976.

STAGE SOUND

Collison, David, *Stage Sound*, Studio Vista, London, 1976.

DESIGN

Hainaux, René, *Stage Design Throughout the World, 1970–1975*, Harrap, London, 1976.
Powell, Kenneth, *Stage Design*, Studio Vista, London, 1968.
Warre, Michael, *Designing and Making Stage Scenery*, Studio Vista, London, 1966.

COSTUME

Cunningham, C. W. and P. E., *A Dictionary of English Costume*, A. & C. Black, London, 1960.
Hanson, Henry Harold, *Costume Cavalcade*, Eyre Methuen, 1972.

MAKE-UP

Buchman, Herman, *Stage Make-Up*, Pitman, London, 1972.
Perrottet, Phillipe, *Practical Stage Make-Up*, Studio Vista, London, 1975.

GENERAL AND REFERENCE

Baker, Hendrik, *Stage Management and Theatrecraft*, Garnet Miller, London, 1969.

Brook, Peter, *The Empty Space*, MacGibbon & Kee, London, 1968.

Esslin, Martin, *The Anatomy of Drama*, Temple Smith, London, 1976.

Grotowski, Jerzy, *Towards a Poor Theatre*, Eyre Methuen, London, 1975.

Hartnell, Phyllis, *A Concise History of the Theatre*, Thames & Hudson, London, 1968.

—— (ed.), *The Oxford Companion to the Theatre*, Oxford University Press, 1967.

Hayman, Ronald, *The Set-up: An Anatomy of the English Theatre*, Eyre Methuen, London, 1973.

Nicoll, Allardyce, *World Drama from Aeschylus to the Present Day*, Harrap, London, 1976.

Roose-Evans, James, *Experimental Theatre*, Studio Vista, London, 1970.

Sweeting, Elizabeth, *Theatre Administration*, Pitman, London, 1969.

Taylor, John Russell, *A Dictionary of the Theatre*, Penguin Books, Harmondsworth, 1970.

Willett, John, *The Theatre of Bertolt Brecht*, Eyre Methuen, London, 1967.

PERIODICALS

The Amateur Stage.
Gambit.
Plays and Players.
The Stage.
Theatre Quarterly.

DIRECTORIES

The Spotlight Casting Directory.
Contacts. (An indispensable source of information for all requirements and contacts. Published by *The Spotlight*.)

Index

170